THE FLESH OF ANIMATION

The Flesh of Animation

Bodily Sensations in Film and Digital Media

SANDRA ANNETT

University of Minnesota Press
Minneapolis — London

Portions of chapter 5 are adapted from "What Can a Vocaloid Do? The Kyara as Body without Organs," *Mechademia* 10 (2015): 163–77, https://doi.org/10.5749/mech.10.2015.0163.

Published by the University of Minnesota Press
111 Third Avenue South, Suite 290
Minneapolis, MN 55401-2520
http://www.upress.umn.edu

ISBN 978-1-5179-1158-4 (hc)
ISBN 978-1-5179-1159-1 (pb)

Library of Congress record available at https://lccn.loc.gov/2024000427

Printed on acid-free paper

CONTENTS

ACKNOWLEDGMENTS

This book is about the interconnections between our embodied experiences of the world and our perceptions of animated images, so it behooves me to acknowledge that I live and work on the traditional territory of the Neutral, Anishnawbe, and Haudenosaunee peoples, the stewards of this land in the past, present, and future.

This research was supported by the Social Sciences and Humanities Research Council of Canada. I would also like to thank Wilfrid Laurier University for providing institutional resources such as free access to paywalled journals and time off during my first sabbatical to conduct research.

My deepest thanks to the community of scholars who have made this book possible through their encouragement and corrections. I am especially grateful to the attendees of the Mechademia conferences in Minneapolis and Kyoto, who gave me feedback on almost all of the material in this book as I delivered conference papers on each case study throughout the years. To those who read early drafts of the Introduction or individual chapters, including Jing Jing Chang, Russell Kilbourn, Deborah Levitt, and Mihaela Mihailova, my deepest gratitude for volunteering your time and energy (during a global pandemic, no less!) on my behalf. An extra special toast to my coeditor at *Mechademia* and dear friend Frenchy Lunning, who was the first person to read through this manuscript in its entirety. Much gratitude as well to Melissa Brennan for preparing the notes. Any mistakes remaining in the text are my own.

Finally, I thank Jason Weidemann and Zenyse Miller at the University of Minnesota Press for their expert editing and support in preparing the manuscript.

INTRODUCTION

Toward a Phenomenology of Animation

This book is about animation and embodiment. It is about how bodies—including human, animal, object, and virtual bodies—are evoked, experienced, and perceived through animated media, following the approach of film phenomenology, which attempts to describe the structures of the "film viewer's *lived experience* when watching moving images in a cinema or elsewhere."[1] As such, I would like to begin with an experience of watching animation in which body and image are both brought vividly into play.

This is an account of my experience watching Jérémy Clapin's 2019 film *I Lost My Body (J'ai perdu mon corps)* on Netflix. I chose to watch this animated art film one cold, lonely evening in January 2020 after noticing that the title seemed to reflect concerns around the loss of embodiment in the digital era, a theme that echoes through film and media theory of the late twentieth and early twenty-first centuries. I had a vague idea that it was about a dismembered hand trying to find its way back to the body from which it came, which certainly sounded like a parable for disembodiment to me. However, upon watching the film, I discovered a richly layered, multisensory world of somatic experiences. I found myself thinking, *this film is not about losing your body at all!* Just the opposite: it is a deep dive into the body from a defamiliarized perspective that forces attention onto the parts of ourselves that usually fade into the background of the overall body schema as mere extensions of our immaterial will (that is, until these parts fail to work). Rather than watching as a detached scholar safely bracketed off in an observational mode, I found myself at several points violently thrown back into my own body and into a doubled state of sheer visceral experience and uncomfortable self-perception.

I began following the film with some amusement, watching as the disembodied hand "awakens" and escapes from a laboratory by such macabre means as climbing up a skeleton and leaving a disembodied eyeball (the mighty eye of Film?!) behind on the floor to be stepped on like a stray grape. The darkly comedic strangeness of seeing a hand crawl around on its own like the Addams family's Thing was quickly overtaken by a more immediate corporeal recognition of how the hand moves: running on its fingertips, the nails tip-tapping on the floor, scrabbling at edges and slipping on smooth tile. It reminded me of the times when, as a child, I used to pretend my hand was a dinosaur (four fingers for its feet, middle finger for its long neck) and make it walk around the back seat of my parents' car on long trips to amuse myself. The way the film uses flashbacks to the childhood of the hand's former owner, Naoufel, framed in a subjective mode with many point-of-view shots, made my own connection to a child's imaginative, corporeal way of apprehending the world seem natural.

Then there comes a scene in which the runaway hand falls off a subway platform and lands next to the tracks, just barely avoiding the wheels of a slow-moving train. It is splotched with tomato sauce from the discarded pasta can in which it has been hiding, red sauce that looks like blood, making me wonder if the hand had been cut by the sharp edges of the tin can—a sensation so painfully familiar that I had to reassure myself, "No, it's just tomato sauce." The hand has fallen and needs to reorient itself in its environment. When it does, it sees that there is a rat in the darkness under the edge of the platform. The rat stretches its head out from the shadows to sniff at the hand. Close-ups, crosscuts: the rat's twitching nose, the hand's surface splattered red, the fingers reaching out to let the rat sniff, the rat tentatively licking at the fingers—

—and oh, oh, oh, here I am, cringing and ducking under the blankets, half-closing my eyes and squirming because I am certain that any minute now the rat is going to bite the hand, that all the rats will swarm out and bite it and tear it to shreds! My own sensitive skin prickles, feeling in advance the sharpness of teeth. I have been bitten by a rodent before; the feeling is evoked from memory and from some primal instinct that screams, *no, danger, abort, get out!* I am suddenly very aware of this instinctive reaction in me. I cannot see the TV screen anymore because my eyes are closing of their own accord to cut the tension back. I become aware of my eyes, of my hands clutching the blanket on my lap to pull it up and my face burying itself into the saving softness. I struggle to feel and to escape the feelings of ten-

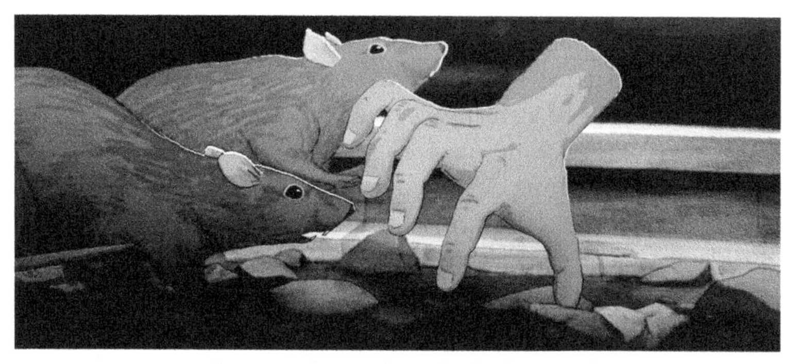

FIGURE 1. A scene of rats attacking a disembodied human hand may evoke prickling skin and shudders of fear in viewers of *I Lost My Body* (2019).

sion that are aroused by the vulnerability of the flesh with which I cannot help but empathize. When the rats do attack, it is almost a relief, because now the hand has to fight back, the narrative action is progressing, and I can watch again unselfconsciously. The moment of suspense—and of my perception of my body in suspense—is over (Figure 1).

For most of the film, I am able to watch by partaking of the various sensations of the hand's travels. The sounds of its fingers tapping on hard surfaces are familiar to me from everyday life. The sensations of falling into a frozen river and scrabbling at the underside of the ice are easy to imagine from my knowledge of the effects of water and ice and currents and breathlessness. The slight pressure of a baby's tiny hand wrapped around large adult fingers, that soft infant palm skin so supple that it feels damp and a bit sticky even when dry, is readily evoked. All of this I can follow with the comfortable immersion of "normal" film viewing.

At the film's climax, however, there comes another one of those moments of tension so acute as to pierce the viewing experience and make the body perceptibly react. In a flashback, Naoufel is working in his mentor Gigi's woodshop with his two whole, healthy hands intact. He is hung over and dull-witted after a late-night party. Then a housefly lands on the electric band saw he's using to cut wood. The fly has been a motif throughout the entire film. I have been thinking (consciously, analytically) at various points throughout the film that the fly represents failure. Naoufel cannot catch a fly with his bare hand in the film's opening flashback to his childhood, despite his father's coaching. At other points, I think that it signals missed opportunities. Frustration and irritation arise from the sounds of its buzzing and the extreme close-ups of its furtive leg-rubbing motions. It has collected associations of foreboding. As soon as that fly lands on the equipment, I know what is coming. My shoulders tense, going into high alert. Naoufel starts to reach clumsily after the fly, not noticing the running saw blade, though the camera frames it deliberately and makes the viewer keenly aware of the danger. It is the simplest possible setup for dramatic tension, but it has me hooked, and here I am again, closing my eyes and peeking out to see if it has happened yet, hiding my face, dancing between wanting to see and not being able to look. I do not think I actually saw the shot where his hand is cut off, if it is even shown graphically. I only remember the brief glimpses I had while I was viscerally moved and literally moving, anticipating the pain and acutely conscious of my own embodied reaction.

The dance between immersion and self-consciousness that I experienced while watching this film should be very familiar to viewers (and scholars) of horror and other films classed as "body genres."[2] After all, it is very common to squirm, close your eyes, hold your breath, or cry out while watching all kinds of movies. So, what is the difference in *I Lost My Body*? One difference is that this is a cel-style animated film, created using 3D and 2D animation tools available in the free software program Blender. The visual style is one in which the world is made of flat planes of color and thin black lines rather than photorealistic textures. It is a cartoon world with an impossible and strangely invulnerable protagonist: a hand with the miraculous ability to survive events that should break its bones or tear its skin. And yet, the body genre effect of sensory evocation still persists. This is in part because the hand seems to possess a full range of senses, along with the usual tactile sense associated with a hand. Even though it has no eyes, the cinematography and editing clearly suggest that it can see. Subjective point-of-view shots of far-off objects that the hand wants to grasp, like doorknobs and windowsills, are followed by shots of the hand making its way unerringly in the right direction, giving the impression that the hand can navigate its environment visually. The hand also responds to sounds like a dog barking from out of frame, suggesting that it can hear with no ears. There is no direct evidence that it can smell or taste; at least, it does not visibly react to the smell of garbage in a dumpster or the taste of tomato sauce on its skin. But still, I imagine the smell and heat of the garbage as part of my engagement in the film's mise-en-scène, and I attribute this experience to the hand as the focal point for my expectations of how things in the world look, feel, smell, or taste.

The hand in this film thus becomes a metonymic figure standing in for the whole of the human body. It both searches for its "lost body" and reincorporates all the senses of that body into a new, independent agent. It is a broken-hologram hand, where each fragment contains the whole. Despite the cel-like 2D style and the dismembered hand's impossible "life-in-death," it still evokes all of my embodied experiences, especially the tactile experience of my own hands feeling their way through a world filled with sensations. At its moments of greatest intensity, it also makes me perceive my own body engaged in the act of spectatorship. My interpretation of *I Lost My Body* springs from my own internal physical experiences and from the film's gesture of reaching out to me, or even at points seizing me violently, bringing me into a momentary awareness of its effects on me. I will describe this process as "evocation": a form of bodily recall and incitement that is present in all the arts, including animated films. The evocation of sensations or perceptions is a process created by the intersection of three factors: (1) the actually existing film or media object, with all its material, technical, stylistic, and authorial properties; (2) the conditions of its exhibition; and (3) the spectator's own unique, intrinsic embodiment. Along with the physical, material qualities of spectators' bodies, embodiment also includes things like subjective body image; physical and mental abilities; different modes of sensory processing and neurodivergence; socialized bodies (the social relations encoded in race, gender, sexuality, etc.); and memories of past bodily traumas, pleasures, or life experiences. For instance, I reacted strongly to the rat scene in *I Lost My Body* because of my past experiences of being bitten and my overall sensitivity to violence in films, but a less squeamish viewer may not find the same scene as viscerally affecting as I did. While reading this book, you may find my descriptions of how particular films or media texts appeal to my senses unrelatable or unconvincing because your relation to your body, your mode of sensory processing, or your tastes and experiences are different from mine. However, as a baseline, I contend that films are perceived by the spectators who engage with them through their senses and that films can evoke embodied sensations, however varied, subjective, or partial each spectator's individual perceptions may be. This book is an exploration of the processes by which animated films and digital media evoke embodied experience, even when they depict virtual or nonexistent figures like sentient disembodied hands.

I have analyzed *I Lost My Body* at length because it is reflective of a larger turn toward embodiment in scholarship and public discourse. As I will show, there has been a cultural shift from the postmodern discourses about how information "lost its body," common in the 1980s and 1990s (as critiqued by N. Katherine Hayles in her 1999 book *How We Became Posthuman*[3]), toward a burgeoning interest in embodiment's persistence as a vital property of contemporary life, even in the age of digital media. Research on embodiment and digital media is taking place across a wide range of disciplines, including (but not limited to) philosophy, psychology, sociology, and computer sciences. However, because my area of expertise is film studies, including new media studies and animation studies, this book focuses primarily on scholarship from that discipline. My interpretations of philosophical texts also come from a film and media studies perspective, following the work of other scholars of film phenomenology rather than the traditions of philosophy as a discipline. For the rest of this Introduction, then, I place the arguments I have outlined about the evocation of sensory experience in the context of existing scholarship on film, animation, and embodiment.

The Body in Film and Animation

When scholars of cinema wrote about animated characters and digitally generated actors in the 1990s and 2000s, digital formats were often seen as visible manifestations of information—that is to say, *not* photochemical traces of real bodies, as in analog film, but rather the result of a codified configuration of ones and zeros. Writing on motion capture in 2009, Scott Balcerzak described how digital technology "removes the physical reality of the body and replaces it with something or someone digital."[4] Digital characters, like the version of King Kong played by Andy Serkis in 2005, appear when "filmmakers remove 'flesh and blood' and allow 'presence' to exist as pure kinesis."[5] This strand of thought retains currency among scholars of "post-cinema," such as Shane Denson, who argues that "moving images have undergone what I term their 'discorrelation' from human embodied subjectivities and (phenomenological, narrative, and visual) perspectives."[6] This postphenomenological approach has its roots in Vivian Sobchack's pioneering work on film phenomenology, which contrasts the embodied nature of photochemical cinema with the disembodying effects of electronic media. Of particular note is her chapter "The Scene of the Screen: Envisioning Photographic, Cinematic, and Electronic 'Presence,'" from *Carnal Thoughts,* which uses the same scare quotes on "presence" that Balcerzak does to signal skepticism about the possibility of the body's presence in electronic media.[7] This chapter is also reproduced in the edited collection *Post-Cinema,* in which Denson cites Sobchack's work to support his theory of discorrelation in twenty-first-century digital cinema.

In recent years, however, a number of scholars from both film studies and animation studies have stepped forward to contest such discourses of digital disembodiment and postmodern historical rupture by drawing on examples of animation that demonstrate the virtual image's potential to express and incite embodied experience. In the course of my previous research on anime fan communities, I observed many instances when fans engaged physically with animated media, from shouting at the screen during a tense moment to enacting their favorite character through cosplay.[8] Even when they are sitting motionless and apparently unaffected, it is common for viewers to report an internal sensation of imagined or mirrored motion that corresponds to the movements of animated images, a phenomenon that some scholars attribute to the capacity in human and primate brains for "neuronal mirroring,"[9] or to perceptual processes resulting from evolutionary biology.[10] Following from my observations and those of other scholars working on digital film and animated media, this book draws its inspiration from what might be termed an "embodied turn" in film theory. This turn began as a feminist counterargument against the prevailing postmodernist discourses of digital disembodiment in the 1990s and grew to a veritable flood in the late 2010s, with no fewer than six books published on the topic of film and the body between 2017 and 2019 alone. Seminal works, such as Sobchack's 1992 book *The Address of the Eye* and Laura U. Marks's 2000 book *The Skin of the Film,* have inspired an entire subfield of film philosophy that continues to promote queer, feminist, and posthumanist interventions into film theory. The late 2010s saw the release of a number of publications on film, feminism, embodiment, and phenomenology, including book-length studies by Kate Ince, Katharina Lindner, and Saige Walton, to name a few.[11] *The Flesh of Animation* follows in this tradition, right down to the titular references to Marks's *The Skin of the Film* and French phenomenologist Maurice Merleau-Ponty's conception of the flesh.

This book does deviate from previous scholarship in one major regard, however, and that is in its attention to the apparatus of animation through media theory. Almost every work of film phenomenology cited earlier is founded on the primacy of traditional live-action cinema. That is, the ontological grounding for the "body of film" in most of these studies is the apparatus of the celluloid film reel and the analog camera recording indexical traces of the world. The audience's viewing conditions are tacitly imagined to be a traditional screening set in a darkened theater and targeted to mass audiences. And the genres considered tend to fall within the cinematic "supergenre" of live-action narrative cinema, which assumes that "fictional films are live action films, i.e., they largely consist of unmodified photographic recordings of real events which took place in real physical space."[12] In fact, the very conceptual underpinnings of film phenomenology rely heavily on the Bazinian tradition of reading film through its photographic ontology. Spencer Shaw describes how film and phenomenology coincide by noting that film is a medium through which "we are presented with the raw materiality of life," which is captured through indexical recording.[13] It thus has a direct connection to the "life-world" Merleau-Ponty propounded. In his 1964 article "Film and the New Psychology," Merleau-Ponty argues that film "directly presents to us that special way of being in the world, of dealing with things and other people, which we can see in the sign language of gesture and gaze and which clearly defines each person we know."[14] In contrast to the "raw" or "direct" nature of film, however, animation is an essentially "an-ontological" medium. As Deborah Levitt explains, in animation "everything is shadowed by its possible metamorphosis, erasure, and resurrection—there is thus no ontology."[15] Animation is predicated on the "animatic," defined as "any aspect of image production—from animation as such, to digital special effects to extreme camera angles—that does not deploy the cinematic reality effect of the index . . . as it produces a pro-filmic real."[16]

Although animation may be anontological in its visual content (nonexistent characters, settings, etc.), scholars like Levitt and

Thomas Lamarre also recognize that animation is not immaterial as a medium. Like all media, it cannot exist without some physical means through which to convey images to viewers. It must circulate in a relationship between "viewer, image, screen; or, user, content, platform," as Lamarre has argued in his work on "platformativity."[17] And once it has reached the viewer, an animated image cannot be understood without the operations of perception that refer us back to the tactile, physical world of our experience (the weight of characters in motion, the textural depth or planar flatness of settings, etc.). Therefore it is still necessary to frame a phenomenology of animation as the attempt to describe embodied perceptions of anontological images. To this end, I argue that animation presents heretofore unknown or overlooked ways of considering embodiment in its digital and posthuman dimensions. Indeed, animation reveals the paradoxical necessity of material embodiment to digital media. Animation is by definition an illusory, artificial format: it must either create the illusion of motion in objects where no motion has occurred (for instance, in stop-motion and traditional hand-drawn cel animation) or create the illusion of a new object where motion has taken place (for instance, in rotoscoping and motion capture). However, this fundamental illusion is just as fundamentally created within particular material conditions, and its intentions are always directed back toward the tangible world, creating the entwinement or reversibility of object and beholder that Merleau-Ponty identified as crucial to our perceptions of the world.

To be more concrete, every animated image is created through repeated, and often rigorous, physical practices, such as drawing and painting, clicking and typing, or moving objects and bodies in space. These practices take place through some material infrastructure, such as an animation stand, a Wacom tablet, or a miniature set for puppets. The results of all this labor are, for the most part, visual, aural, and tactile reproductions of human sensorimotor experiences, even when other animals, plants, objects, or alien creatures are the diegetic subjects of the work. And most important, animation is consumed by viewers who enliven the images with their own physical impulses and perceptions. As Lamarre argues, paying attention to the effects of the apparatus does not necessarily affirm technological determinism or fall into essentialist declarations about the true nature of animation and its viewers. We are neither determined by our biology nor forced by our technology to experience the world in a certain way through any given medium. Rather, we each perceive the worlds of animation through the interaction of material media technologies and the nonindexical images they produce with our physical abilities, neurological differences, and sociocultural experiences of embodiment in all its many dimensions.

The production techniques, visual styles, and consumption methods of film and animation have certainly changed with time and technology. But the difference between analog and digital animation is not essential. That is to say, it is not a matter of technological determinism or physical essentialism, as if digital technology were inherently unable to capture preexisting "real bodies" because of its nonindexical, information-based nature. If strict indexicality were our sole measure of contact with reality, animation would always already be a disembodied medium. I propose to look at it another way. Rather than relying on a materialism of the body based in determinist and essentialist thought, I argue that animation encourages us to perceive the world through varying intensities, modes, and qualities of embodiment as a dynamic experience, one that is not dependent on the ontological presence or absence of "the body" as a singular, monolithic object. As such, it is my contention that cinema does not degenerate from "more" to "less" real or from "presence" to "absence" of embodiment as technology shifts from analog to digital or as images shift from indexical to anontological. Instead, cinema presents different levels of intensity or qualities of experience that a viewer may have, ranging from visceral connection to disorientation to sensory overload. As Shaviro argues, the twenty-first century has seen a "multiplication of technologies for controlling perception and feeling on the most intimate level, and its play of both embodiment and disembodiment."[18] The variations in intensity that any given viewer experiences spring not only from the technology itself and the pressures it exerts but also from each viewer's situated knowledge of many factors, including their background knowledge of filmmaking and animation techniques, their relation to their own body and to images of bodies like their own (for instance, in cases of highly sexualized or racialized imagery), where they are positioned in the world, what media they can access, and how they came to see that particular image in the first place.

Overall, the main task of this book is to trace some of the variations in animated embodiment that have come about mainly, though not exclusively, since the 1980s, for viewers of both mainstream commercial film and cult or experimental media in North America, Europe, and East Asia. These examples do not pave the way for a totalizing, fixed, transcendent, or universally applicable theory of "the body" or of "perception" in the abstract; rather, they are instances of animated embodiment seen as a situated, ongoing process of (mostly) human beings living in mediated worlds and encountering images that provoke undeniably physical reactions despite their evident virtuality. In the coming pages, I tease out the strands of thought that explain how we can experience animation as an embodied medium and weave them together with critiques of the ways in which some bodies are erased, recast, manipulated, privileged, commodified, or otherwise subjected to the workings of biopower through animated and digital media of the late twentieth and early twenty-first centuries.

Embodiment in Film (Theory)

What does it mean to say that a film "has a body" or that it can "touch" viewers in reality? Using commonsense definitions of the body as the physical structure of a human, animal, or object, all film seems to fall short of true embodiment owing to the unavoidable fact that its most attractive component, the visible image, exists only as a 2D play of light or as pixels on a screen. No matter how much you may wish to touch or be touched by a cinematic image, it will always remain intangible. At best, if you are a collector, you may be able to get your hands on a framed cel, a stop-motion puppet, or a hard drive full of digital production files. But these inert objects and dull machines hardly seem to embody that which most viewers would desire to touch: the alluring figure of an animated character or the sensuous experience of living in a fantastic world full of colorful creatures. What we commonly refer to as "the film"—the ensemble of image, sound, narrative, character, and cinematic style or technique visible on a screen—remains intransigently untouchable for audiences and only partially accessible even for the film's cast and crew, who work on just a few specific aspects of a vast, intricate production. And yet, there is clearly something with which we interact when we watch a film: something that exists as both an object that must be activated (a film projector, a DVD player, a device for accessing streaming video sites) and a virtual experience of a fictional world that we apprehend through our sensory perceptions, intellects, memories, and other situated knowledges. To understand how film, world, and experience connect, we must delve deeper into philosophical and theoretical understandings of film's body.

In *The Address of the Eye,* Sobchack makes an argument for the existence of the "body of the film" using a phenomenological mode of inquiry. Her motivation for selecting this approach at the time was to move beyond the mainstream currents of psychoanalytic and Marxist film theory that reigned in the 1970s and 1980s, which focused on film as a patriarchal expression of male desire and female lack, such as Laura Mulvey's 1975 theory of the male gaze,[19] or as a deceptive illusion that lulls audiences into passive consumption while eliding the material base of its own production, such as Jean-Louis Baudry's 1975 critique of the ideological effects of the cinematic apparatus.[20] In contrast, Sobchack argues that film is neither lack nor elision but is itself a form of perception that is grounded in our embodied reality and cocreated with various actors, including both humans and machines. She does this by drawing on the work of Merleau-Ponty, who argues that "perception, like the structure of consciousness, is never empty but always a perception of something"[21] and is always necessarily perceived from the limited, finite viewpoint of an embodied subject. Far from being restrictive or solipsistic, the process of perception that takes place between the embodied subject and the world is intersubjective, mutually constitutive, and reversible, because the world informs the body as the body informs or "intends toward" the world through its perceptions. Through Merleau-Ponty's articulation of phenomenology, Sobchack is able to demonstrate how film itself has a body that is "partially mechanical and inhuman—and as well, partially intentional and human," involving viewers' bodies as well as the cinematic apparatus of camera, projector, screen, and theater.[22] In this view, "the film's body functions to visibly *animate* perception and expression in existence," as the viewer's body likewise animates, or gives life to, the images by imbuing them with human experience.[23] Although Sobchack does not consider the medium of animation in depth in this particular book, her theories have had widespread implications for the study of cinema and other media.

On the basis of the work of Sobchack and others in the phenomenological tradition, twenty-first-century scholars like Scott Richmond have examined "cinema as a technology for the modulation of perception" based in a "proprioceptive aesthetics."[24] In *Cinema's Bodily Illusions,* Richmond describes cinema as a technical system and an artistic medium that utilizes "the set of perceptual processes whereby we orient ourselves in the world."[25] In this view, cinema is a form of "technics" that engages viewers in a coproduction that happens across the film, environment, and body. Following Bernard Stiegler's work in *Technics and Time,* Richmond defines technics as "the pursuit of life by means other than life," arguing that, unlike the repressive visions of *technology* found in classical apparatus theory or Foucauldian biopower, "technics is not a domain over against life, but rather life's manifestation in 'organized inorganic beings.'"[26] This approach recalls Bruno Latour's career-long articulation of actor-network theory (ANT), in which humans and nonhumans are considered equally to be actors that have impacts within a given field. A "body" in ANT is no longer limited only to a human's physical form but includes inorganic bodies as well. Cinema, as a form made jointly by machines and humans, frequently draws on human-embodied intentions and experiences like proprioception: our sense of movement and spatial orientation based on input from the nervous system, inner-ear fluids, and so on. Our sense of proprioception may be enhanced or altered by mechanical means, for instance, when the camera depicts motions that would be impossible or highly unusual for the human body to perform. However, we still respond physically to simulated stimuli based on our embodied knowledge of the world. Richmond vividly describes his experience of watching the opening long take of Alfonso Cuarón's 2013 film *Gravity,* in which an astronaut, played by Sandra Bullock, becomes untethered during a space walk and tumbles headlong into the void. In his words, he felt "a sensation of my own body moving through onscreen space, at once weightless and frictionless, terrifying and illusory."[27] I assume that Richmond has never been on a space walk, and neither have most viewers of *Gravity* (at least, those who are not astronauts). But, like Richmond, I also find that I am capable of imagining the sensations of weightlessness and disorientation evoked in this scene on a very visceral level, in the same way that I am capable of imagining myself as a disembodied hand scrabbling under the ice of a frozen river as the current pulls me away. The illusion is tolerable because I know it to be fiction, but it has a thrilling impact because it plays with proprioception, evoking and disordering my usual perceptions.

Along with Merleau-Ponty's work on perception and embodiment, film scholars have drawn on the work of Continental philosophers Gilles Deleuze and Félix Guattari to articulate the virtual dimensions of embodiment, which are no less real than the body's physical dimensions. Of particular interest is the concept of the "Body without Organs" (BwO), which extends the body from its purely material, empirical, or essentialist connotations to include the virtual dimensions of desire, flow, intensity, and quality. In this view, the body is not something that one has or is, like a possession or a fixed subjectivity, but something that one *does* by acting, changing, and becoming. Steven Shaviro's *The Cinematic Body* (1994) provides one example of how Deleuze and Guattari's concepts may be applied to film, and particularly to films that deal with desire, queer subjectivity, and a masochistic embrace of the abject. Like Sobchack, Shaviro rejects Lacanian and Marxist film scholarship. He argues instead for "the notion of cinema as a technology for oxymoronically intensifying corporeal sensation, for affecting and transforming the body, for at once destabilizing and multiplying the effects of subjectivity."[28] He explores "the relations between the cinematic apparatus and the life of the body," aiming to "suggest that these two realms are not alien or extrinsic to one another: their more-than-marriage, their symbiotic and parasitic interpenetration, is an inescapable feature of postmodern culture, which is to say of late capitalist social and technological relations."[29] Shaviro's attention to subjectivity and late capitalist social relations here points to a larger dimension of the body: the body as lived within a system of power that stratifies experiences and relations along various hierarchical lines. In this case, power is not purely a repressive or controlling mechanism but a means of inciting desire, directing its flow, and managing its energies, as in Foucault's conception of biopower. However, Deleuze and Guattari also suggest that the BwO provides the mechanisms by which power subverts itself through a proliferation of desires in various forms of "becoming" that run counter to hierarchical organization or stratification, from "becoming-woman" to "becoming-animal" to "becoming-imperceptible."[30]

Of course, the tenets of these twentieth-century French philosophers have not gone uncontested, and they are now considered by some to be old-fashioned and patriarchal. As Elizabeth Grosz points out, feminist scholars have leveraged many criticisms against Deleuze and Guattari, noting the ways in which they depoliticize women's movements and unwittingly follow phallocentric and teleological patterns of thought by making "becoming-woman" just another stage in the greater journey toward "becoming-imperceptible."[31] Likewise, Judith Butler has famously critiqued Merleau-Ponty's works, arguing that "feminist theory has both something to gain and something to fear from Merleau-Ponty's theory of sexuality" as put forth in *The Phenomenology of Perception*.[32] On the positive side, he refutes ideas of sexuality as "natural" or as a blind drive without intentionality and conceives of it as coterminous with existence itself, a mode of choice. But on the negative side, he assumes that the desiring subject is male and the desired object is female. This leads him to consider asexual males as abnormal and to overlook females as desiring subjects. Normal, correct male desire is associated with perception as viewing of the desired object leading to arousal as a natural effect. As such, "*The Phenomenology of Perception* reveals a cultural construction of the masculine subject as a strangely disembodied voyeur whose sexuality is strangely non-corporeal,"[33] an image that strongly recalls the (implicitly male) disembodied subject of postmodern digital theory.

The traditional dependence of film theory on Western male thinkers in general, whether it be Lacan and Marx or Merleau-Ponty and Deleuze, has tended to marginalize women's voices and non-Western philosophical traditions, while granting Western "filmosophy" the highest privilege in terms of its perceived rigor and intellectual sophistication. Still, Grosz sees some value for feminist scholars in the aspects of Deleuze and Guattari's works that disrupt binary thinking, refuse Lacanian constructions of desire as lack, and work against the hierarchical classification of identity categories. For the purposes of my book, the specific value I find in these French philosophers is the vocabulary they have developed for understanding embodiment as a material and virtual entanglement, coprocessing, or becoming, rather than a monological, essentialized being. The BwO is not about refusing physical practices and perceptions so much as it is about refusing the kind of organization that requires the body to exist in one unified, coherent, and implicitly masculine ideal way. Likewise, Butler's critique of *The Phenomenology of Perception* only acknowledges Merleau-Ponty's later work in *The Visible and the Invisible* in passing, when it is there that many scholars find the very concept that would rejoin the perceiving subject and the bodily senses: the flesh.

"The flesh" (or in French, *le chair*) is not simply the body seen as "meat," as the term might suggest, but is rather the joining point or "chiasm" of the touching and the touched, a hyphenated "subject-object."[34] This conjoining extends not only to touch but to vision as well. In *The Visible and the Invisible,* Merleau-Ponty stated:

> We must habituate ourselves to think that every visible is cut out in the tangible, every tactile being in some manner promised to visibility, and that there is encroachment, infringement, not only between the touched and the touching, but also between the tangible and the visible, which is encrusted in it, as conversely, the tangible itself is not a nothingness of visibility, is not without visual existence. Since the same body sees and touches, visible and tangible belong to the same world.[35]

This kind of embodied encroachment, this intimacy of the tangible and the visible, is an approach that some contemporary feminist and queer film scholars have revisited in productive ways.

One apt example of a feminist approach to Continental philosophy is Marks's aforementioned book, *The Skin of the Film.* There Marks explores "the way vision itself can be tactile, as though one were touching a film with one's eyes."[36] This is what she terms "haptic visuality." In contrast to "optical visuality," which "depends on a separation of the viewing subject and the object," haptic visuality evokes a "combination of tactile, kinesthetic, and proprioceptive functions," inviting "a bodily relationship between the viewer and the image."[37] For Marks, haptic visuality is grounded in the analog documentary image, in which "light reflected by an object makes contact with the witnessing material of film,"[38] providing it with an indexical connection to an event that happened in the world. This approach is particularly evident in the generation of female diasporic filmmakers who migrated to North America and Britain from the "Third World" (as it was called then) in the 1970s to 1990s. Across the numerous examples of intercultural film and video Marks cites, there is a common focus on images of the tactile: hands stroking fabric or touching skin, for instance. These images are often self-reflexive of film itself, as the contact of light with a sensitive recording surface creates a tangible connection between image and life, grounding the artist's intercultural experiences of belonging, displacement, remembering, bodily agency, and desire in a kind of mediated memento.

Along with vision and touch, Marks considers cinematic uses of taste and smell, such as the scent of magnolia that is evoked in Shani Mootoo's 1994 video poem *Her Sweetness Lingers.* Although Marks found the image evocative of scent based on her own memories of magnolia blossoms, images like these also bring to our attention the subjectivity of sensory depictions on film. There is an ambiguity about what happens when a filmmaker visually depicts a sensory experience of smell, taste, or touch that a viewer does not share or for which one has different associations. I had never knowingly encountered a magnolia tree when I first read *The Skin of the Film,* and with no opportunity to find one blooming in the dead of winter, I was fascinated instead by the experience of having to mentally "reach" for some imagining of a scent I did not know. (I address further such subjective and imaginary sensory experiences in chapter 1 of this book.) Suffice it to say, Marks makes a valuable contribution to the study of embodiment in cinema, as she suggests the ways in which film can evoke a range of human senses through its record of physical experiences and objects in the world, along with its virtual dimensions of memory and imagination.

Much in these works has influenced my own arguments in this book. I employ the vocabulary of perception and experience, of desire and BwOs, of proprioceptive aesthetics and haptic visuality, though not because I agree with everything Merleau-Ponty or Deleuze has written. I employ these concepts because they are useful terms with which to think and from which to develop new vocabularies. That said, one troubling current underlies the arguments of many of the authors discussed here that I must contest from the start: the idea that digital media are somehow less embodied, less ethically grounded, and less invested with presence than analog, indexical cinema.

This discourse is particularly evident in Sobchack's founding work on film phenomenology. In the conclusion to *The Address of the Eye,* she states in no uncertain terms that "electronic space disembodies," as there is a kind of "free float" or "free fall" or "free flow" in cyberspace that "seems to belong to no-body."[39] In *Carnal Thoughts,* released twelve years after *The Address of the Eye,* Sobchack expands this argument into a critique of the particular strand of disembodiment imagery found in the work of postmodern theorists like

Jean Baudrillard and cyberpunk authors like William Gibson, which she describes as "the millennial discourses that would decontextualize our flesh into insensate sign or digitize it into bits of information in cyberspace."[40] She goes on to quote a 1990 article by John Perry Barlow from the cyberculture magazine *Mondo 2000* that crystallized this discourse in his famous description of cyberspace: "it's like having had your everything amputated"—though Sobchack's own lived experience of an actual leg amputation leads her to add that her "enthusiasm for being a virtual 'no-body' is somewhat limited."[41] While critical of cyberpunk, this chapter also reveals the extent to which Sobchack was working from within the postmodern conception of new media and in some ways replicating its discourses on nonindexical formats.

Although Sobchack was responding more to print media than to film, critics of digital cinema have expressed a similar lack of enthusiasm for the virtual. In his 2012 chapter "Tracing an Ethics of the Moving Image," Markos Hadjioannou uses an existentialist approach to argue that, whereas traditional cinema allows the viewer to engage with the world through indexical images, digital cinema—as a mathematical, calculated, and nonindexical medium—cannot evoke the same kind of connection with the real. In his words:

> celluloid film links the viewer with the continuous powers of change that take place simultaneously across corporeal, spatial and temporal fields within reality. How, then, can the digital conjure up such an implicating relation to reality as a constant force of change when its own formal bond to reality is missing, or at least strongly deemphasized? How can the digital recreate the existential experience of film, thus emphasizing the subject's ability to respond to reality as an ethical implication?[42]

This is a genuine inquiry on Hadjioannou's part, not merely a series of rhetorical questions. Through a comparative reading of several Hollywood blockbusters of the digital age, such as *The Matrix* (dir. Lana Wachowski and Lilly Wachowski, 1999), along with several art films that utilized digital technology, such as Agnès Varda's *The Gleaners and I* (2000), Hadjioannou establishes some criteria for problematic versus ethical uses of digital cinema. A problematic use of digital cinema, such as that found in *The Matrix,* is one that "expresses the potential of an active involvement in the world in what seems like the total abandonment of any reality whatsoever in favor of an absolute digital control."[43] That is to say, digital media can engage viewers, but only in the use of more digital media. By contrast, he finds an ethical use of digital video in Varda's documentary film about "gleaning," the practice of collecting discarded food that would otherwise be wasted. In Varda's film, Hadjioannou argues, "the act of capturing images with a digital camera is [depicted in the film as] an activity through which the world is continually archived, through the immediate ability to glean images and to subsequently encounter the subject-world relation as a creative activity."[44] The key actions the digital camera performs here are *gleaning from* and *archiving* the world to allow creative engagement, an approach that is based more in the film's documentary techniques than in any property of digital media itself. So, despite the digital documentary's ability to "make possible different responses" to the world, Hadjioannou still concludes that "digital's mathematical codification or generation of an image of the world confronts the individual decisively with the abysmal absence of existence when she or he does not respond to the world, when involvement in reality is not an ethical response to living as the continual creativity of change."[45] Hadjioannou values films that demonstrate touch or contact with reality (literally, in Varda's case, the image of hands digging in the earth and finding a heart-shaped potato), a propensity that has precedents in Laura Marks's valuation of the indexical connection to touch in diasporic film and video. In his negative counterexample of *The Matrix,* however, Hadjioannou echoes Sobchack's critique of cyberpunk literature and postmodern theory in affirming that the digital format is nothing but information and that information is inherently disembodied.

While I do not contest the problematic nature of disembodiment discourses in postmodern theory, I do contest the ways in which Hadjioannou (and to some extent Sobchack, in her earlier work) slips into attributing disembodiment to the technology itself and not to the discourses that have developed around it. In *How We Became Posthuman,* Hayles illustrates "how information lost its body"[46] through a process that was as much discursive as it was technological. Hayles argues that "embodiment has been systematically downplayed or erased in the cybernetic construction of the posthuman" ever since Wiener declared that "information is information" and

Claude Shannon defined information as "a probability function with no dimensions, no materiality, and no necessary connection with meaning."[47] Hayles, however, wishes to "mix things up enough so that the emphasis falls not on the separation of matter and information but on their inextricably complex compoundings and entwinings."[48] In her view, "information, like humanity, cannot exist apart from the embodiment that brings it into being as a material entity in the world; and embodiment is always instantiated, local, and specific."[49] She is careful to avoid essentializing the body and making it a new universal. She draws a distinction between the body as an inscribed normative figure and embodiment as an "incorporating practice, an action that is encoded into bodily memory by repeated performances until it becomes habitual."[50] So, "in contrast to the body, embodiment is contextual, enmeshed within the specifics of place, time, physiology, and culture."[51] This argument echoes Donna Haraway's concept of "situated knowledges," which works to avert the patriarchal "god-trick" of "infinitely mobile vision," or the assumption of an all-seeing, masterful objectivity that claims access to the entire truth of the world, and instead takes "the view from a body, always a complex, contradictory, structuring and structured body, versus the view from above, from nowhere, from simplicity."[52] Likewise, Hayles emphasizes an "embodied knowledge"[53] of the material practices that are necessarily entailed in electronic and digital communication and that are elided by discourses that claim that we can live purely in the mind or as "information." The important point here is that the elision of the body is a function of the discourse of disembodied information, not an essential property of digital technology itself.

Through her critique, Hayles was among the first to signal the need for an alternative approach to posthumanism that emphasizes the mutually constructing nature of body and information, humanity, and technology. This approach was eagerly taken up by feminist theorists of film and digital media starting as early as 2001, when Ingrid Richardson and Carly Harper examined the new technologies of the internet and virtual reality as forms of "corporeal virtuality" dependent on a rich variety of situated, embodied knowledges, refuting the "digital disembodiment" discourses of Cartesian dualism and Gibsonian cyberspace alike. Tellingly, Richardson and Harper's article is directly inspired by Merleau-Ponty's concept of the "body-subject," as expanded upon by a host of authors working in intersectional and corporeal feminism.[54] This current of thought has only grown in the 2010s and early 2020s, as scholars living in a world dominated by labor precarity, pandemics, wars, and the climate crisis seek ethical ways of connecting media technologies and lived experiences of the world. As a result, they tend to pay more attention to nonindexical media like digital film and animation than have previous generations of scholars.

For example, Jennifer Barker's 2009 book *The Tactile Eye* applies Merleau-Ponty's theories of the flesh, reversibility, and perception to a wide range of cinematic examples, from the live-action films of Andrei Tarkovsky and Buster Keaton to the digital animations of Pixar Studios. The book proceeds through three levels of embodiment: skin, musculature, and viscera. In each chapter, Barker convincingly shows how film operates and engages audiences at the surface level of tactility, the muscular level of reaction and adaptation to the film's world (for instance, in Keaton's physical comedies), and the visceral level of hidden processes and intervallic movements. Although her baseline for understanding film's materiality is celluloid, as she writes of hairs caught in projector gates, she also considers animation and digital cinema at several points throughout the book.

Following Marks, Barker spends a large portion of the last chapter on stop-motion, especially the Brothers' Quay *Street of Crocodiles* (1986). She argues that in stop-motion, "the essential characteristic of cinema—its ability to represent apparently fluid motion—is exaggerated and intensified. In this sense, animation could be called cinema *par excellence*."[55] She does still privilege stop-motion over 2D cel animation in the very next sentence, arguing that "stop motion animation, *even more than cel animation*, draws our attention to the discontinuity inherent in cinema."[56] But she does admit that other animated media, even computer-generated imagery (CGI), can be tactile. In the chapter "Skin," she gives the brief example of *Toy Story* (dir. John Lasseter, 1995), where "both its nostalgic charm and its kid-appeal are inseparable from its tactile allure" in evoking the "smooth flatness" of army men or the "tumbling weight" of a coin in a piggy bank.[57] In her theory, then, indexicality is not necessary for tactility.

Barker also shows that digital films can create muscular engagement in their speed and movement, for instance, in the virtual camera movements of *Fight Club* (dir. David Fincher, 1999) or the swinging flight of Spider-Man. Here she argues that films like these in fact "transcend the world of human bodily potential for minutes at a time" and "mark an insurmountable difference between film's body and viewer's body, leaving us slack-jawed and amazed."[58] This discourse of transcendence might seem to echo the digital disembodiment discourse of other critics, such as Sobchack and Denson. But in the context of this chapter, digital cinema's ability to exceed the viewer's bodily limits is not essentially different from mounting a camera on a train, as was done in the 1890s Cinema of Attractions; that is, it is different in *intensity* but not in essence. And it does not mean that digital (or digitally inspired) films like *Run Lola Run* (dir. Tom Tykwer, 1998) cannot "exaggerate their own muscular limitations"[59] as well by imitating human stumbles, hesitations, and curiosities. Overall, Barker places animation, digital, and celluloid film on a much more level playing field than past critics have, providing a way of considering digital media and animation in light of embodiment theory.

That said, the most thoroughgoing book-length consideration of this topic as of 2022 is Sylvie Bissonnette's book *Affect and Embodied Meaning in Animation*. Drawing on both Merleau-Ponty and Deleuze, Bissonnette coined the term *becoming-animated* to describe "the idea that animation can bring out the permeability of our sensory boundaries and manifest our readiness to be extended by the interface."[60] Unlike Deleuze (but more like Merleau-Ponty), Bissonnette is not content to remain within the abstract realm of theorization and instead argues for the materiality of the senses and technology alike, applying concepts drawn from neuroscience to explain how we can feel motion that is only seen. She explicitly "distinguishes the embodied spectator from the abstract spectator of traditional film theory," arguing that "unlike abstract spectators, biological spectators experience animated media with their perceptual systems. From this perspective, the spectators construct meaning through their tangible engagement with the world viewed instead of decoding semantic cues that emerge from the cinematic text."[61] She goes on to argue that the perceptual system is shaped by the mechanisms of our nervous systems, including change-blindness, motor schemas, mirror neurons, and other neuroscientific explanations for the ways in which animated images have physical effects on viewers. In this regard, Bissonnette's work is on a continuum with both Merleau-Ponty's interest in Gestalt psychology and works like Torben Grodal's *Embodied Vision: Evolution, Emotion, Culture and Film*, which explains film spectatorship using the scientific discourse of evolutionary biology, and Dan Torre's *Animation—Process, Cognition and Actuality,* which usefully combines Deleuzian concepts and process philosophy with theories of cognition.[62]

While I admire the application of advances in fields like biology, psychology, and cognitive science to film spectatorship, I am ambivalent about applying discourses that privilege the brain or mind, and that are methodologically reliant on objectivity and systematized knowledge, to embodied, subjective, and immanent experiences. In the work of Haraway and Hayles, biology and computer sciences are discussed as knowledge systems that promote the "god-trick of vision" or the transcendent, disembodied viewpoint of the scientist or the philosopher, as we see in Butler's critique of Merleau-Ponty's uses of psychological case studies. I do not dispute the facticity of the accounts in Bissonnette's, Grodal's, and Torre's works, nor do I believe they themselves adopt the viewing position of the transcendent patriarchal scientist (far from it, especially in Bissonnette's case!). However, I seek another way into this problem through the path of immanence and experience—modes of knowledge that are traditionally looked upon with suspicion in academia but that can be upheld through the strategic application of queer and feminist phenomenologies of embodiment, along with a solid grounding in scientific research to avoid the solipsism of personal opinion.

Rather than seeking the common cause of our experience of film primarily in the structures of our brains or our evolutionary biology, I wish to argue that digitally animated imagery, as a combination of cinema and information technologies, engages audiences in a complex entwinement of physical behaviors, material platforms, intangible images, and imagined or remembered haptic and proprioceptive sensations that are unique to each lived experience. A similar argument has been made about film (though not animation) by Francesco Casetti, who argues that cinema has not "died" with the coming of digital platforms but has simply been "relocated" and presents a new kind of experience. He "use[s] the word relocation to refer to the process by which the experience of a medium is reactivated and repurposed elsewhere than the place in which it was formed, with alternate devices and in new environments."[63] The technological base certainly changes the kinds of actions in which we engage when watching a film, just as it changes the aesthetic traits and the range of experiences possible within any given image. However, change is not erasure. Embodiment does not disappear simply because we experience its screen presence in another way than was previously commonplace. Rather than going away, the body becomes *reanimated*—albeit sometimes in challenging ways, as I discuss at more length later.

A second way in which I diverge from some of the theorists introduced heretofore is in my approach to issues of representation and ethics. I do not believe an ethical stance on media representation can only be grounded in the indexical truth, as Hadjioannou suggests. That said, I must also acknowledge that digital media are not always or inherently helpful in addressing "real-world" issues, particularly where representation and identity politics are concerned. Existing hierarchies based on physical differences can be perpetuated through digital platforms in disturbingly exaggerated ways that are somehow rendered acceptable by their obvious artificiality. Through photorealistic digital retouching and filters in apps, highly sexualized and impossibly idealized bodies have become the norm for representations of straight, cisgender femininity in the mediasphere, as the most readily commodifiable form of fantasy embodiment. Racial representation in North American media even in the 2000s and early 2010s continued to be disproportionately in favor of historically white-coded styles of gesture and speech, even in animated works that use animal or robot characters as protagonists. Films that depict the idiosyncratic vision of independent producers or the experiences of marginalized peoples are still at a disadvantage in the "attention economy" of digital media, in which filtering algorithms, ad revenues, and corporate sponsorships determine what global audiences can access first and most easily. Despite Hollywood's recent efforts to include more Black, Indigenous, and Queer characters (among other marginalized identities), films that promote the commodification and manipulation of bodies for biopolitical purposes continue to be made as of the early 2020s. I address this in more detail in chapter 3, on "phenopower," or the shaping of our perceptions of embodiment for disciplinary purposes in live-action remakes of animated films.

In short, I feel I must address the ongoing issues of representation in mainstream commercial film if this book is to find any possibility of ethical engagement in a digital age. Of course, it is always possible to shift the focus to non-Hollywood works in a search for alternative examples of embodiment. Scott Richmond takes such an approach by focusing primarily on the experiences evoked by avant-garde works and the most experimental moments within commercial works like *Gravity* and *2001: A Space Odyssey* (dir. Stanley Kubrick, 1968). However, Richmond's approach also entails looking only at works or scenes that play with the proprioceptive experiences of embodiment, while "bracketing" issues of representation as peripheral.[64] Though bracketing is a foundational technique of phenomenology, and it may work well in more formalist studies, when it comes to considering audiences, it is just as problematic to bracket the representation of racialized, gendered, and otherwise stratified bodies as it is to focus too strongly on representation at the risk of reifying the dominance of mainstream commercial cinema's visual codes. This book will thus continue to give due consideration to the stylized representations of bodies depicted at the diegetic level in mainstream commercial cinema. However, it will also open up the range of possible perspectives to include nonmainstream and even noncinematic texts and characters, such as online music videos and virtual idols, from national contexts outside of the American mediasphere. This inclusive—though by all means not exhaustive—approach to selecting texts is meant to suggest, however partially, the range of embodied experiences that animation can provide both within and outside of dominant discourses and to attempt to describe the contexts in which new experiences become possible. This book does not bracket off "ugly feelings"[65] or "messy" issues of racial and gendered representation but instead tries to offer a range of different perspectives. However, I acknowledge that these perspectives will inevitably be filtered through my own positioning as an academic from the "Global North."

A third way in which I diverge from the theorists who have inspired me is in my refusal to privilege live-action cinema—and, in particular, the documentary genre—as the most grounded, ethical, and "real" medium for expressing embodied experience. In most studies of the film body (excepting Bissonnette's once again), animation is typically subsumed within practices of experimental or digital cinema or used as a figure of speech meaning "to bring to life," as in Sobchack's assertion that film's body functions to "*animate* perception."[66] I will happily take her figures of speech at their word, as they are quite evocative of what animation does in fact do, that is, bring perception to life. However, it is my overall contention that animation can make use of proprioceptive aesthetics and haptic visuality to evoke embodied experiences and encourage viewers to engage actively in the world, and so it deserves due consideration in the study of film phenomenology. To explain how animation has historically engaged with embodiment and look at how the approaches of analog animation have been relocated into digital media, it is necessary to turn to animation studies.

Animating the Body

In the academic subfield of animation studies, much scholarly work has been done on animated bodies using a huge variety of methodologies and disciplinary approaches—indeed, more than can be summarized here! Entire books and essay collections have been devoted to cultural studies–style analyses of race, gender, and class in Disney films alone.[67] Other authors draw on the disciplines of philosophy, psychology, or biology to consider the representation of bodies in works ranging from the Fleischer Brothers' Betty Boop series[68] to contemporary Japanese anime films like *Spirited Away* (dir. Hayao Miyazaki, 2001).[69] In terms of laboring bodies, scholars have also paid close attention to the material dimensions of the craft of animation and the ways in which they reflect bodily practices and technologies of production, from the hands of cameramen captured during cel photography to labor issues in motion and performance capture.[70] Many of these issues are considered in chapters 1, 2, and 3, which deal, respectively, with embodiment in cel, hybrid, and digital special effects animation.

That said, in this Introduction, I would like to engage with scholars who consider issues of media specificity, spectatorship, and perception from a phenomenological and Deleuzian perspective. One key scholar who addresses how we perceive objects and bodies in animated film is Suzanne Buchan. In her article "Animation Spectatorship: The Quay Brothers' Animated 'Worlds,'" Buchan ably demonstrates how the poetic stop-motion films of the Brothers Quay, which bring to life such diverse objects as screws, dandelion puffs, and porcelain dolls, can affect spectators deeply with their sensuous, haptic qualities. Crucially, Buchan does *not* depend on an argument that the sensuous qualities of the Quays' films are due to their indexical nature as stop-motion films based on photochemical impressions of existing objects. She refutes the notion that animation can or should depict a single objective "reality," as modernist thinkers like Stanley Cavell, author of *The World Viewed,* would have it. Instead, she draws on Merleau-Ponty to argue that animation does not depict "the" world but rather "a" world, one that we know to be impossible or inaccessible but that at the same time is not quite hyperreal or divorced from any reality whatsoever. According to Buchan, Merleau-Ponty gives an example of a man looking at a room in a mirror placed at forty-five degrees to him and imagining the virtual body that could inhabit the spectacle of that space. To give an example that is somewhat less philosophically freighted for cinema than the mirror, I can recall as a child lying with my head upside down over the edge of a couch or a bed and looking at the ceiling as if it were the floor of "a world" that I could explore. I could only go there through my virtual sense of my body moving around each light fixture or lintel because I could not, in fact, walk on ceilings. But the longer I looked, the more it seemed that I was somehow walking around, right side up, in the upside-down world above. This is similar to the experience of "a world" we have when immersed in a film. In Buchan's words, the Brothers Quay are particularly skilled at evoking "a cinematic world" that "allows us to experience spaces and haptically to possess material objects that, in our physical world, are inanimate, but through the 'special powers' of animation, are endowed with a semblance of life."[71] The power of these films, like the value of phenomenology according to Sartre, lies not in explicating levels of reality but in "allowing one to delineate carefully one's own affective, emotional, and imaginative life, not in a set of static objective studies such as one finds in psychology, but understood in the manner in which it is meaningfully lived."[72]

If the haptic visuality of the Quays' films is dependent not on an indexical connection to reality but on an affective and imaginative connection to embodied experience, then there is no reason why haptic visuality should not be present in digital animation. Consider, for instance, a digital animator like Chris Landreth, whose signature style of "psychorealism" literally embodies affective, emotional, and mental states in characters who *look* the way they *feel,* the way they should look in "a world" where inner experiences are fully externalized. This style is evident in his 2004 film *Ryan,* in which an animated version of Landreth interviews former National Film Board of Canada animator Ryan Larkin (Figure 2). The plastic and haptic qualities of his character's bizarre physical features, along with the narrative and conceptual dimensions of the films, give Landreth's

FIGURE 2. Visual embodiments of mental states in Chris Landreth's *Ryan* (2004).

work its visceral impact. Commercial CGI animation has also grown increasingly rich in textures and particle motions, some of which are mapped from photographed objects, others of which are wholly generated through mathematical algorithms that apply the laws of physics to moving objects within a virtual space.[73] These textures allow audiences to experience the same kind of imagined tactile engagement in a computer-animated world that they would find in stop-motion or, indeed, in live-action film.

That said, animation does not only impact audiences when it most closely imitates the haptic dimensions of cinema. As its own medium, animation presents various kinetic possibilities for delving into illusions of cinematic depth or playing with the flat, stylized planes of layered images. The complexities of animation as a medium are explored by Thomas Lamarre in *The Anime Machine: A Media Theory of Animation* and *The Anime Ecology: A Genealogy of Television, Animation, and Game Media*.[74] Together, these two books elucidate the effects of the production and distribution of animated media, mainly in a Japanese context. In *The Anime Machine,* Lamarre describes how technologies like the animation stand, the multiplane camera, and the processes of limited animation have led to the creation of "cinematic" and "animetic" styles of animation based on depth and flatness. In *The Anime Ecology,* Lamarre turns more to the ways in which distribution platforms like television impact audience reception, examining the "Brain-Screen Apparatus" by citing the case of the infamous

"Pokémon incident" of 1997 in which animated flashing lights caused seizures in susceptible viewers—a physically impactful encounter with animation if there ever was one!

Lamarre demonstrates that the material properties of the anime machine and the larger forces of the anime ecology are crucial for understanding the ways in which animation can be perceived. As I argue in chapter 1, the "movement through depth" that is a property of cinematic animation can enhance the viewer's somatic engagement with scenes of flying, floating, and falling, which are precisely the kinds of images on which Richmond focuses in his examination of proprioceptive aesthetics. An emphasis on textural density can also encourage experiences of haptic visuality, as Marks argued. However, the fact that cinematic animation can evoke embodied experience does not necessarily mean that the animetic style cannot. Embodiment is simply evoked in a different way, through surface and virtuality rather than depth and mimesis. As Lamarre notes:

> there is a long line of efforts to think in animation the disembodied mind—a ghost that can move from shell to shell. . . . If animation frets a great deal about the connection between the body and the soul, it is because the centrality of compositing—and this is where cel animation and digital animation continue to overlap and intersect—forces a confrontation with the animetic interval in the bodies of characters.[75]

When the animetic interval is strongly present, as in limited animation, it "tends toward the creation of 'soulful bodies,' that is bodies where spiritual, emotional, or psychological qualities appear inscribed on the surface."[76] In this passage, Lamarre draws a comparison between the animetic interval and Deleuze's theory of the time-image from *Cinema 2,* in which it is inaction, and not action as in movement-image-based films, that crystallizes the character's (and viewer's) experience of the flow of time.[77] In Lamarre's emphasis on the surface of the character, however, I also find an echo of the BwO as a plane or surface that enables the flow of desire. The connections between the layered or composited properties of the time-image and the BwO are drawn out more in chapter 4, on "reanimation" in electro swing music videos, and in chapter 5, on Hatsune Miku and the Vocaloid phenomenon.

What Lies Ahead

This book explores various forms of animated experience in the late twentieth and early twenty-first centuries. It is not limited to one national or cultural experience, though it is limited to the national cinemas with which I have the most cultural familiarity and linguistic facility, namely, North America, French-speaking European nations, and East Asian nations like Japan and China. To capture how embodiment may be expressed through the various styles, technologies, and spatiotemporal manifestations of animation, this work is organized in a loose progression through the dimensions of the image, from the flat, "2D" images of cel animation to the 3D modeling and stereoscopic projection of digital cinema and beyond to the temporal, multiplanar, and multidimensional aspects of new media arts, such as streaming video, "holographic" or "2.5-dimensional" virtual idol concerts, and immersive video art installations. In a way, this book moves from the most clearly material dimensions of animation to the most virtual or abstract in that it traces a path from hand-drawn works of cinematic animation that use haptic visuality to encourage spectator identification toward purely digital works that reflect on issues of time and virtuality. Following Deleuze, one might say there is a shift from movement-image to time-image, or from works based on sensorimotor actions to ones that use purely optical situations, throughout the book. However, I aim to show that embodiment, as a process of perception, does not vanish with this shift but only transforms in its potentials and manifestations.

In chapter 1, "Haptic Visuality in Cinematic Anime," I address how sensory experience can be evoked in 2D, hand-drawn cel animation. In particular, I examine the contrast Lamarre identified between the stylized "animetic" style of flat, layered Japanese anime and the realistic, "cinematic" style based on full animation, rounded character design, and "movement into depth" as pioneered in Golden Age Disney films and works by early Japanese animators like Seo Mitsuyo. Although the cinematic style of animation is sometimes associated with the transcendence of aerial views and bodiless camera movements, or even with the "ballistic vision of the camera" critiqued by Paul Virilio,[78] I argue that the cinematic style can also be used to highlight the immanence of embodied experience through what I term the *flesh of animation,* which dynamically connects visuality with haptic sensations like tactility and proprioception. As examples of this argument, I compare several East Asian coming-of-age fantasy films that evoke sensations of floating, falling, and (sometimes monstrous) physical transformations. Using the examples of *Howl's Moving Castle* (dir. Miyazaki Hayao, 2004), *A Letter to Momo* (dir. Okiura Hiroyuki, 2011), and *My Beautiful Girl Mari* (dir. Lee Sung-Gang, 2002), among others, I show how cinematic anime films, even those that depict mutable bodies and humanly impossible actions like magical flight, can engender a form of haptic visuality in that they convey through vision the body's tactile, proprioceptive, and motile senses using a combination of hand-drawn and computer-generated effects. This chapter defines the titular concept of the flesh of animation and lays the theoretical basis for examining other works that use supposedly "fantastic" or "unreal" imagery—that is, animated or digital images—to convey embodied experiences.

Chapter 2, titled "Liveliness in the Hybrid Film," complicates the previous chapter's exploration of cinematic animation by examining works that self-reflexively combine animation and live-action film. In contrast to films with a single unified style, such as the examples of cinematic anime in chapter 1, in chapter 2, I explore films that use heterogeneous or hybrid styles to create a sense of corporeal engagement between animal cartoon characters and human characters played by actors shot in live action. Examples include mainstream American films from before the digital age, such as *Song of the South* (dir. Harve Foster and Wilfred Jackson, 1946) and *Who Framed Roger Rabbit* (dir. Robert Zemeckis, 1988), along with independent productions of the late twentieth century, such as *Twilight of the Cockroaches* (dir. Yoshida Hiroaki, 1987) and *Joe's Apartment* (dir. John Payson, 1996). These examples demonstrate the relations between different kinds of bodies and worlds, which are foundational to phenomenological philosophy. However, they also create a kind of paradox in that they encourage viewers to build a narrative equivalence between lively animated characters and living human actors (that is, we think of humans and cartoons as equally "real" or "alive" within the film's diegesis), while highlighting the ontological disjunction between "real" people and "toons" (that is, we recognize that they are not made of the same "stuff," as the animated characters have different capabilities and material bases, both within the diegesis and in the practical production of the film). Often this disjunction is used to address ideas of racial or species-based segregation in ways that can be more or less problematic. As such, I argue that hybrid films can generate what Sianne Ngai calls "ugly feelings": ambivalent and highly embodied affects like envy, irritation, and (most importantly for this chapter) animatedness. The social impact of these films is not always positive, as some of them enable viewers to reaffirm deeply embedded racist and sexist stereotypes, as in the case of *Song of the South*. However, actively discussing hybrid animation as such can also make viewers aware of how such animatedness is constructed in ways that live-action filmmaking alone cannot do. As such, this chapter sets the stage for considering visual effects in live-action films to come in the following chapters.

Chapter 3, "Phenopower in Live-Action Remakes," considers a more contemporary approach to combining live-action and animated imagery in the trend for so-called live-action remakes of American and Japanese animated films and television series. Case studies in this chapter include Disney's live-action remakes of *The Lion King* (dir. Jon Favreau, 2019) and *Mulan* (dir. Niki Caro, 2020) as well as live-action adaptations of Japanese anime and manga by American studios, such as *Pokémon: Detective Pikachu* (dir. Rob Letterman, 2019). These films are based on the underlying idea that CGI animation, with its textural, physics-based, and hypernaturalistic qualities, can be seamlessly composited together with live-action footage to create what Stephen Prince has termed "perceptual realism," or "the replication via digital means of contextual cues designating a three-dimensional world."[79] Unlike hybrid films, these films create diegetic worlds in which there is no ontological difference between cartoon bodies and the bodies of live-action actors. While the lush texture mapping and "weighty" animated bodies in these films may seem to promote haptic visuality, this chapter argues that live-action remakes privilege the mainstream discourse that equates realism with (the appearance of) indexical cinema and elides the "anontological" quality of animated effects. As such, these films tend to approach bodies more as digital assets used to generate spectacle than as evocations of lived experience, as felt from the inside. The case studies of live-action remakes in this chapter demonstrate how mainstream digital animation can be used to perpetuate a form of sensory training that I describe as *phenopower*.

Chapter 4 is titled "Time and Reanimation in Electro Swing Music Videos." This chapter expands my consideration of 2D and 3D animation into the fourth dimension of time by looking at a contemporary media genre based on layering imagery from different eras, namely, electro swing music videos. Electro swing is a subgenre of electronic dance music that combines swing jazz and big band music from the 1920s–1940s with techno beats and digital editing from the 2000s and early 2010s. This chapter examines the ways in which the music videos created for electro swing songs remediate silent-era and Classical Hollywood animation and musical films. Electro swing videos create an uncanny sense of "lifedeath,"[80] as long-deceased actors and deathly cartoon characters of the 1920s–1940s, such as the skeletons from Disney's *The Skeleton Dance* (dir. Walt Disney, 1929), appear to "come back to life" and dance to techno beats. To explore this strange phenomenon, this chapter draws on Deleuze's concept of the time-image, which describes the layering and folding of time that take place in films that simultaneously evoke the past, the present, and the future. In particular, it focuses on the ways in which the human and inhuman dancers in electro swing videos reanimate silent-era and Classical Hollywood film in their bodily "gest," a form of movement that, in Deleuze's words, "puts the before and the after in the body."[81]

Chapter 5, "Virtual (Idol) Corporeality and the Posthuman Flesh," examines the global popularity of multidimensional media experiences, including those of popular 2.5D performers like the Japanese virtual idols known as Vocaloids and the installation works of Shanghai-born new media artist Lu Yang. These examples carry the visual or stylistic hybridity observed in earlier chapters to the "other side of the screen" in that they encourage physical audience interaction in "real-world" settings. The virtual idol Hatsune Miku, for instance, is commonly represented as a flat, 2D, anime-style *kyara,* or iconic character, but she also appears as a 3D "holographic" projection in concerts and can even inhabit fans' homes through various augmented reality devices and apps. Lu Yang's art installations of the 2010s also carry the body into posthuman dimensions as he creates vibrantly colorful, hypermediated installations in which participants can dance before a screen that translates their motions into the figures of Buddhist gods representing parts of the brain or play video games as *Uterus Man* (2013), a queer embodiment of the female reproductive organ. This chapter reads multidimensional media experiences through the philosophies of Deleuze and Merleau-Ponty to explore the shifts in consciousness and perceptions of the body that new media engender.

Through the course of these chapters, I show that digital animation is not a purely virtual or disembodied medium but possesses a body of its own, one that is cocreated through the labor of animators who produce anontological images, the technical apparatus of animation, the platforms of the media ecology, and the perceptions and embodied experiences of viewers, which are my primary focus. This chiasmatic interrelation is what I term the *flesh of animation.*

CHAPTER 1

Haptic Visuality in Cinematic Anime

In a famous thought experiment, medieval Islamic philosopher Avicenna (Ibn Sina) once imagined what would happen if a "Floating Man" were to come into existence without any awareness of his body. He wrote:

> One of us must suppose that he was just created at a stroke, fully developed and perfectly formed but with his vision shrouded from perceiving all external objects—created floating in the air or in the space, not buffeted by any perceptible current of the air that supports him, his limbs separated and kept out of contact with one another, so that they do not feel each other. Then let the subject consider whether he would affirm the existence of his self. There is no doubt that he would affirm his own existence, although not affirming the reality of any of his limbs or inner organs, his bowels, or heart or brain or any external thing. Indeed, he would affirm the existence of this self of his while not affirming that it had any length, breadth or depth. And if it were possible for him in such a state to imagine a hand or any other organ, he would not imagine it to be a part of himself or a condition of his existence.[1]

When this thought experiment was proposed in the early 1000s, it was an impossible situation imagined to demonstrate the independent self-awareness of the soul. However, by the 1980s and 1990s, similar states of existence without embodiment had been theorized and even reportedly experienced by postmodern philosophers, cybernetics researchers, and cyberpunk authors, who first imagined and then came to see the real-world development of cyberspace. "It's like having had your everything amputated," wrote one early "devotee" of cyberspace in the magazine *Mondo 2000*.[2] "Simulation is no longer that of a territory, a referential being or substance. It is a generation by models of a real without origin or reality: a hyperreal," wrote Baudrillard on the first page of *Simulacra and Simulation*.[3] "Information is information, not matter or energy," wrote Norbert Wiener forty years earlier in *Cybernetics; or, Control and Communication in the Animal*.[4] Although these authors do not affirm the existence of a transcendent, self-aware soul as Avicenna does, they do affirm a virtual space, a hyperreal, or a pure state of information that can exist in an immaterial form, infinitely mobile and transferrable, weightless, and disembodied.

At first glance, animation may seem to present a similarly abstracted, hyperreal state of being quite unlike the material, embodied state we inhabit in daily life. Fully developed cartoon bodies can be created "at a stroke" (or at least using lines or data points) by their animators, and they can be de-formed and re-formed, turned from one thing into another, or dismembered and reconstituted with impunity. Images of weightlessness, such as floating, flying, or walking on air, are also pervasive in animation, from Walt Disney's flying elephant Dumbo to Miyazaki Hayao's soaring heroines. At first glance, animated bodies may seem as abstracted as Avicenna's thought experiment of the Floating Man and as hyperreal as Baudrillard's conception of Disneyland, that is, "models of a real without origin or reality."[5]

That said, if we approach animation phenomenologically, then the gap between virtual and lived experience may not be as wide as it first appears. After all, an animated film is also a perceived phenomenon that results from material labor practices, just like other phenomena in this world. And film watching is also an experience in which we engage not just the distance senses of sight and sound but all the senses of the body. This chapter explains how embodied experience can be evoked by the medium that might seem the most removed from it: 2D cel animation, with its obviously stylized and artificial images. It does so by contemplating the balance between what Thomas Lamarre describes as the cinematic and animetic tendencies within the "anime machine" and, in particular, the cinematic tendency that evokes sensorimotor experiences like weight, balance, proprioception, and movement through depth in various ways, including depictions of floating, flying, and falling. Following Lamarre, I examine cinematic anime from Japan, looking specifically at coming-of-age fantasy films, such as Miyazaki's *Howl's Moving Castle* and Okiura Hiroyuki's *A Letter to Momo*. As a comparison, I also consider a South Korean animated film, Lee Sung-Gang's *My Beautiful Girl Mari.* These films all use a combination of hand-drawn cel animation and computer-generated effects, along with a mix of cinematic and animetic elements, to show young characters in liminal moments of transformation. They demonstrate the mutability and fantastic capabilities of the animated body, without losing touch with the kinds of embodied sensory experiences that viewers might experience in their own lives. They engender a form of haptic visuality, conveying through vision the body's tactile, proprioceptive, and motile senses, even as they highlight the "anontological" nature of animation as a medium based on the nonindexical apparatus of recording hand-drawn images frame by frame. These case studies thus illustrate what I am describing as the flesh of animation: an "indirect ontology" based on Merleau-Ponty's concept of *la chair,* or the "flesh," which ecological philosopher David Abram describes as "the mysterious tissue or matrix that underlies and gives rise to both the perceiver and the perceived as interdependent aspects of its spontaneous activity."[6] In these films, animation itself acts as the underlying tissue or (im)material network through which embodied experiences of the natural world are evoked in audiences. Though they are culturally specific and reveal imbalances in power between the animation industries of Japan and South Korea, these coming-of-age stories are linked by a common concern with burgeoning sensuous experiences of world and body.

The Flesh and/of Animation

If we are to think about animated films phenomenologically, it is important to recognize that the indexical, photochemical recording of living beings—that is, live-action cinema—is not the only means of conveying embodied sensation in cinema. As mentioned in the Introduction to this book, film scholars often associate Merleau-Ponty's work on cinema with neorealist and documentary styles of filmmaking, following the Bazinian tradition that valued the direct, objective, mechanical recording of reality. Some of this emphasis on the direct recording of the lifeworld or *Lebenswelt* derives from various film scholars' interpretations of the "father of phenomenology," Edmund Husserl, who believed that "if the intentional object exists, the intention, the reference, does not exist alone, but the thing referred to also exists."[7] Photochemical cinema, with its direct reference to an existing object in the world, has often been read as the phenomenological experience of film par excellence—hence the emphasis on documentary and live-action film in the works of phenomenological film scholars such as Laura U. Marks and on stop-motion animation in phenomenological studies of animation by scholars such as Suzanne Buchan and Jennifer Barker. In stop-motion, as in documentary, the haptic quality of the world is grounded in the material reality of the actual objects being photographed.

By contrast, Vivian Sobchack has pointed out that embodiment does not just go away when we enter the virtual world of CGI. In her article on Pixar's *WALL•E* (dir. Andrew Stanton, 2008), she argues that "each technology [used for animation] not only differently mediates our figurations of bodily existence, but also constitutes them. That is, each offers our lived bodies radically different ways of 'being-in-the-world.'"[8] For her, even a CGI character like WALL•E can embody the material, analog traces of cinema, demonstrated in the little robot's love of a classic Hollywood musical on videocassette and in the tactile appeal of his rusty, mechanical frame. Through digitally rendered images, Pixar's film places different senses on-screen for us to experience, visually and haptically. However, it is the evocation of indexicality that Sobchack most values, and at the end of the essay, she still concludes that "much as I find *WALL-E* easy to love, much as I admire its formal achievements and narrative complexity . . . , my preference in animated films has always been for those that visibly labor,"[9] such as Willis O'Brien's *King Kong* (1933) (which she prefers over Peter Jackson's 2005 CGI-animated version) and the works of Jan Svankmajer and the Brothers Quay. In short, she prefers animation that makes apparent the apparatus of the camera and the presence of indexical objects, such as puppets with visible marks of wear or use that strike us with their poignant imperfection. One might compare this to "the lacerating emphasis of the *noeme* ('that-has-been')" in Roland Barthes's concept of the "punctum" in photography.[10] Sobchack describes these noematic stop-motion films as "animation that speaks to its (and our) existence."[11] This perception of existence once again returns us to Husserl's *Lebenswelt* and Bazin's photographic ontology.

That said, the ways in which animation can speak to both its own apparatus and the lifeworld in which we are all enmeshed are rich and various, as Sobchack recognizes here and in some of her other work on animation. Placing too much emphasis on the noeme of cinema in stop-motion, as many scholars have done to date, overlooks the phenomenological potentials of the nonindexical image in cel-style and digital animation. As recent scholarship has shown, Merleau-Ponty himself did not base his theory of cinema on indexical images of existing things or even on a realist cinematic style. By contrast, he was sympathetic to formalist and montage-based film styles in which postproduction effects play a vital role. Daniel Yacavone, in an illuminating reinterpretation of the philosopher's 1964 article "The Film and the New Psychology," writes that

> Merleau-Ponty, by contrast [to Sobchack's emphasis on the cinematic apparatus and the photographic process of filming] directly associates the existential phenomenological possibilities of cinema with (a) the creative and transformative use of montage, and thus (b) the editing stage of filmmaking; (c) a fundamentally audiovisual presentation to the senses of viewers (in the case of the sound film); (d) presented and experienced time; and (e) overall cinematic rhythm—as all resulting in a highly (and necessarily) stylized presented world, "finer grained" and "more exact" than actual reality, and constituting (f) a perceptual, expressive, and distinctly aesthetic object-experience as the direct product of a filmmaker's artistic vision, choices, and intentions (including those related to narrative).[12]

Here we see that the evocative power of film lies not in its indexical photographic ontology or in capturing the existence of an object before the camera but in the editing stage, which today includes the addition of digital effects and animation. It is here that the audiovisual perception of the image is created through time, rhythm, and intention. Yacavone goes on to add that "phenomenological meaning or expression is instead an aesthetic potential of cinema, which certain features of the medium and its technology certainly may aid but, by definition, neither determine nor guarantee."[13] In support of his argument, Yacavone draws comparisons with Merleau-Ponty's writings on modern art. He notes the philosopher's admiration for the post-impressionist paintings of Cezanne, which "do not show how [objects] look at a given moment, in a single view, but how we construct what we regard as their independent reality from an indefinite, dynamic series of perspectival, spatiotemporally distinct views," allowing for the representation of "subjective phenomena . . . rather than things apart from, or following, this primary perception."[14] An ideal work of phenomenological cinema, then, might be described as one that evokes subjective experiences of the body and the world, even if that representation diverges from conventional realism and goes into the realm of stylization, including manipulations of perspective and unusually flattened, exaggerated, or multiplied points of view created through editing.

Whereas Merleau-Ponty's published work on cinema is minimal, his final philosophical project provides much fodder for film and animation scholars. In *The Visible and the Invisible,* a work left unfinished upon his sudden death in 1961, Merleau-Ponty sketched out his concept of the flesh or *la chair.* Here Merleau-Ponty does not use the term *flesh* to indicate the material human body, as in Cartesian dualist accounts that would divide the mind from the body; rather, he states that

> the flesh is not matter, is not mind, is not substance. To designate it, we should need the old term "element," in the sense it was used to speak of water, air, earth, and fire, that is, in the sense of a general thing, midway between the spatio-temporal individual and the idea, a sort of incarnate principle that brings a style of being wherever there is a fragment of being. The flesh is in this sense an "element" of Being.[15]

This point is reiterated a few pages later when he writes:

> Once again, the flesh we are speaking of is not matter. It is the coiling over of the visible upon the seeing body, of the tangible upon the touching body, which is attested in particular when the body sees itself, touches itself seeing and touching the things such that, simultaneously, as tangible it descends among them, as touching it dominates them all and draws this relationship and even this double relationship from itself, by dehiscence or fission of its own mass.[16]

As in Marks's concept of haptic visuality, the flesh entails a coiling over or intertwining of the visible and the tangible. It should be noted here that haptic visuality and the flesh are not immutable, universal properties of vision or touch, nor are they inherent properties of a particular type of film imagery. There is no guarantee that any given shot will always evoke the same sensation (or any sensation) for every viewer. For instance, a close-up of a hand stroking velvet, accompanied by a slightly rough brushing sound, might evoke sensations of smooth, luxurious softness or, for those with dry, rough hands, sensations of the ridges of one's fingertips catching against the fabric's fibers. The sensations that arise while viewing the image are created partly by the viewer and partly by the image, as cues within the image direct the viewer toward some sensations and rule out others. No one, upon seeing a shot of a hand touching velvet, is likely to imagine the touch of rusted metal or snail's slime. However, not everyone will touch the same velvet with their eyes because, just as the flesh is not matter, it is not literal, material velvet. It is the evocation of the perception of one's own hand touching velvet, born from each viewer's embodied experience of both their hands and the fabric of their world. As such, it is neither a predetermined code in which a given image will create a predictable reaction nor a mere effect of solipsistic subjectivity where each person wholly fabricates their own experience in their mind. Rather, the flesh is processual and relational, being based on a simultaneous mutual exchange between the perceiving subject and the perceived object, in which there is both a dehiscence (splitting) and an intertwining of the senses. As such, the flesh can be described as a "chiasm": a point of crossing over, comparable to the Deleuzian baroque fold.[17] What is most significant here, however, is that the flesh is not purely matter nor purely mind but a category of experience that bridges the subjectively perceived individual self embedded in its particular space and time and imaginative mental perceptions like abstract ideas, daydreams, or fantasies. Abram describes daydreaming as an "intersubjective phenomenon," using Husserl's term designed to avoid the critiques solipsism leveled against his earlier iterations of transcendental phenomenology based on "a wholly mental dimension, an immaterial field of appearances."[18] For Merleau-Ponty, likewise, the flesh is not simply the objective body, nor our fully subjective imaginary experiences of the body, but (as mentioned earlier) "the mysterious tissue or matrix that underlies and gives rise to both the perceiver and the perceived as interdependent aspects of its spontaneous activity."[19] This can be referred to as an "indirect ontology" because it hinges not merely on existence but on the *perception* of what exists (both objectively and subjectively), a perception that necessarily takes place as a mutually creating and reversible feedback loop between the perceiver and the perceived.

When it comes to film and spectatorship, animation introduces an element of *anontology* into the chiasmatic relations of the flesh. In *The Animatic Apparatus,* Deborah Levitt introduces the concept of the "an-ontology" of animation. In her work, "an-ontology" (or anontology, as I will spell it henceforth) is somewhat similar to Suzanne Buchan's concept of "a world": it is a way of being with no grounding model or physical real, "no necessary limiting features, no essential finitude."[20] This is based on the animatic quality of animation, where "the animatic is any aspect of image production—from animation as such, to digital special effects to extreme camera angles—that does not deploy the cinematic reality effect of the index . . . as it produces a pro-filmic real."[21] Animation is anontological because it is not indexical and there is no death; rather, "everything is shadowed by its possible metamorphosis, erasure, and resurrection—there is thus no ontology."[22] What there is, however, is a relation between the "Body-as-Image" and the "Image-as-Body," in which each mode influences and mutually creates each other. A similar argument can be found in Sylvie Bissonnette's *Affect and Embodied Meaning in Animation,* in which she coins the term *becoming-animated* to describe "the idea that animation can bring out the permeability of our sensory boundaries and manifest our readiness to be extended by the interface."[23] These are all excellent conceptual tools that I will also employ when speaking of the specific theories, concepts, and examples that these authors use. For the purposes of this study, however, I return to Merleau-Ponty's term to describe the "flesh of animation," not solely in terms of ontology or anontology, nor in terms of the physiological processes of mirror neurons and motor schema set out in Bissonnette's neurobiological account, but as an experience that is "midway between the spatiotemporal individual and the idea,"[24] that is, a chiasmatic relation between the individual viewer's body, the fantastic or virtual animated bodies the viewer inhabits as they watch, and the medium of animation itself.

The Cinematic and the Animetic

Having laid the groundwork for understanding the flesh, I would now like to turn to animation and, in particular, East Asian anime, which will be the focus of the case studies in this chapter. In pop culture and the art world alike, anime has become associated with the "superflat" style of matte colors, bold outlines, and exaggerated or stylized bodies capable of humanly impossible feats. Western animation, on the other hand, has been linked to a persistent drive toward realism or, as Paul Wells calls it, "hyperrealism,"[25] born from the classic 1940s Disney style of cinematic depth of field and naturalistic body movements based on life drawing and rotoscoping from recorded footage. However, it is a false opposition to say that all anime is superflat, while all American animation is hyperrealistic. In *The Anime Machine,* Thomas Lamarre notes that Japanese anime contains at least two stylistic tendencies: the animetic, which features flattened, stylized, planar movement, and the cinematic, based on movement into depth. Importantly, these are *tendencies,* not essential properties of a given nation or media technology. American animators may take the historical credit for inventing the rotoscope and the multiplane camera, but Japanese animators from the 1940s, such as Seo Mitsuyo, and onward have also created cinematic anime films with striking depth and naturalism. Furthermore, the cinematic is not itself a monolithic concept opposed to the animetic but is rather a complex approach to space and physicality that supports internal contradictions and aesthetic mixes, much like the flesh described earlier. In fact, it has been explained in different ways by theorists who have noted similar tendencies but frame their arguments differently.

In a 2002 article, Thomas Looser theorizes an opposition between what he calls the cinematic and the "anime-ic." The cinematic form, he argues, is dominated by an urge toward panoramic vision, like the vista of a city viewed through a telescope, which "implies a spectatorial distance from that which is meaningfully ordered . . . that which is distanced from the observer [and] can be seen with stability and clarity. Distance and depth thus allow for a static, meaningful order (distance and depth allow certainty of place that provides stability of meaning)."[26] He finds evidence of this style of vision in Japanese literature and film as early as the 1920s and 1930s. The anime-ic, on the other hand, is not bound to the optical perspectives of the lens or indexical photography. Animation can be composed of "multiple layers, consisting of mixed styles and mixed media each with their own particular orientations, brought together on a single plane without any one point of origin that would fix the relations between them."[27] Anime achieves this by drawing on the flattened perspectives of Japanese artforms like *ukiyo-e* woodcuts. However, while Looser finds moments of anime-ic flatness in Miyazaki's work, like the tapestry shown under the opening credits of *Nausicaä of the Valley of the Wind* (1984), he argues that "for the most part . . . Miyazaki is careful to provide three-dimensional perspective" and "maintains a camera-like point of view throughout most of the movie."[28] Miyazaki's work thus serves as an example of cinematic anime.

A similar, but differently articulated, argument can be found in *The Anime Machine,* in which Thomas Lamarre argues that cinematic anime are those that rely on "movement into depth."[29] Like Looser, he aligns cinematism with Cartesian perspectivalism and distanced subjectivity. But instead of focusing on a static viewpoint, Lamarre draws on Jean-Louis Baudry's critique of the mobility of the camera as "a disembodied eye, an eye unfettered by a body, shoring up the illusion of a transcendent subject who stands over and above the world, separate from it."[30] He also references the work of Paul Virilio to argue that this subject is not just transcendent but aggressive, because it is aligned with the ballistic vision of the camera, a perspective comparable to a missile's line of sight. By contrast, the animetic draws attention to movement across the planes of an image, especially the multilayered surfaces of the cels that make up animation. While Miyazaki favors cinematism overall, Lamarre also notes that in some parts of *Nausicaä* "Miyazaki clearly prefers animetism over cinematism. He favors the sliding sensation of speed. . . . He avoids both linear progressive movement and cyclical regressive movement. . . . At every level he strives to produce animetism, not cinematism."[31] Basically, Lamarre and Looser both argue that *Nausicaä* is a film with some cinematic and some animetic tendencies.

In recent years, other scholars have expanded this discussion of the relations between animetic and cinematic tendencies in anime to include what Crafton has termed "figurative acting" in animation based on the repetition of conventional codes and "embodied acting" based on individualized gestures that physically express a character's psychology.[32] For instance, Stevie Suan notes in his book *Anime's Identity* that "embodied and figurative performances are not opposites but tendencies that go in different directions . . . with each tendency keeping traces of the other in each performance."[33] So, following Looser, Lamarre, and Suan, the question now becomes, what are these tendencies *doing*? How do cinematic and animetic bodies, or figurative and embodied performances, interrelate in animated coming-of-age feature films? And do those images confirm or disrupt the kind of optically created transcendental subject cinematism is supposed to create?

I would like to make a start on answering these questions by giving an example from Miyazaki's film *Howl's Moving Castle,* which uses a predominantly cinematic style to explore themes of flight, movement, and transformation that draw the viewer into "a world" of haptic sensation. This film depicts the journey of an eighteen-year-old hatmaker, Sophie, who is transformed into an old woman by the jealous Witch of the Waste. She is taken in by the wizard Howl—or, more accurately, by his moving castle, which is "animated" by the fire demon Calcifer—and initially joins the castle staff as a cleaner and cook. Over the course of the film, she becomes a mother figure to Howl's young assistant Markl and a confidante and eventual lover to Howl himself. The wizard has his own dilemmas as he tries to avoid being pressed into service as a monstrous living weapon in a war between the heads of two rival countries, both of whom he serves under different aliases. Lamarre points out that Miyazaki's later films have been received as more technologically "deterministic and less nuanced"[34] than his earlier works, and at some points in *Howl's Moving Castle,* we do get a direct association between technology, warfare, and ballistic vision.

In *Affect and Embodied Meaning,* Bissonnette analyzes several scenes from this film in which bird's-eye-view shots of Howl flying over the city in flames are cut with point-of-view shots of the burning buildings, establishing "a sense of empowerment over the situation by simulating a totalizing gaze."[35] Bissonnette links such shots directly to Virilio's ballistic vision and Lamarre's cinematism. Although she goes on to argue that the function of these scenes is to "align the viewer with Howl's perspective" and to "strengthen the exchange between spectators and the protagonist," there are also scenes in which, as Lamarre says, "the eye becomes one with the bomb, and everywhere in the world becomes a target."[36] As I noted in a presentation delivered in 2014 at the Society for Cinema and Media Studies conference, there is at least one literal instance of ballistic vision in this film, in a sequence in which Howl, in his monstrous avian combatant form, saves Sophie from a barrage of incoming missiles. Here dozens of blunt-nosed missiles are shown from a low angle, as if falling down from above against a menacing, smoke-filled sky. The camera then cuts to an image of Sophie shot from a high angle, staring up in terror at the bombs. The next shot shows Howl swooping down from above to save them. One could assume that the point-of-view shot is Howl's view of Sophie as he swoops down to block the incoming missiles, as in the earlier scene Bissonnette describes where subsequent shots confirm a subjective shot to be Howl's view of the burning city. However, for a viewer who is caught up in the moment (especially during their first time watching the film), it seems just as likely that the subjective shot looking down on Sophie is from the *bombs'* point of view. Indeed, at this point in the film, Howl himself has become engulfed in his own spell and subsumed in his role as a weapon, in a commentary on the ways in which participating in warfare, even for righteous reasons, can corrupt the soldier. His dark gray coloration, pointed tail feathers, and angle of descent match the color, shape, and trajectory of the missiles almost exactly (Figure 3). As a result, the point-of-view shot in this sequence hovers ambiguously between technological vision and character vision, placing the audience halfway between identifying with the protagonist and—in a dangerous moment of ambivalent power—identifying with the weapons themselves and the technological apparatus they represent. In the age of drone technology, where both stunning aerial cinematography of landscapes and bombs that destroy those landscapes are delivered by the same mechanical means, such smooth, unfettered movements through depth take on an even more sinister air.

That said, Drew Ayers argues in his book *Spectacular Posthumanism: The Digital Vernacular of Visual Effects* that even drone cams do not perforce create a destructive form of ballistic vision. Looking at nature documentaries based on drone footage, he asserts that they can promote "an ecological form of humanism, using nonhumans to facilitate the production of human affect"[37] and encourage the protection of nature (however complex and potentially problematic this approach may be). *Howl's Moving Castle* also offers an alternative vision of flight than the ballistic point of view. Alongside technological motion, we also have a kind of magical mobility that is created not

FIGURE 3. Visual parallels between Howl and the missiles create ballistic vision in *Howl's Moving Castle* (2004).

just visually but haptically, enabling an escape from the gravity of war through movements of floating and weightlessness. This occurs much earlier in the film when Howl rescues Sophie from a group of frightening blob-men controlled by the Witch of the Waste, leading to an iconic sequence in which Howl literally sweeps her off her feet and takes her on a magical stroll through the air above town.

The visual style in this scene still tends toward the cinematic, as described by Looser and Lamarre. To start, a fast tracking shot down a narrow alleyway creates a strong sense of movement into depth through linear perspective. Once the virtual camera soars up out of the alley and into an aerial shot of the town, the perspective between buildings in the midground and tiny little people in the distant background is maintained in a unified way. The viewers, along with Sophie, are snatched out of obscurity and given a perspective that is above and away from everything: a transcendent point of view. And yet, it is *not* a disembodied sensation. The movement depicted is not one of flying straight ahead like an airplane: it is specifically a sort of buoyant gait, as if walking underwater. Sophie still has to move her own feet. She keeps her legs curled up protectively underneath her body at first, and her motions are hesitant. There is a moment of uncertainty, even vulnerability, before the walk begins. This creates a sense of embodiment that is fantastic yet somehow familiar: the process of learning to move in new ways within a new environment. We can clearly see Sophie going through the stages of apprehension, tentative testing, and growing confidence as she lowers her feet and begins to stroll through the air in Howl's arms, matching his bounding steps. By the end, their graceful, weightless movements are evocative of a dance, an impression strengthened by the lilting orchestral waltz that rises on the soundtrack. The proprioceptive aesthetics of weightlessness here point us away from the optics of animation's virtual camera-eye and toward a haptic experience of the embodied world, half-imagined, half-remembered—a "style of being" that reflects lived experiences of balance and weight in the form of an idea brought to life in a fantastic, impossible, yet familiar image. As an alternative to ballistic vision, it points us toward the flesh of animation, and that is the direction toward which the rest of this chapter travels.

The Floating Girl in *A Letter to Momo*

The films of Studio Ghibli are among the most frequently studied anime features, particularly when it comes to depictions of realism, the natural world, and gendered bodies.[38] While Studio Ghibli is the most highly visible producer of films with such themes, it is not the only studio to make skillful use of anime's cinematic tendencies when creating fantastic or magical-realist imagery. Other cinematic anime films of equal caliber from East Asia have not received as much attention as English-language scholarship. In the following sections, I consider one alternative case study of cinematic anime from Japan, *A Letter to Momo,* and one example of an animated film from South Korea, *My Beautiful Girl Mari.* These two coming-of-age fantasies will allow us to explore both the cultural and national grounding of each film's expressions of embodiment, as well as their shared appeal to sensory and tactile experience.

Compared to Studio Ghibli's releases, *A Letter to Momo* did not receive much mainstream media coverage outside of Japan after its premiere at the Toronto International Film Festival on September 10, 2011. Scholarly considerations of this film have been even more lacking. However, it deserves wider recognition as an example of cinematic anime that retains a commitment to a painterly, rather than photographic, visual style. It was directed by Okiura Hiroyuki, best known as the director of *Jin-Roh: The Wolf Brigade* (1999) and as a key animator on such acclaimed films as Ōtomo Katsuhiro's *Akira* (1988) and Kon Satoshi's *Paprika* (2006). Along with directing *A Letter to*

Momo, Okiura developed the script and drew highly detailed storyboards for the film in between other projects. It ultimately took seven years to complete. The animation was done at Production IG studio by a seasoned staff of animators and designers renowned for their "mature, cinematic realism."[39] These included key animation supervisors Ando Masashi (former character designer for Studio Ghibli) and Inoue Toshiyuki (key animator on *Akira*), art director Ono Hiroshi (background artist on Miyazaki's *Kiki's Delivery Service* [1989]), animation director Kusumi Naoko (key animator on Oshii Mamoru's *Ghost in the Shell 2: Innocence* [2004]), and color designer Mizuta Nobuko (who worked with famed Studio Ghibli color designer Yasuda Michiyo on Miyazaki's *My Neighbor Totoro* [1988]). As a sentimental family comedy and drama, *A Letter to Momo* is certainly a departure from Okiura's dark, violent, and politically complex *Jin-Roh.* However, it was familiar territory for many of the animators, who had worked on other features with similar cinematic tendencies. In the end, the creative contributions of the entire staff combined produce a richly textured animated film that draws on both contemporary Japanese life and traditions of animistic folklore.

In terms of narrative, the film follows an eleven-year-old girl named Momo whose father has died in an accident at sea. The only thing Momo has left of him is a letter he began writing to her, with the words "Dear Momo" at the top and nothing else. As the film opens, Momo is moving with her mother Ikuko from Tokyo to an island in the Seto Inland Sea called Shiojima, a quasi-fictional setting based heavily on the island of Osaki Shimojima off the coast of Hiroshima prefecture. There they stay with Ikuko's aunt and uncle in an old, traditional villa. Momo is left alone in her new home for much of the day while her mother takes summer courses. However, she is not alone for long. After discovering a book of Edo-period prints of monsters in the attic, Momo begins to hear strange sounds and voices in the house. She soon discovers that three otherworldly creatures have appeared in the attic, looking exactly like the monstrous "goblins" (in the English translation) or *yōkai* illustrations from the ancient book she found. The creatures call themselves "Iwa" (Rock), "Kawa" (River), and "Mame" (Bean), and they are incorrigible troublemakers with no respect for anyone else's privacy or personal property. Remaining invisible to everyone but Momo, they wreak havoc in the village by stealing food from the farmers, fighting with wild boars, and taking any item that happens to catch their eye, from a child's yellow raincoat to Ikuko's sentimental hand mirror. To maintain the peace, Momo must learn to work with the yōkai, who have a deeper connection to her deceased father than expected.

A Letter to Momo is hardly the first anime to represent Japanese folktales through animation. Mischievous yōkai have been represented on-screen since the 1920s and 1930s, initially appearing in numerous short films featuring haunted houses and forest-dwelling monsters. For instance, in the 1935 short *Ban Dan'emon's Monster Hunt at Shōjōji (Shōjōji no tanuki-bayashi ban dan'emon)* by Kataoka Yoshitarō, a famed samurai named Ban Dan'emon breaks into a haunted house to find a beautiful woman captured by a monster. What follows is a classic narrative reversal found in many traditional yōkai stories: as the hero watches, the damsel's lovely face melts like wax to show a hideous, inhuman face beneath (Figure 4). This moment of upset, in which the apparent victim becomes the menacing monster, uses a visible transformation to depict the slippage between the ordinary and supernatural worlds, a core feature of the fantastic tale both in the West and in Japan.[40] It is not a cut from human to inhuman but an animated morphing effect that highlights mutability. According to Michael Dylan Foster, "the notion of mutability provides an important key to the ontology of the mysterious" in yōkai stories.[41] Ideas of deception, doubt, instability, and transformation appear in every Japanese term for monsters, including *yōkai,* which is made up of two characters meaning "doubt" or "suspicion": *bakemono,* which means "changing thing," and *mononoke,* which Foster translates as "the instability of the thing."[42] In Kataoka's short film, the body of the yōkai woman is rendered visibly unstable, and it is the power of cel animation, with its animetic slippage between layers, that lets the transformation become manifest on-screen. As Sergei Eisenstein observed in the 1940s, metamorphosis is at the heart of both animation and the yōkai illustrations found in Japanese woodblock prints, so they are a natural combination.[43] It is no wonder, then, that metamorphosis and monsters have been linked in subsequent films from later decades, such as Isao Takahata's *Pom Poko* (1994), which featured *tanuki* (racoon dog spirits) that not only switch from wild animals to cuddly protagonists but transform visually from naturalistic creatures into animetic or "iconic" caricatures.[44] The transforming body is thus at the heart of Japanese anime, especially when yōkai are the subjects.

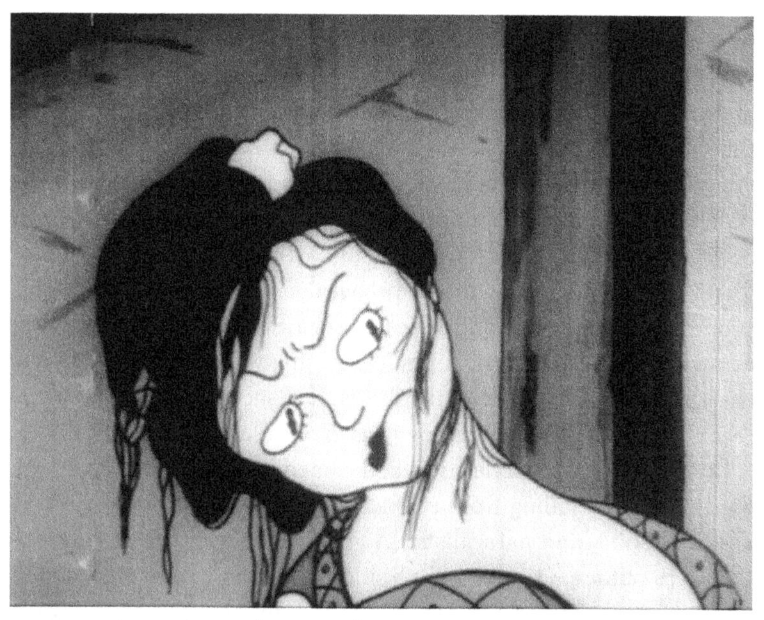

FIGURE 4. Plasmatic transformation from woman to monster in the early anime short film *Ban Dan'emon's Monster Hunt at Shōjōji* (1935).

Like its cinematic forebears, *A Letter to Momo* shows creatures that have the ability to transform their bodies. The opening aerial shots of the film follow three round, liquid shapes falling through the clouds from a great height. They have irregular, constantly changing edges and appear at the start more like abstract, liquid-patterned geometrical shapes than like representations of identifiable objects. After a few seconds, the camera plunges past them to dive into a very solid and carefully animated world: a sparkling ocean, lush green islands, a ferry full of cars seen from high above, and finally, our heroine, Momo, with the titular letter in her hand. The three drops of water, one large, one medium sized, and one small, fall onto her head, then roll away like balls of mercury. These drops will become the three yōkai: large Iwa, medium-sized Kawa, and tiny Mame. Their initial depiction as liquid forms introduces the traditional associations between yōkai, metamorphosis, and the plasmatic body, as they are literally little balls of primal protoplasm. The audience is also placed in a state of doubt and uncertainty as to what the yōkai really are throughout the film. They initially tell Momo that they came out of an Edo-period picture book of yōkai in the attic, where they were imprisoned by an ancient lord. However, it is clear from the opening shot of the film that they have actually fallen from somewhere above the earth and crawled into the book after their arrival. Later, they claim to come from somewhere that they call the "Sky," an equivalent of heaven complete with divine rules and punishments, though without being bound to any specific set of religious tenets. So, it seems these beings have come to Earth on behalf of an obscure force of divine justice and that they have taken on forms that seem appropriate for accomplishing their task, using the pictures in the book as models for their physical bodies. In this way, the unpredictable changeability of the traditional yōkai is introduced but also somewhat recontained through a cosmology based on rules and order.

In terms of visual style, as well, the opening shot of the film shows the three yōkai falling from plasmatic abstraction into a world that is stable, solid, and naturalistic. A great amount of care and attention were put into rendering the world of the film in evocative detail. True, it opens with a view of the islands from above, seen in a vast, transcendent aerial panorama, but the perspective quickly shifts, moving closer to give us a more intimate view of the world through haptic visuality. In a "making of" documentary included with the film's American DVD release, Okiura points out that the deck of the ferry where Momo stands was carefully textured to match the rough, grainy antislip paint of the actual ferry on which he sailed while doing research in the Seto Inland Sea area. The backgrounds in general are lush, deep, and painterly, with computer-generated 3D modeling used for architecture in exterior scenes of the town and softer, paper-grained painted backgrounds for scenic views of the Seto Inland Sea. Okiura mentions in the same documentary interview that he wanted to attain a kind of beauty in these nature scenes that is not possible with digital imaging—that is, an organic beauty created with physical paint on paper. So, both the textures of the world that Okiura experiences and the material media with which it was created are on display at various points in the film.

Character action is handled with equal care and commitment to realism. When Momo's hair and clothing blow in the wind of the ferry's passage, each lock of her hair or fold of her skirt moves independently on its own course. As Ikuko gets off the ferry, the weight of her long skirt, the drape of the fabric, and how it sways against the backs of her legs as she walks all combine to evoke the small and often overlooked tactile sensations of life. Each character has her own style of movement, expressed through embodied acting. Significantly, these motions are not created using cycles, a technique in which the same few frames of hair or cloth going back and forth are repeated multiple times so that animators can conserve their time and labor for more demanding sequences. In *A Letter to Momo,* even the smallest motions are rendered in full animation with close attention to the flow of movement. And because the plasmatic beings from the Sky enter into this naturalistic world, they take on a naturalistic form.

Looking closer at how the metamorphic yōkai take on solid bodies in the human world, let us consider the scene in which Momo first encounters them. This pivotal scene takes place in a Shinto shrine in a forest during a thunderstorm, where Momo is sheltering from the rain. As in *Ban Dan'emon's Monster Hunt at Shōjōji,* it is a moment of revelation in which the ordinary becomes supernatural. Unlike the visible metamorphoses of the prewar short, however, this transformation takes place through a transitional process of light and shadow. The yōkai do not transform from, say, statues into creatures. Instead, they shift from amorphous shadows to solid beings when a flash of lightning reveals them, in a literal trick of the light (Figure 5). Although they may seem like illusions at first and remain invisible to the villagers, the audience quickly learns along with Momo that they are decidedly solid, with their own physical mechanics and naturalistically moving bodies. When the yōkai eat a bowl of green mandarins left as a shrine offering, Iwa tosses them into his perpetually wide-open mouth with a fleshy, mobile tongue, and the folds of Kawa's gullet convulse as he swallows, his scalp moving under his hair with the working of his jaw. These shots help the audience feel, on an intuitive, prereflective level, that the yōkai are not just immaterial spirits or figments of Momo's imagination but physical beings who interact with the solid objects in Momo's world. In the final shot of this scene is a surprisingly beautiful image of Mame's foot and the hem of his yellow slicker framed beside a still life of spilled mandarins glistening in the rain, as if to say, yes, the yōkai are real, and they are hungry!

The impact of the yōkai's hunger and the way their invisible yet tangible bodies affect the human world become the key sources of conflict for the rest of the film. The very weight of their existence

FIGURE 5. The yōkai "transform" from shadowy figures to embodied beings through the revelation of lighting in *A Letter to Momo* (2011).

impacts the villagers and alienates Momo from others in the village. For instance, when Iwa gets tired of walking home, he sits on the back of a delivery man's motorcycle, causing the vehicle to sink under his weight—much to the puzzlement of the poor driver! More seriously, the fact that Momo must constantly police a gang of rowdy yōkai causes her to break promises to meet new friends and makes her seem "crazy" in others' eyes as she screams or pulls at nothing. And yet, the disturbance the yōkai cause comes, not from supernatural tricks or transformations, as in yōkai legends, but from their physical existence in a physical world. As they become more integrated, the yōkai's body language even mirrors that of humans. For instance, when Kawa settles in to watch television, he casually lounges on the tatami mat in a comic imitation of an ordinary man watching baseball. Visually, the yōkai lose their plasmatic, transformative abilities. As the film progresses, they are increasingly tamed by the narrative as well.

As one might imagine, the yōkai that at first drive Momo to distraction turn out to have some endearing and helpful qualities. They are fun loving where she is sullen and sad. They open her eyes to the natural beauty of the landscape around her. Finally, they also have a higher protective purpose. Directly after the scene of the encounter in the shrine, Momo runs home soaking wet and is taken in by her grand-uncle. As she warms up over a cup of tea, she notices a scroll above the door with pictures of yōkai. Her grand-uncle then casually tells her that his father collected these images of beings he called "Guardians" (O-mamori-sama) and even claimed to see them. It is a family secret, and Momo is cautioned against telling it to anyone else. Significantly, however, this mention of the Guardians foreshadows a kind of reverse transformation of the yōkai. Instead of being attractive humans who turn into monsters, like the lovely lady in *Ban Dan'emon's Monster Hunt at Shōjōji*, the initially grotesque yōkai are narratively transformed into protective beings with a connection to family tradition. They link Momo to both her mother's side of the family and her deceased father. As it turns out, they did not find their way to Momo by accident but were sent to Earth by the soul of her still-protective father to watch over her and send reports about her well-being back up to him in the Sky. In this way, the film deals with transformation of the kind that Foster claims underlies yōkai stories at their deepest level: the transformation of humans in the afterlife or the question of what becomes of us after death and how the influence of the dead persists for the living. However, there is also a reassertion of lost paternal authority, exemplified by a girl's attempt to regain the stability of a past based on her father's approval and protection. In the service of stability, the yōkai are also reined into a traditional protector role. They are turned from troublemakers into do-gooders who succeed by following the rules of an unseen authority in the Sky that demands that they watch out for Momo, even though they admit to her that they would much rather be sucking humans' livers out through their mouths. In this way, the yōkai are tamed through a "frame of reassurance," like the ones that recontain the supernatural's transgressive potential in many tales of the fantastic.[45]

It might seem, after all this, that *A Letter to Momo* is ultimately patriarchal and conservative in its political orientation in that it contains the transformative power of the yōkai and reaffirms the power of a transcendent, disembodied father-in-the-Sky over his wife and daughter on Earth. However, the final scene of the film does not place Momo back in the traditional home together with her surviving family but rather emphasizes Momo's own personal growth and bodily experience using an image of floating. In an epilogue to the main narrative, the final scene shows how Momo finally works up the courage to do something she has been too afraid to attempt since early in the film: jumping off a bridge into the water with the other children of Shiojima. Once she has overcome her grief, fear, and alienation by resolving the loss of her father, she is finally free to jump back into living her own life. Although this is still a fairly pat ending, it is beautifully rendered in terms of haptic visuality and the aesthetics of proprioception. A low-angle shot from below the surface shows Momo plunging into the water in a rush of bubbles, then drifting slowly up toward the surface. Unlike Avicenna's Floating Man, this image of a floating girl is not a disembodied one. It is profoundly evocative of the sensations of motion through water: exhilaration, breathlessness, buoyancy, and drifting serenity. The yōkai may be gone, returned to their liquid forms, but Momo's embodied engagement in the sensory world—and the audience's imaginative, haptic experience of that world through her—continues to change and evolve. Along with providing narrative resolution, this final floating scene shows how the lifeworld of embodied experience can be perceived through the elemental quality of fluid transformation that defines both yōkai and the flesh of animation.

The Haptic and the Animetic in *My Beautiful Girl Mari*

So far, I have discussed how the cinematic tendency in anime can be used to evoke embodied sensations. Now, as an alternative example, I would like to consider a film that relies more on the animetic tendencies within feature film animation, even as it evokes subjective, haptic sensations of embodiment. This example is Lee Sung-Gang's debut film *Mari iyagi* (The story of Mari), translated into English as *My Beautiful Girl Mari*. Like *A Letter to Momo*, it is a coming-of-age tale that reflects on themes of childhood loss and grief by mixing dreamlike fantasy with daily life in a small coastal town. When it was released in 2002, *My Beautiful Girl Mari* won the Contrechamp Grand Prix for Feature Film at the twenty-sixth Annecy International Animated Film Festival. However, it has since received even less critical attention abroad than Okiura's film. This may be because, as Joon Yang Kim points out, South Korea has long been relegated to the role of subcontracting *(hacheong)* in the global animation industry, with Korean animators doing much of the in-betweening for Japanese anime and American television, while producing relatively few original feature films—and fewer still that secure international distribution.[46] Whereas *A Letter to Momo* was overseen by accomplished key animators, character designers, and color designers from major studios, Lee's animation director, Kim Moon-Hee, previously worked almost exclusively as an in-betweener for Japanese anime productions, such as *Ghost in the Shell* (dir. Oshii Mamoru, 1995) and *Perfect Blue* (Satoshi Kon, 1997). As a result, "the animation journalist Kakizaki Shundō evaluated . . . *My Beautiful Girl, Mari (Mari iyagi)* as the result of the simple combination of an outstanding director, with animators trained through subcontracted production."[47] As Kim argues, this discourse of creative genius and manual labor is often framed in corporeal terms as a division between the creative "brain" and the laboring "hand" in animation.[48] Drawing on Kim's work, I discuss this labor situation as part of the imbalance between Japanese and South Korean animation. However, I would also like to examine *My Beautiful Girl Mari* as an exception to this trend, as an original, creative work of South Korean animation and a stand-out example of a film that values the haptic, the embodied, and the touch of the hand. It may occupy a minor position within the unbalanced circulation of world cinema distribution, but—perhaps for that very reason—it is also a film that perfectly demonstrates the flesh of animation in a culturally specific visual style.

The main character in *My Beautiful Girl Mari* is Kim Nam-woo, who is introduced in a frame narrative as an absent-minded, awkward young man working in a gloomy office in Seoul. After he meets with Jun-ho, a childhood friend whom he has not seen in years, he begins to reminisce about their early days together. The main part of the film subsequently plays out as a long flashback to one summer in Nam-woo's youth, showing him as a clumsy boy on the cusp of his teenage years who feels abandoned on all fronts. His father has died (like Momo's) in a storm at sea, his mother has a new boyfriend whom he dislikes, his grandmother is ailing, and his best friend, Jun-ho, will soon be leaving their small seaside town to study in Seoul. In short, Nam-woo recalls being at a transitional moment in his life. Just as everything is poised to change, Nam-woo dreams of entering a surreal world of enormous plants and solid clouds, which is inhabited by a silent floating girl he calls "Mari." The lines between dream and waking reality are quickly blurred as his friend Jun-ho also starts to see Mari and enter her world. Following the structure of many classic tales of the fantastic, the boys most often enter her world by passing through a liminal portal with the aid of a magical talisman. In this case, the portal is a half-ruined lighthouse (a space between sea and shore), the broken lights of which can only be activated by a mysterious marble with a tiny figure resembling Mari inside. As with Momo in *A Letter to Momo,* the boys' connection to the supernatural world proves crucial in defending their town and family members against a natural disaster: a raging typhoon. Okiura's and Lee's films may share some similar plot elements, but their visual styles could not be further apart. While Okuira embraces the cinematic in his painterly, fluid, and naturalistic style, Lee's approach draws more on the animetic tendencies of animation's layered and multiplanar apparatus, an effect that persists in the film's use of digital imaging.

One of the most striking features of *My Beautiful Girl Mari* is the way in which it presents a world of depth and texture inhabited by flat, planar, digitally animated characters, while simultaneously suggesting the relation between the two. In terms of character design, this film is unlike anything found in mainstream Japanese anime or Western cinematic feature animation. Rather than using black outlines to separate character from background and to delineate body

FIGURE 6. Minimalistic character designs in *My Beautiful Girl Mari* (2002).

parts, Kim Moon-Hee and his animation team use only the faintest outlines when absolutely necessary to make the image legible. For instance, a close-up of a character's closed hand may have fine colored lines a few shades darker than the character's skin tone to indicate the fingers and prevent the hand from looking like a shapeless blob. Otherwise, however, figures are without any outlining, even around key facial features like the eyes, placing the emphasis instead on planes of color and geometrical form. Although backgrounds are often shaded with gradients that suggest light, shadow, depth, and texture, the characters are shaded very simply with matte areas of darker color, in a minimalist approach to digital cel shading (Figure 6). Some reviewers, such as Theron Martin of the *Anime News Network,* have complained that this approach "leaves the characters devoid of texture and is too obviously computer-rendered to sit well with fans of cel-based animation."[49] However, there are moments when the world and the characters impinge on each other, bringing together the cinematic and animetic tendencies of animation and suggesting a phenomenological entwining of digital stylization with evoked bodily experiences. This is particularly evident in moments of transformation or transition between the "ordinary" diegetic world of Nam-woo's town and the fantastical space of Mari's world.

The first time Nam-woo enters into Mari's world is a key example of transition into a new kind of sensory experience. In this scene, Nam-woo goes to the ruined lighthouse alone, where he finds his cat

Yo chasing a strange flying creature, something like a fat, round flying fish with tiny wings that constantly flutter to keep it afloat. Nam-woo is not afraid of it, as Momo was when encountering the grotesque yōkai, but approaches it like a boy seeing an interesting new kind of animal. He lets it hover near his hand and talks softly to it. When it takes off, he follows it to the top of the lighthouse. He circles around an elaborate, volumetric, 3D-modeled reflector looking for it. Just then, there is a shimmer of light within the reflector, followed by a brilliant flash from the lighthouse, framed in a long shot. The view cuts to a low-angle shot of Nam-woo's best friend, Jun-ho, running up the lighthouse stairs while calling Nam-woo's name. Arriving at the top, all Jun-ho finds is the mysterious marble, which sits gleaming on the reflector. Jun-ho's arrival into the empty lighthouse confirms for the audience that what has happened is not a childish fantasy: Nam-woo is really gone.

Nam-woo's transition from the ordinary world of the lighthouse into Mari's parallel world is bridged by both sound and camera angle. First, the audio track introduces the sound of Nam-woo screaming over a bird's-eye-view shot of a puzzled Jun-ho holding the marble, framed from high above through a hole in the lighthouse roof. Next, there is a cut to another bird's-eye-view shot, this one showing Nam-woo falling from the sky into a sea of soft, dense, gray clouds. The realism of the shot is amplified by motion blur and unsteady camera movements that evoke the sensation of an uncontrolled fall. Suddenly, there is a hard cut to a close-up of Nam-woo's torso and raised arm as his outstretched hand is caught by some unknown agent off-screen. The audience, like Nam-woo, is denied a full view of what is happening as the action unfolds through fragmentary, fast-moving close-ups. He gets only a glimpse of his rescuer's white-clad body before he is tossed face first into a cloud, which seems to have the soft density of a mattress. His rescuer is glimpsed once again in extreme long shot as a tiny white curve soaring away through the blue sky, resembling the figure in the marble.

Following this transition, Nam-woo drifts on the back of a now giant-sized flying fish into a panoramic view of Mari's world. In contrast to the flatness of the character shading, this world is lushly textured with hair, grass, and immense flowers that blossom wildly. The textures even proliferate into objects where they should not exist. For instance, some of the clouds seem to be made of fur, while trees take on the pink color and branching forms of staghorn coral. However,

FIGURE 7. Mari's textural world in *My Beautiful Girl Mari*.

in contrast to earlier aerial shots set in the "real" world that moved through clouds as if through a space of 3D depth, the movement in Mari's world is more animetic. The camera does not penetrate deeply into any of these objects but lets them slide across the surface of our vision, almost as if we are stroking the film (or being stroked by it) with our eyes (Figure 7). Nam-woo also literally feels his way through this world in exploration, rather than approaching it through the mastery of vision. He is repeatedly shown reaching his hand out to touch things or even falling bodily into them as he grasps at the ephemeral strings that bind a cloud to the ground or tumbles down a slope of tall, golden grass while looking for the mysterious girl he will come to call Mari. In his daily life, Nam-woo is made fun of for constantly stumbling over his own feet and tripping, but in this world, falling forward becomes a means of physical connection with another being who allows him to experience her way of moving through the world. The first scene of their meeting comes to a head as Nam-woo careens down the grassy hill and comes to an abrupt, precipitous stop on the edge of a cliff just in front of Mari, who drifts backward as if pushed gently by the momentum of his fall. Although she has a human face and expresses emotions like surprise and curiosity through stylized gestures, she never speaks, and her body is covered in white fur, which may be either clothing or her own natural pelt, placing her also in a liminal position between human and animal or (given how she floats) between natural and supernatural.

As with all opposing modalities in this film, there is a crossover or relation between the two youths and the human and inhuman realms they inhabit. In later scenes, Nam-woo and Mari communicate by touching each other's faces, which allows Nam-woo to begin to float like her. This allows them both for an instant to share a way of feeling and moving through the world that is based as much on mutually exchanged touch as it is on seeing and possessing. Contrary to the English-language title, however, Mari does not become Nam-woo's "beautiful girl" in the sense of ownership that adding the word "my" implies. They do not have a romantic relationship, and she does not join Nam-woo in the "real world" at the end of the movie. Unlike the yōkai in *A Letter to Momo,* who are revealed to be the Guardians of Momo's family, Mari is not aligned with any formal system of divine justice or any human social institution like the family or the romantic couple. A comparison of the climactic scenes in *A Letter to Momo* and *My Beautiful Girl Mari* is instructive in this regard. In the climax of Okiura's film, the three yōkai summon a horde of nature spirits who help Momo cross a bridge in a dangerous storm to fetch a doctor for her mother; however, they do it on behalf of her father, to avoid a terrible punishment by the rulers of the Sky. In this way, their plasmatic natures are recontained by systems of law and order designed to serve humanity and continue the line of the immaterial yet powerful father.

In *My Beautiful Girl Mari,* by contrast, Nam-woo and Jun-ho scale the broken-down lighthouse during a storm to light the beacon and guide home Jun-ho's father, who is caught at sea in a fishing boat and is in dire need of rescue (that is, in a position of powerlessness). Even then, Mari does not help the boys through a feat of physical daring or a confrontation with nature, like Momo and the yōkai crossing the bridge; rather, she enables a momentary interweaving of her world and the small Korean coastal town. Once the boys bring her talisman, the marble, to the top of the lighthouse, it emits a brilliant flash. Then, in a lyrical long shot, flowers are shown growing up to the roof of the lighthouse, appearing in the same outsized scale, tableau-like planar framing, and textural dimension as they do in her world. A series of reaction shots follows from other people in the town, including Nam-woo's mother and grandmother, who witness otherworldly vines twining through the ordinary streets and homes of their seaside village. With the emergence of Mari's serenely cloud-filled world, the storm is dispersed and the ocean calms. This scene acts as the final point of chiasmus or crossing over between Nam-woo's world and Mari's world, as both are present simultaneously, overlapping and mutually influencing, without either being effaced. Mari is not precisely Nam-woo's love interest, nor is she his divine savior. She is rather the embodiment of her own elemental, animetic realm of unnatural nature, an inhuman being who presents a radically different way of "being-in-the-world" that nonetheless connects with Nam-woo's own clumsy embodiment and small-town life.

This film is unique in the way it traces the multiple crossing-over points between Mari's and Nam-woo's worlds and styles of embodiment. As audience members, we are invited to participate in this experience through haptic visuality, in the proprioceptive sensations of Nam-woo's falls and Mari's flights and through the tactile dimensions of the different worlds and styles through which they move. This invitation is extended through the film's animation, with its combination of flat stylization and deep, textured tactility, which acts as the tissue or flesh of the encounter. Spencer Shaw, in his chapter "Merleau-Ponty's Embodiment," has argued that though the philosopher felt that "the traditional description of depth [namely, linear perspective] resulted in artificial abstraction," he still believed that a sense of "interconnectedness and depth is fundamental to lifeworld experience as the unseen founding presence that subtends everything."[50] *My Beautiful Girl Mari* provides precisely this sense of interconnectedness, utilizing a form of depth that is based not solely on the Western tradition of linear perspective but on a mixture of perspectival styles and approaches to space of the sort more often found in East Asian art.

In depicting both movements into depth and planar movements across the layers of the image, *My Beautiful Girl Mari* provides an exploration of the potential of animation to express world, body, and motion in ways unique to its apparatus, as the digital nature of the image is so apparent. This is part of what Joon Yang Kim describes as the kinaesthetic aspect of South Korean animation. In looking at the discourse of the "brain" versus the "hand" in animation production, Kim says, "The fact is that we can immediately experience something emotional or mental from a series of subtle bodily gestures in an animated character, even if we 'know' it to be merely composed of pixel-based . . . images or flat, discrete, hand-drawn pictures. Such experience tells us that our sensation of animated visuals is not determined simply by cerebral intelligence."[51] Rather, animation, like the broader medium of cinema, can be understood through what film theorist Rudolf Arnheim has described as "isomorphism," in which different levels of perception—psychological, electrochemical, mechanical, and geometrical—come into resonance with each other through structural similarities and create a mutually informing, nonhierarchical holistic expression, such as when a dancer's gesture evokes an emotional state through the similarities of physical rise and fall with emotional lift and drop. As Kim says, "in a phenomenological sense, an observer can experience the kinesthetic and other isomorphic levels of the expressing person's body, through resonance with its geometrical shape and movement."[52] In his article, Kim is concerned primarily with the isomorphism experienced by animators themselves, who often physically perform the gestures that they draw into animated characters' bodies. But we can also see the resonance between the simple, geometrical forms of flat characters in *My Beautiful Girl Mari* and the audience's perception of embodied gestures, which create resonance between the stylized images and the lived gestures and experiences they evoke. As Bissonnette has shown, the isomorphic effects of the image's "becoming-animated" for audiences are not merely theoretical; they have a neurochemical basis in the brain's mirror neurons and in the muscular and visceral actions of the entire body. And as Lamarre also shows, the properties of the apparatus itself—animation, as a medium made from layered images—can form a "screen-brain apparatus,"[53] which I would say also extends throughout the body as a nervous *system* or network operating within the broader material network of media images and platforms.

Conclusions: Weighing Imbalance in Japanese and Korean Animation

When watching animated films, it is easy to say that we as viewers "identify with" or "relate to" bodily sensations like weight and texture, as if embodied experience is an essential, universal property that all of humanity experiences in the same way. But for Marks, haptic visuality is not a universal or stateless quality; rather, it is a socially constructed quality found most often in "intercultural cinema." "'Intercultural,'" in her words, "indicates a context that cannot be confined to a single culture. It also suggests movement between one culture and another, thus implying diachrony and the possibility of transformation."[54] This is not a blissfully frictionless process but involves engaging with histories of imperialism and the contemporary state of globalized "economic neocolonialism."[55] Likewise, Miyazaki's, Okiura's, and Lee's films all use images of floating and falling, or weight and weightlessness, to grapple with imbalances in the global network of media.

Studio Ghibli's films have been extensively studied as examples of the tension between Japanese source materials and the globalized media environment. Susan Napier reads Miyazaki's 2001 megahit *Spirited Away* as a clash between the discourses of *kokusaika,* or internationalization, and *furusato,* or the uniquely Japanese, culturally bounded sense of home. She finds the film progressive because it both critiques the commercial trappings of globalization and defies bounded concepts of identity. For her, *Spirited Away* "suggests the fundamental permeability of boundaries, evoking a liminal world of uncertainty, loss, constantly changing identities, and abandoned simulacra, where old truths and patterns no longer seem to hold and where the deep-seated desire to return home may never be fulfilled."[56] But can we say the same for *Howl's Moving Castle*? In this case, I would say no. Despite that this film is an adaptation of a British novel, I think we do see a subtle return to a bounded cultural subjectivity in the weight and trajectory given to home and family in the final shots of the film. Once the war is over and Sophie has broken her curse, the characters she has met along the way—from the little boy Markl to the now-senile Witch of the Waste—are gathered together in Howl's castle as a harmonious, intergenerational family. The castle that literally fell apart under their feet at the film's climax is restored to safe, whole solidity. What is more, we finally get the soaring, purposeful flight that Sophie's first hesitant walk in the air was lacking. The castle's flight may represent the culmination of confidence and freedom, but along with that smoothness of movement, we lose all sense of active bodily engagement with the world. The camera frames the castle's backyard from a high angle in an extremely long shot, then pulls back through deep space, away from Sophie and Howl's posed final kiss. Balance is restored and, along with it, optical visuality. This ending also reaffirms Miyazaki's auteurist mastery over his foreign source material, because unlike Diana Wynne Jones's book, his vision of "home" shows three generations united in one household under a stronger and more mature Howl. Similarly, as I have shown, Momo's family finally returns to the stability and fixedness of patriarchal protection, as the yōkai become stylistically and narratively naturalized or recontained when they are made into Guardian figures working under Momo's father and the punitive justice of the Sky.

My Beautiful Girl Mari, on the other hand, does not rely on closure to frame its ending. Lee's film might seem at first like an assertion of specifically South Korean identity, mainly because the film is so grounded in its rural, historical setting. But it was important for Lee to show Korean life because Korean animators have struggled for decades to produce original films about their own culture in an industry built on American and Japanese outsourcing contracts. At the end of his article, Kim quotes Yoo Sun Young's argument that "many Korean audiences in the early twentieth century seem to have been possessed by gestural ghosts invoked in the new medium of film" as "their bodies were imbued and animated with the gestures of Hollywood actresses or actors."[57] In terms of animation styles, the regional supremacy of Japanese anime becomes imbued in many Korean feature films, even Lee's own subsequent release of *Yobi the Five-Tailed Fox* (2007), which uses clear-lined, rounded, big-eyed, and altogether more anime-like designs for both the cute magical fox protagonist and the schoolchildren with whom she interacts. In *My Beautiful Girl Mari,* the idiosyncratic character design and detailed South Korean settings could be seen as another attempt to establish "cultural boundedness" or a "uniquely Korean" film style. But in the handling of weight and embodied experience, Lee's film finally refuses to return to stability.

This final scene of the film returns to the frame narrative in which Nam-woo, now grown up and working in Seoul, remembers the strange summer of his youth. Sitting on a city bus, he explains in voice-over that he went back to his childhood town as an adult but was left with a sense of alienation, as if everything was "the same but somehow strange and different." During his monologue, we see nothing but a close-up of his hand from his own point of view, hanging outside the bus window and collecting snow that seems oddly dry and cottony. When he gets off the bus, the city is transformed into the cloudscape of Mari's world. Rather than floating off blissfully, however, Nam-woo trips, falls over, and then stands up while looking around sheepishly. Even in an extreme long shot, the image remains haptic, filled with the texture of solid clouds and the stubborn, clumsy embodiment of falling. There is no clear resolution, no explanation as to why Mari's world has reemerged or confirmation of whether anyone else in Seoul can see it. The film remains poised in the act of crossing over, neither bounded nor fully transcendent in its imagery. In this way, it embodies the elemental qualities of the flesh of animation, hovering halfway between the individual and the idea.

I do not want to reassert another binary at the end of this chapter between the "heroic underdog" of South Korean animation and the "soft-power dominance" of Japanese anime, nor between "innovative animetic anime" and "traditional cinematic anime." I argue that the films discussed in this chapter offer several different visions of weight, texture, balance, and movement, illustrating how animation can contain multiple elements of optical and haptic visuality or of cinematism and animatism. All these sensory and stylistic elements are entwined by the flesh of animation as a network of material and labor practices, industry discourses, moving images, mediating screens, and bodies in reception. As such, all three films play an important, if unequal, role in circulating animated media within East Asia and beyond it to the rest of the world. Finally, however, the value of these films lies in their ability to make us question received notions of the dominance of visuality in animation, whether it be hand-drawn on cels or digitally produced, and see the animated character's body as more than an abstract, suspended "floating man."

CHAPTER 2

Liveliness in the Hybrid Film

Writing on the "illusion of life" in animated film, William D. Routt remarks:

> One of the first things which might strike one about the ideas of "life" clustered under *anima* is their invisibility. Who has seen the wind? Or breath or soul or mind, for that matter? Perceptions of these things are matters of feeling, not really of seeing or even of hearing. Indeed, it seems that life cannot be apprehended with the physical senses at all. . . . Common sense says that there is a distinction that makes a difference between a dead body and a live one and that the life in the latter may be something we cannot see or hear or smell or taste or touch. It is no wonder, then, that the imagination has filled this void with dreaming. Or, put in another way, life cannot be present in and of itself. It can only be represented, mediated—incorporated—in its effects, like breath. . . . If what seems is what is, then the perception of the effects of life is sufficient evidence of life itself.[1]

In this passage, Routt follows scholars like Alan Cholodenko in considering how it is that an animated image might be alive. Routt's approach overall is idealist. Life is not a material quality detectable by the physical senses, he argues. It can only be perceived through some other, more ephemeral sense, such as "feeling" or "imagination," or through the observation of secondary physical effects, such as breathing, which act as evidence of life but do not present life itself. Putting aside for now the question of what Routt thinks "life itself" actually is, I would like to delve deeper into his comments on the perception of life.

Here Routt explains the process of perception very briefly, saying that to be perceived, the effects of life must be represented, mediated, and incorporated. However, these three terms are given with no further gloss. The distinctions between them are not made clear, nor is it evident whether this list is meant to suggest a linear process or a collocation of different, independent operations. The distinction between these modes of perception is crucial to my phenomenological study, however, because how perception is framed as taking place makes all the difference for considering the embodied dimensions of animation. Life may well be *represented* in animation through figurative techniques based on the reduction of sensory detail, such as stylized graphics, stereotypes, and visual symbolism. In this sense, animation does indeed present life in its immaterial or ideal dimensions. But these representations cannot be *mediated* without a medium, that is, some physical substance, instrument, apparatus, or platform that transmits the effects of life to the perceiver, be it the air that resonates with the sound of a breath or the sheet of celluloid upon which an animator traces the image that, with repetition, will move. Likewise, the impression of life cannot be *incorporated* into someone's worldview without the corporeal senses that allow the perceiver to relate their feelings, imaginations, or observations about life's effects to their own embodied knowledge of how it feels to be alive, what living things do, and which other things may or may not be alive. This chapter builds on Routt's proposition that "if what seems is what is, then the perception of the effects of life is sufficient evidence of life itself" and explores exactly how "what seems" becomes "what is"—that is, how we perceive or imagine the effects of life in animation. Coming from a phenomenological position, I argue that the perception of life—even as an effect or illusion—is an inherently intersubjective, relational, and embodied process that takes place between the perceiver and the world, not an abstract operation of the mind or imagination divorced from the physical senses. We may make contact with life only through our perceptions, but even our most ephemeral forms of perception, such as intuition, are still necessarily channeled through certain physical faculties and technologies for engaging with the world, which bridge the gap between being and seeming without collapsing one into the other. This is especially evident in films that present the interval between the "illusory" cartoon and "real" photographic footage directly by combining live action and animation.

Animation is at its base a process for creating the "effect of life" in images by using various combinations of representation, mediation, and incorporation. The "effect of life" is not the same thing as biological life conceived in scientific, utilitarian, and anthropocentric terms—what Giorgio Agamben terms "bare life."[2] Rather, like the flesh of Merleau-Ponty's theory, it is the perception of a living quality created by the interaction between an individual perceiver and something in the world, be it an organic being, an object, or an image. To distinguish this perceived living quality from biological life, I will call the effect of life that animation creates *liveliness*. Kenny Chow has defined *technological liveliness* in the context of digital media as "the perceptual quality of animated phenomena reminiscent of life."[3] This term captures the metaphorical, representation-based aspect of animation (its "lifelikeness"), which separates cartoon characters from the literal "bare life" of organic being. At the same time, *liveliness* suggests a vital, mobile, and engaging quality that exists in many things, some of which are biologically alive (a lively child) and some of which are not (a lively tune), so that we cannot immediately discount the animated character as *only* metaphorically alive. Whereas the term *live action* implies the photographic capture of life itself in action, in keeping with Bazinian theories of film's indexicality, animation's "liveliness" evokes that dimension between the organic and artificial where humans interact with perceptibly unreal images and, through their effects, with the existing bodies and machines that made those images.

Some of the best examples of liveliness in animation can be found in hybrid films that overtly and purposely combine animated and live-action elements. The primary goal of these films is to create the impression that both the "toons" and the human actors with whom they star are equally alive and can touch each other, despite their differing ontologies. This genre has a long history, from silent-era short films, such as the Fleischer Brothers' Out of the Inkwell series (1918–29) and Disney's Alice Comedies (1923–27), to full-color feature films, such as *Who Framed Roger Rabbit* and *Chip 'n Dale: Rescue Rangers* (dir. Akiva Schaffer, 2022). Relatively little research has been published on films like these compared to wholly animated (or wholly live-action) films, though there has been some excellent work done on the formal classification of hybrid films into various categories and on the representation of space in films that mix animated and live-action worlds, on which I build in this chapter. After all, if we are to consider the ways in which animation may be phenomenologically experienced as alive, then the hybrid film is an essential genre. Hybrid films explicitly frame the representation of animated characters as lively yet artificial beings, the media through which they are created, and their incorporation into the world of physical things and bodies. As such, they self-reflexively illustrate the process by which liveliness is created in animation.

If we are to take seriously Routt's assertion that animated images can display the "effects of life" and even be considered active agents within a mediated world (as the proponents of ANT might suggest), then it is instructive to look at cases in which artificially created image-beings—namely, animated characters—interact with indexical recordings of live human actors and, in doing so, reveal the similarities and differences between their forms of liveliness. Live-action actors inhabit a realm of indexical recording that is in turn grounded in a human existence in the world. Animated figures, on the other hand, exist in an "an-ontological" sense[4]—or at least a *differently* ontological one—in that their materiality is not entirely organic but composed of paint, celluloid, and the artist's gesture. In this chapter, I address the disjunctions and connections between animated and live-action cinematic bodies. I consider the abstract social categories or representations of racialized and sexualized images of bodies, along with the material medium of the animation apparatus through which we perceive these bodies, and some of the embodied affects that audiences may experience when we perceive the meeting of different forms of liveliness. Following Sianne Ngai's work on the "minor affects" of "animatedness" and disgust in *Ugly Feelings,*[5] I argue that animated characters in hybrid films can create not only the "effects of life" but also the affects and visceral sensations of liveliness, as a sometimes uncomfortable "in-between" state. In contrast to the previous chapter, which looked at pleasurable and empowering sensations like walking on air or floating in water, this chapter focuses on the negative or ambivalent affects that animation can create. I examine cases in which animated figures are both "too alive" and "not alive enough," thus creating a sense of physical repulsion or abjection. Examples include the racialized figure of the "Tar Baby" in Disney's notorious 1946 feature film *Song of the South,* as well as sexually charged images of cockroaches that evoke both desire and disgust in the 1996 gross-out comedy *Joe's Apartment* and the uncanny anime on which it was based, *Twilight of the Cockroaches.* Although these are by no means "good" films, they are just as important to understanding the haptic, embodied experience of animation as films that depict more uplifting sensations. In these cases, it is possible to grasp how animation can act as a body genre, like horror or pornography, by evoking physical responses of discomfort, disgust, or arousal—or an ambivalent mix thereof. Here the flesh of animation works as a bridge between "what seems" and "what is" by provoking the body of the viewer into action in response to the body of the lively character—a relation that the hybrid film narratively models in depicting the interaction between toons and humans.

Defining the Hybrid Film

The hybrid film has proven somewhat difficult for authors to define and classify. Specialized technical knowledge is required to grasp how animation and live-action film can be combined in the first place. The production process is often complex, and it varies from film to film according to the kind of animation being used (hand-drawn cel animation, stop-motion, CGI) and the method of combining the animated images with photographic footage (on-set projection, in-camera compositing using mattes and multiple exposures, optical printing, digital compositing, etc.). Even for those who understand the production process and appreciate the technical mastery involved, the apparent interaction between cartoon characters and actors can still come across as jarring, distracting, or unsettling.

For example, a 1944 article in *Popular Science* magazine described the technical wizardry involved in making Disney's package feature *The Three Caballeros* (supervising dir. Norman Ferguson, 1944) with a strange mixture of enthusiasm and apprehension. The author describes the technical process positively enough, explaining how drawings of characters were carefully timed to accord with recorded dialogue and then painted on cels which were photographed using a multiplane camera. This animated footage was then combined with live action through "process projection," a technique by which actors performed against a translucent plastic screen measuring fourteen by twenty feet on which the animated footage was projected using specially ground quartz lenses for optimal clarity, so that all the elements of the scene would appear equally vivid when captured in Technicolor by a motion picture camera.[6] The entire apparatus of hybrid animation is impressively illustrated with diagrams and photographs. In the end, however, the author expresses skepticism regarding the possible results of this production process, asking, "Will mystification outweigh story interest: or will Disney's genius make plausible the mingling of animated pictures with equally lively people?"[7]

The generally negative critical reaction to this film (and to similar Disney features of the period, such as *Song of the South*) suggests that audiences were not just mystified by the technique but made uncomfortable by it. To see a cartoon character sexually pursue a human actress, as Donald Duck lustily chased the actresses Dora Luz and Aurora Miranda in *The Three Caballeros,* is to confront the material gap between them. Both appear "equally lively," as the *Popular Science* writer claims, in that both create the "effects of life" in their behavior: they appear to move with internally generated intention, respond to stimuli in their environment, and interact with each other. They compel us, as viewers, to respond to them physically and emotionally. And yet, it is also apparent that the animated and live-action characters should not be able to touch one another "in reality." It is difficult to suspend one's disbelief because there is a visible difference not just in the gender or race or species of the main players (though there is that as well) but in their *dimensionality.* Donald Duck remains his usual 2D self—flat, clean-lined, and minimally shaded—while the actresses appear fully fleshed in 3D by contrast, with their contours, textures, and gestures all captured by photographic cinema. When bodies with such markedly incompatible origins and capabilities coincide, the resulting film threatens to transgress the categories of reality and fantasy, of genre and medium, of child and adult target audiences, and, most importantly, of the kinds of liveliness we are familiar with seeing in cinema. The transgression is often glossed over in mainstream films with some diegetic frame that justifies the juxtaposition of different styles, such as showing a live-action child who enters the world of animation in her dreams, as in Disney's Alice Comedies, or establishing a world like that of *Who Framed Roger Rabbit,* where toons and humans coexist. Still, hybrid films can also call up ambivalent sensations or "ugly feelings," as Sianne Ngai has described them.

When confronted with the violation of categories, some scholars have responded by creating new categories with which to classify hybrid film. For instance, Frederick S. Litten has categorized the different

Type	Description
1	Animation and live action do not appear in the same frame but are shown in separate sequences, either with pretended interaction between the two created by crosscutting (1a) or without any interaction at all (1b).
2	Animated characters appear in a real (photographic) environment. Either animated and human characters interact in a real environment (2a) or animated characters appear in the real environment but do not interact with it (2b).
3	Photographed actors appear in an animated environment and interact with animated characters, as in *Bedknobs and Broomsticks* (dir. Robert Stevenson and Ward Kimball, 1971) and *Mary Poppins* (dir. Robert Stevenson, 1964).
4	This is a combination of types 2 and 3, most often seen in "package features" with more than type 1 hybridity, such as *Fun and Fancy Free* (dir. Jack Kinney, Hamilton Luske, and William Morgan, 1947).
0	This has a combination of more than two kinds of animation/media, as in *Tron* (dir. Steven Lisberger, 1982), which featured cel animation, CGI, stop-motion, and live-action film/special effects.

FIGURE 8. The five types of hybrid film according to Frederick S. Litten.

types of hybrid animation depending on the media elements present and the level of interaction between them. His main stipulation is that, "in general, a hybrid film or TV episode recognizably combines animation and live action, or different types of animation, such as puppet animation and drawn animation."[8] On the basis of this definition, he divides the hybrid film into five major types (Figure 8). I will refer to these categories throughout the rest of this chapter, as they are useful for quickly indicating exactly what type of hybridity is present in a given scene.

Franziska Bruckner, in the 2015 article "Hybrid Image, Hybrid Montage: Film Analytical Parameters for Live Action/Animation Hybrids," likewise takes a formalist approach to hybrid films, with the aim of expanding Litten's focus on American feature films to address combinations of animation and live action across a wide range of national cinemas, genres, and media, including short films, music videos, advertisements, and experimental works in analog and digital media.[9] Like Litten, she sets one main standard that qualifies a work as hybrid: there must be some detectable difference between the live-action and animated effects, even if the effect is only detectable because the audience knows it to be impossible to photograph. However, rather than focusing on content, such as how animated characters interact with live-action backgrounds or the like, Bruckner focuses purely on visual qualities and analyzes hybrid films descriptively, noting the types of animation combined, the method, the frequency, and the duration of different kinds of images, as well as how images from different sources are edited together. Using these results, she creates a series of categorical types that are similar to Litten's, but more complex than can be summed up in a single table.

Although these formalist approaches are valuable for classification purposes, they tend to overlook the challenges that hybrid films pose for film viewers and scholars alike. Both Litten and Bruckner depend for their definition on audience recognition of the different media in hybrid films, but they do not address how it is that audience members perceive distinctions between different kinds of images, nor do they take into account the difficulties that can arise when a viewer is not familiar enough with filmmaking techniques to notice the sometimes subtle differences between, say, a practical special effect filmed live with puppets and one created with stop-motion. What becomes of hybridity when an audience member does not mark the distinction between one medium and another? Can we still call a work a "hybrid film" when the animation is so photorealistic as to be indistinguishable from live action even for an expert, as is sometimes the case with contemporary CGI special effects? And what is it that makes viewers assign *significance* to the mixing of techniques in the film and so come to perceive the work as a clear hybrid film, rather than as a live-action or animated film that happens to have visual effects or isolated scenes in another format? Hybridity, like liveliness in a character, is a rather subjective quality at times.

That said, there are films in which hybridity is made inescapably obvious to everyone in the audience. These are films that self-reflexively comment on their own production processes by overtly drawing attention to the ontological differences between the animated and live-action elements. *Who Framed Roger Rabbit* is a perfect example. Writing on this film, Alan Cholodenko argues that the "frame" of the film's title in fact refers to the act of framing animation itself, in a kind of postmodern mise-en-abyme in which "*Who Framed Roger*

Rabbit frames the very nature of the frame as its subject. The frame is always already the frame of the frame."[10] In this film, live-action cinema and animation are highlighted as such, enabling both a distinction between the two media and a transgression of their borders. For instance, Cholodenko points out that the scene introducing detective Eddie Valiant begins with a slow tracking shot across a series of framed photographs on his desk in which the younger, happier Eddie of yesteryear can be seen eating a carrot with his brother and making "rabbit ears" with his fingers behind his girlfriend's head. These rabbit references create a concordance between the young Eddie and Roger Rabbit, foreshadowing the collapse of boundaries between human and toon performances that takes place at the climax of the film, when Eddie takes on Roger's comic persona by doing a looney dance with cartoon props. In his attention to the framing and transgression of ontological boundaries, Cholodenko reveals how this film draws the viewer's attention to the film's various media, including the photograph, live-action cinema, drawing, and animated cinema.

Erwin Feyersinger describes the techniques found in *Roger Rabbit* and other hybrid films as a form of "metalepsis," a classic rhetorical technique in which there is "a fictional and paradoxical transgression of the border between mutually exclusive worlds that cannot be transgressed in our actual world. The hand of the animator reaching into the diegesis of his creations as well as characters communicating with the audience, escaping to the world of their creators, or altering their own worlds are all different types of metaleptic transgressions."[11] Following this definition, the article elaborates on some of the forms of metalepsis found in animation, such as extradiegetic interference in the diegesis, as exemplified in *Duck Amuck* (dir. Chuck Jones, 1953), and cases where characters appear in paratexts like the credit sequence of a film, such as in the end credits of *WALL•E*. In pointing out the metafictional nature of metalepsis, in which the text is both fictional and true in its representation of itself, Feyersinger's argument parallels my focus on the quality of "liveliness" in animation as both a metaphorical lifelikeness and an experienced living quality. Although the use of metalepsis alone is not sufficient grounds to classify a film as a hybrid work, we might say that the most effective hybrid films are those that use metalepsis to draw audience attention to the combination of animation and live action as distinct planes of liveliness that interact without becoming fully integrated or identical. Given this working definition, I have chosen for the rest of this chapter to look at hybrid films that use metalepsis to draw attention to the disjunctions and uncomfortable conjunctions between animation and live-action footage. Films that attempt to elide the differing ontologies of their various media sources and seamlessly integrate animated elements into the live-action mise-en-scène—as is the case in most Hollywood films with CGI special effects made since the 1990s—are not considered as hybrid films here but are examined in chapter 3, on seamless compositing.

Representation, Mediation, and Incorporation in *Song of the South*

Thus far, I have argued that animation creates a sense of "liveliness" that is particularly remarkable in hybrid films, where animated characters or worlds are brought to life through metalepsis and the visible disjunction of layers of media. However, the issue of how it is that audiences perceive this liveliness still remains. In this section, I return to my proposition that animation evokes embodied experience through a combination of representation, mediation, and incorporation. I use Disney's hybrid film *Song of the South* to illustrate all three, because this film is notable for its problematic racial representations and the "ugly feelings" that have arisen around both the actors' and the animated characters' bodies as a result of its hybrid style.

Representation, as a form of "standing in" or "standing for," encompasses all those processes by which bodies are evoked through signs, symbols, idealized images, and stereotypes. As such, representations depend not just upon what is perceived through the senses but also upon conventional codes of language and graphic depiction that re-present what we experience in life with a greater or lesser degree of abstraction. For instance, there is a certain capacity for abstraction—or, as Routt would say, imagination—that allows us to perceive a cartoon figure like Roger Rabbit as a "rabbit," even though he lacks many of the physical properties of actual rabbits, such as richly textured fur and a four-legged, hopping gait. That is not to say that representations have no basis in reality whatsoever, as in Jean Baudrillard's description of the hyperreal, or that "there is nothing outside the text," as Jacques Derrida's famous maxim (in Gayatri Spivak's translation) would have it.[12] Rather, representation is the tip of the iceberg of perception, as the most highly stylized (and academically commented upon) aspect of a much larger process of embodied engagement with the world. The concept of representation has a long, complex intellectual history, as its nature and processes have been defined, debated, and reimagined through various philosophical and critical lenses. For the purposes of this chapter, however, representation will be understood as referring to the idealized, symbolic, or stereotypical depiction of a body or world, particularly as perceived through visual and auditory markers of identity categories like gender, sexuality, class, race, ability, and nationality. To date, the lion's share of scholarly attention paid to hybrid films has focused on representation and its effects on audiences. Especially in the subfield of Disney studies, entire volumes have been devoted to identity politics in animated films, including hybrid films like Disney's Alice Comedies, *The Three Caballeros, Song of the South,* and *Mary Poppins* (dir. Robert Stevenson, 1964), which are seen as active agents in the social construction of race, nationality, gender, and class.[13]

Song of the South, in particular, has long been singled out for its harmful and stereotypical racial representations, which are seen as among the most egregious within the Disney canon. Based on Joel Chandler Harris's Uncle Remus book series, this film was intended to promote interracial harmony by showing the heartwarming friendship between a seven-year-old white boy, Johnny (played by Bobby Driscoll), and a kindly old Black man, Uncle Remus (played by James Baskett), who tells Johnny comical tales about Brer Rabbit and Brer Fox. The animal tales are rendered in cel animation under the direction of longtime Disney animator Wilfred Jackson. There are also several bridging scenes between the live-action and animated segments that make use of what Litten calls type 3 hybrid animation, in which Baskett's character appears to interact with cartoon animals in an animated environment. For instance, in the famous musical number "Zip-a-Dee-Doo-Dah," Uncle Remus sings to "Mr. Bluebird on my shoulder" as the animated bluebird lands on his shoulder and tweets along. These hybrid transitional sequences seem to reinforce the ideological message of harmony between characters of different races or, in this case, ontologies. That said, Disney's vision of utopian racial harmony has been widely criticized by contemporary viewers of the 1940s and later critics alike as an outmoded and stereotypical representation of race relations in America.

As Kheli R. Willetts has pointed out, the representation of African Americans in Disney films stems from a "discourse of difference," begun as early as the mid-fifteenth century, in which paintings, etchings, and later satirical newspaper cartoons "continued to highlight the differences between Africans and Europeans and create a dichotomous relationship that presented Europeans as good, pretty, intellectual, refined and driven, commonly articulated as whiteness, juxtaposed against bad, ugly, emotional, savage and lazy Africans, representing blackness."[14] These traits were used to justify the slave trade between Europe and the United States and persisted in popular discourse, becoming common tropes in comic strips like Winsor McCay's *Little Nemo in Slumberland* (1911) and from there into early animated cartoons by Bray Productions, Pat Sullivan Studios, Fleischer Studios, and Disney's earliest films. A quality of excessive "animatedness" pervades depictions of Africans and African Americans in these works. In *Trader Mickey* (dir. Burt Gillett and David Hand, 1932), Willett notes that the "wild-eyed Africans" are depicted as savages with "swirling eyeballs" and "over-exaggerated lips" who "communicate through grunts and babbling . . . that is when they are not laughing."[15] For Willett, these representations left a lasting mark on her experience of film spectatorship. As she writes:

> Growing up I searched for characters who mirrored the people in my community and reflected the values and aesthetics of the Other, in this case, African, Latino, Asian and First Nations Diasporas. Instead, Disney gave me caricatured representations of the diversity of my world.[16]

Even more apparently positive portrayals drawn from African American culture, such as the inclusion of the diasporic tales of Brer Rabbit and Brer Fox in *Song of the South*, have been seen as generating a sense of negative self-image within Black communities. Willett harshly critiques "the bastardization of characters taken from traditional African folktales that survived the Middle Passage and were transformed by enslaved Africans in this country," arguing that "Disney's re-interpretation of these treasured folkloric characters is so offensive that it forever changed how African Americans view them. . . . These centuries-old characters, born in ancient Africa as animal metaphors for crafty, sage survivalists, have been silenced and are no longer an active part of African American folklore and culture."[17]

Clearly representation matters a great deal when it comes to racial stereotyping. And yet, representation is only the first, and arguably the most abstract, level of perception in film and animation. Indeed, to draw attention back to the perception of film as such and its sensory impacts, some phenomenological film scholars, such as Scott C. Richmond, have opted to "bracket" representation in their analyses of film and embodiment. On one level, I agree that there is some merit to moving beyond a form of analysis in which every character must be reduced to a symbol of its gender, race, historical, or national context. While some consideration of representation is clearly necessary in studies of animation, analyses based solely on what the characters stand for can quickly decay into reductiveness. This is apparent in the strand of scholarship on Japanese anime that reads animated characters as mere ciphers of the anxieties and hopes of contemporary Japan. Though the tendency was strongest in the 1990s, it was still common in the mid- to late 2010s to find articles that focused primarily on how "the 'bodies' of . . . female heroes symbolically represent idealized fantasies about the past, fears about the present and, to a smaller extent, hopes for the future."[18] The use of scare quotes around the word "bodies" in this quotation renders the female cyborg bodies of anime purely notional and metaphorical. In arguments like these, the body becomes nothing but a proxy for a monolithic notion of Japanese national and ethnic identity. As a result, this approach to representation tends to reify the very techno-Orientalist stereotypes it should critique. Likewise, reducing all Black characters in American animation to either "bad" or "good" representations simplifies both the depictions of those characters and the rich diversity of Black identities in North America and around the world. That is not to say that we should avoid talking about representations of race, nationality, gender, and other identity categories altogether. For instance, I cannot bracket the ways in which my experiences of embodiment are inflected by the powerful representations that since childhood have contributed to my sense of how I should look, move, and speak as a woman—a condition also remarked upon by phenomenological feminist scholars like Iris Young.[19] In solidarity with scholars like Willets and Young, I must continue to ask hard questions about how animated texts create stereotypes and promote dominant ideologies.

However, instead of phrasing the question as "what does this character represent?" I propose to ask, How is this character embodied? How do I perceive its image-body to interact with my own? and How is this relation enabled by the flesh of animation itself?

To answer such questions, we need to consider more than just representation. We also need to consider mediation, including the platforms and materials through which animation is created and accessed, and the various strategies films may use to prompt a recognition of the medium itself. In *Animating Space: From Mickey to WALL-E,* J. P. Telotte pays close attention to the mediation of space in Disney and Pixar films. He argues that when film critics have analyzed *Song of the South,* ideological criticisms of the film's representations of race (such as Willetts's) have typically taken priority over aesthetic ones. "Yet," he suggests, "emphasizing the links between the animated and real worlds, what we might term a *reciprocity of space* seems like the film's key concern, as its opening and the various packaged cartoon episodes suggest."[20] Here Telotte focuses on the ways in which Disney's skillful deployment of the hybrid animation technique has the potential to undercut the divisive aspects of racial representation in *Song of the South* by visually and aurally emphasizing integration. He argues that the "blurring of boundaries [between animation and live action] was an integral part of the film's visual design scheme," as clever lighting, stylized painted sets, and careful blocking "ha[ve] made it practically impossible to parse out real space from animated."[21] From the very beginning of the film, audiences are instructed to watch for similarities across different categories of beings in a voice-over coda by Uncle Remus:

> Just 'cause these here tales is about critters like Brer Rabbit and Brer Fox, that don't mean they ain't the same like can happen to folks. So them that can't learn from a tale about critters just ain't got their ears tuned for listenin'.

Telotte glosses this line by describing it as "a warning, of course, to 'tune' our ears—and eyes—correctly for what follows, so that we can better appreciate the correspondences between the animated and the real" and goes on to describe the subsequent hybrid scenes as "easily some of the studio's most successful efforts in this area," as they "underscore that linkage [between worlds] in their nearly seamless nature."[22]

These readings are based on a solid assessment of the technical prowess of the Disney studio's deployment of the apparatus of animated filmmaking. The sets do indeed create a light, bright, cartoony quality. The live-action Uncle Remus character is integrated cunningly into these sets by being lit with flattering high-key lighting that minimizes shadows and downplays his depth or dimensionality. And the animation is rendered in a cinematic style that emphasizes movement into depth. In the scene in which Uncle Remus first sees Brer Rabbit hopping down a line of fence posts in masterful linear perspective, it seems entirely plausible that the two inhabit an idyllic world in which "folks" and "critters," or humans and cartoons, can coexist harmoniously. Using examples like these, Telotte convincingly demonstrates that smooth integration was the driving aesthetic intention behind this film. Ideologically as well, the Disney studios may indeed have been trying to depict a world without racial strife in which African American storytellers are respected and honored, as a utopian model for contemporary coexistence. On the level of representation, its depiction of happy Black workers singing in the plantation fields and loyally serving a rich white family has been critiqued for idealizing slavery, despite the studio's insistence at the time of the film's release that it was meant to be set well after the end of the Civil War. But representation is not the only issue here. Looking at mediation, I argue that this film has proven highly divisive because of the subtle but powerful ways in which metalepsis is used to highlight the distinction between the animated characters and the live-action sequences. On a formal level, *Song of the South* undermines the harmonious aesthetic balance it strives to create in its tendency to excessive cartooniness, which at points becomes an uncanny reflection of the medium of animation itself.

This is particularly evident in the Tar Baby scene. A *tar baby* is metaphorically a sticky situation in which the more one fights it, the more difficult it becomes to escape. However, it has also accumulated racial valences as a slur used against African Americans and as a metaphor for the abjection of African American identities. Disney's version of the Tar Baby has done nothing to overcome the ambivalences of Harris's literary Tar Baby story. Indeed, Disney has only enhanced the Tar Baby's "animatedness," or the disturbing ambivalence between its inert passivity and its overexaggerated expressivity, which Ngai argues is indicative of racialized performance styles.[23] The Tar

Baby scene is all the more complicated in terms of racial representation by the fact that all the animal characters, especially Brer Rabbit and Brer Fox, are aurally coded as Black. Brer Rabbit was voiced by African American actor Johnny Lee, while James Baskett provided the voice of Brer Fox in addition to the visible figure of Uncle Remus. The most striking figure here, however, is the Tar Baby itself and the way it is framed through the mixture of live action, animation, and a particular kind of "animatedness."

As a bridge into the fully animated Tar Baby cartoon sequence, there is a hybrid framing scene in which Uncle Remus interacts with a pastoral animated world replete with flowers and animals while singing a song on the theme of saying "howdy" to all the critters around. Cross-fading from Remus's dim, rustic shack and eager audience of boys, the audience sees the old storyteller in silhouette mounting the rise of a brightly lit dirt road, with a fringe of trees and a ramshackle wooden fence receding to the horizon in perfect linear perspective to lend depth to the scene. Remus comes into the light and greets a flock of butterflies, who giggle and scatter around him like flighty schoolgirls. Not long after he passes, a cut shows Brer Rabbit coming down the same road and leaping onto the fence to chat with Remus, even leaning over his shoulder to greet a mother opossum and her babies. This is one of the sequences that most emphasizes harmony and smooth interaction between live action and animated bodies. Brer Rabbit hops off cheerfully, and the transition scene ends with a peaceful scenic shot of an old fishing hole reminiscent of such early Disney shorts as *The Old Mill* (dir. Graham Heid and Wilfred Jackson, 1937), especially because it ends on a multiplane camera shot in which the bobber on Uncle Remus's cast fishing line lands so close in the foreground of the shot that it almost seems to come through the screen in 3D. The peaceful mise-en-scène is not long to last, however, as Uncle Remus and his frog friend both note that Brer Rabbit is heading into trouble and is likely to "put his foot in it" soon—a corporeal metaphor that foreshadows the haptic sensations to come.

A cut to an establishing shot of Brer Fox's den shows the bright blue sky now shadowed with black clouds that stretch out over the hollow, dead branch serving as Brer Fox's lookout. A point-of-view shot from inside the branch shows a distant Brer Rabbit targeted within the Fox's "scope," in an echo of Paul Virilio's remarks on the "ballistic vision" of the camera. An ominous wisp of smoke rises from the den below as Brer Fox scrambles back inside gleefully. A cut to the interior of the den reveals the source of the smoke: the sticky black substance of the Tar Baby, boiling on the fire. Brer Fox gathers up a glob on the end of a stick, fast-chattering about giving the Tar Baby a head and using it to fool Brer Rabbit. The fox's companion, Brer Bear, protests that "it ain't gonna fool nobody. It ain't got no eye!" But with the addition of two round white buttons from Brer Bear's jacket, a nose made of a pipe bowl, and a clump of hair ripped from Brer Bear's backside, Brer Fox proclaims that it is "looking more nat'ral all the time!" The simple running joke in the Tar Baby creation scene is that it looks nothing like a living being due to the ham-handed efforts of the villains. Even when dressed up in a shabby coat and hat, it is still blank eyed and completely inert at the start, lacking the kind of liveliness the animal characters display. Being unable to move, it lacks *animation* and lets the audience in on the trick of its deceptive artificiality.

However, the situation changes when Brer Rabbit encounters the Tar Baby and is fooled into thinking the taciturn thing should respond to his "howdy-do." In a scene of rising narrative tension, Brer Rabbit gives the Tar Baby until a count of three to respond to him, and during the count, "Brer Fox laid low," a phrase that narrator Uncle Remus repeats in urgent tones as the Fox goes into comically animated contortions of anxiety. When Brer Rabbit finally punches the Tar Baby on the chin, the narrative tension is released, and the Tar Baby springs into animation, revealing its gooey, springy, plastic nature. As Brer Rabbit pulls on it, the Tar Baby changes shapes, seeming to suggest first an elephant, as its face is deformed into a trunk, and then a giant clam as Brer Rabbit springs inside it and is engulfed in a body that takes on the appearance of a viscous clamshell "mouth." This kind of deformity falls within the classic Disney tradition of animation in which bodies can stretch, squash, morph, and deform to take on other forms, a quality Sergei Eisenstein praised as a liberating "plasmaticness" or "freedom from once-and-forever allotted form."[24] In the case of the Tar Baby, however, haptic visuality creates an unpleasant sensation of restriction as Brer Rabbit is bound up in the sticky tar. The Tar Baby takes on the uncanny animatedness of an immobile figure that suddenly springs to life as a trap. It is a being with no life or will that binds the protagonist to the will of another, creating a confusion between object and subject. The Tar Baby is not disturbing only because it resembles a stereotypical Black caricature with its pitchy skin and round white eyes; it is disturbing because it also calls up the ambivalent affect of animatedness, in which movement, excess, racialization, and control are mixed in a way that is ostensibly comical and yet profoundly uncomfortable. The liveliness of animation in this film is thus riven with ambivalence.

The profoundly corporeal ambivalence generated in *Song of the South* brings us to final step in generating liveliness in the image: *incorporation*. Unlike representation and mediation, which both have an established presence in philosophy and in film studies, *incorporation* has not been used as a major keyword for film analysis. However, I believe it will prove useful in describing many aspects of embodiment in cinema owing to the rich set of connotations it has accrued over time. According to the *Oxford English Dictionary*, the term *incorporate* derives from the late Latin *incorporāre*, meaning "to embody" or "to form into a body." Its most common contemporary usages are "to combine or unite into one body or uniform substance; to mix or blend thoroughly together," "to put into or include in the body or substance of something else; to put (one thing) in or into another so as to form one body or integral whole; to embody, include," and, in economics and politics, "the formation of a legal corporation or body politic." Historically, *to incorporate* has also carried the meanings of "to take or absorb into the body," as with a taste or smell, and "to furnish with a body; to give bodily shape to." As with *anima* and the many aspects of life or soul that it presents, the term *incorporation* presents a range of meanings related to the formation of bodies, including concepts of mixing, unification, consumption, and even copulation. The bodies in question may be human or animal forms, collections of objects or ingredients, guilds and corporations, or the body politic at large. Perhaps of most interest for the study of animation, however, is the idea of incorporation as giving shape to a body in which a spirit or soul may reside. *Soul* and *incorporation* have been used as opposing but interlinked terms, where *incorporation* means "embodiment" or "an embodied realization." The *Oxford English Dictionary* lists two examples of this usage:

> 1642 H. More *Ψυχωδια Platonica* sig. N6 The self-formed soul may work without Incorporation.
>
> 1645 M. Casaubon *Orig. Cavse Temporall Evils* 2 That opinion

> of the ancientest Philosophers [is] that the Soules of men had a subsistence long before their incorporation.[25]

These examples, while referring primarily to Plato, also echo Avicenna's assertions of the independence of the soul from the body of the Floating Man. I do not presume to speak about religion or spirituality, but when it comes to film, I believe that incorporation is in fact necessary in generating the anima of animation. To make an animated film, many elements (cels, painted backgrounds, etc.) must be combined, layered, or otherwise *incorporated* through an apparatus, such as the animation stand and camera of cel-style animation or the editing software used for CGI, to create a series of unified images that are then projected into a moving picture. To make the images convincing as animation—that is, to create the effect of seeing self-motivated characters or living worlds—the film must depict the movements of some body, be it human or inhuman, with which audiences can engage, for instance, through techniques like haptic visuality and the aesthetics of proprioception. And to feel the effects of life that these techniques create, the audience must incorporate the images into its own perceptions, comparing what it sees with its own embodied knowledge of what it is to be alive and what living things do. Most commercial animators use images of humans or anthropomorphized animals, plants, or objects to create relatable representations of bodies, but experimental animators can embody liveliness in many forms. For example, Norman McLaren's *Boogie Doodle* (1940) is an exceptionally lively film because the movements of lines, dots, circles, hearts, and other geometric shapes incorporate (give form to) the bouncy rhythms of the boogie-woogie piano.

Through the brief example of McLaren's work, I hope to suggest that even my most literal, material usages of the term *body* are not grounded in an anthropocentric worldview or in any form of essentialism that claims that a given body can exist only in one way (for instance, that a woman is inherently female because of the anatomical configuration of her body). By contrast, I use the term to suggest a process of incorporation in which many parts are combined into a whole. This process is distinct from the kind of monolithic unification that Deleuze and Guattari term "organization,"[26] in that the whole does not need to be homogeneous or rigidly stratified but may contain many, ever-shifting layers or planes of images, as we see in the body of the hybrid film. Indeed, one of the most interesting things about hybrid films is that they draw attention to their disparate layers, creating a disjunction that challenges the idea of incorporation as a complete blending or mixing.

In terms of film production, incorporation indicates the layering of many different elements into a single film, often through the compositing of material from various visual and audio sources. In terms of film spectatorship, incorporation describes the intersubjective ways in which audiences take images designed to create the "effect of life" into themselves and, in so doing, imbue those images with a liveliness drawn from their own physical, emotional, and social experiences. This process does not necessarily have the same outcome every time, and neither does it always produce a harmonious impression. Even in the most accomplished efforts at seamless interaction between live action and animation, there are still moments that disrupt the audience's immersion in the narrative by breaking the illusion of perfect coexistence. For instance, there might be a moment when the character does not quite touch the actor convincingly or the actor's performance appears stilted as a result of acting with a screen or a stick as a stand-in for the animated costar. The effect of life in such cases can all too quickly become uncanny and disturbing.

When it comes to understanding affect and embodiment in film, Sianne Ngai's 2005 book *Ugly Feelings* is highly instructive in the way it privileges neither pure affect nor bare life. Deleuzian philosophers and media scholars, such as Brian Massumi, tend to view affect as "a prepersonal intensity corresponding to the passage from one experiential state of the body to another and implying an augmentation or diminution in that body's capacity to act," without yet involving the body's action in the world.[27] Affect is not a personal emotion, nor is it embedded in any particular body. This theoretical branch of affect studies thus skews toward the virtual and abstract dimensions of human experience. On the other hand, film scholars working from the perspective of evolutionary biology tend to see affect as entirely rooted in the nervous system, tracing "how the brain's architecture and the different steps in its processing of audiovisual data support different aesthetic forms, and also how the brain's architecture influences our experiences of the reality of film."[28] This certainly puts the focus on embodiment in film viewing; but at the same time, it can risk becoming programmatic, essentialist, and even deterministic, as all films must ultimately move us in the same way through the "PECMA flow" from perception to emotion to cognition to motor action and the hits of dopamine, oxytocin, and other neurochemical transmitters that result from this process. We may understand the underlying physical processes of film viewing from such an approach, but the nuanced and varied quality of the experience of perception is lost.

Ngai's work is a welcome middle ground between these two extremes. It provides a view of affect that is neither heavily abstracted nor exclusively biological but rather grounded in an attention to the ambiguities of perception in literary and cinematic texts. Looking beyond major affects like horror, sorrow, and ecstasy, Ngai theorizes "minor affects that are far less intentional and object directed, and thus more likely to produce political and aesthetic ambiguities, than the passions in the philosophical canon."[29] Minor affects include ambivalent states of mind and body such as anxiety, envy, paranoia, and irritation. In drawing out the complexities of each concept, Ngai explores cases in which there is a "systematic problematization of the distinction between subjective and objective enunciation," in which one is left wondering whether one's perceptions are caused by something "*out there* or *in me*?"[30] This is at base a phenomenological approach, though Ngai does not name it as such specifically. It is also an approach that is particularly apt for hybrid films because they are generally minor entries in the canon of film studies and call up equally ambivalent reactions in critics.

As described in my reading of the Tar Baby scene, one of the minor affects Ngai addresses is the uncomfortable sense of "animatedness" that arises from the "ambiguous interplay between agitated things and deactivated persons" in mechanical puppets and stop-motion films, which she describes as follows:

> The rudimentary aspect of stop-motion technology parallels the way in which the affective state of being "animated" seems to imply the most basic or minimal of all affective conditions: that of being, in one way or another, "moved." But as we press harder on the affective meanings of animatedness, we shall see how the seemingly neutral state of "being moved" becomes twisted into the image of the overemotional racialized subject, abetting his or her construction as unusually receptive to external control.[31]

Here Ngai makes a connection between physical and emotional movement, and between exaggerated displays of emotion and racial stereotypes in animation, to theorize the concept of "animatedness." Ngai pursues the affect of animatedness through the annals of animated film and television history to arrive at *The PJs*, a television series that aired on the FOX network from 1998 to 2000. *The PJs* was "the first prime-time program in American television history to feature a completely non-white, non-middle-class, and non-live-action cast, as well as the first to depict its characters in foamation, a three-dimensional stop motion animation technique trademarked by Will Vinton Studios."[32] This show about a Black family living in an urban housing project generated a great deal of controversy, as Ngai notes that it was condemned as hateful by Spike Lee and criticized for its ugly, exaggerated African American character designs. However, she points out that the "show also contains the internal references to African-American history and culture that Kristal Brent Zook finds integral to antiracist identity politics of the first black-produced sitcoms in the early 1990s, which, unlike previous white-produced shows about African-Americans, attempted to foreground struggles over the *representation* of blackness within the black community."[33] She feels further that *The PJs* refused sanitized visions of middle-class Black families based on the generic tropes of white sitcoms and openly addressed issues of stereotyping, caricature, and typecasting. In part, it did this by highlighting the animatedness of the characters as dolls whose mouths, hands, and bodies moved in a "slippery," "spasmodic," "overanimated," and antinaturalistic way.[34] Ngai in no way claims that every negative representation in the show is justified simply because it is self-reflexive and parodic. However, she does highlight the ugly feeling of excessive animatedness that overexaggerated racial representation can give audiences, particularly when they hover somewhere between caricature and critique, leaving us uncertain how to respond objectively.

If *The PJs* has any ethical value (a point that is still debatable), it stems from the use of metalepsis, which reminds viewers of the artificial nature of the characters and the construction of representations of Blackness. That said, I cannot help but wonder: what about films in which the effect of animatedness is not part of a deliberate critique but arises through complicit representation, failures in mediation, and dissonant incorporation? For instance, despite her attention to representations of African Americans in stop-motion film, Ngai does not mention the 1940s *Puppetoons* of George Pal, which used a rough and rickety style of stop-motion animation to depict a little Black boy named Jasper who was seen even in the 1940s as an egregious stereotype of a "'razor-totin', ghost-haunted, chicken-stealin' concept of the American Negro."[35] Nor does she mention Disney's *Song of the South*, despite its reputation for animated racism. These are cases in which animatedness is in full force formally, as one cannot help but notice the wooden artificiality of Pal's puppets and the combination of animation and live action in *Song of the South*. However, these films lack the redeeming critical value of parodic postmodern uses of animatedness and, as such, they seem stripped of moral ambiguity. Because they portray stereotypical representations of African Americans, mediated through hybrid film and incorporated through animatedness, they are complicit in a racist system of oppression in America that has lasted for hundreds of years and still has not been eradicated as of the early 2020s, despite the efforts of civil rights activists and contemporary protestors like the Black Lives Matter movement.

Even in the 1940s, when *Song of the South* premiered, ambivalent or outright negative affects were not confined to the screen but also came to the fore in the treatment of live-action bodies and living actors, such as James Baskett. As noted earlier, Baskett is portrayed in a "cartoony" fashion in his role as Uncle Remus through high-key lighting and charmingly rustic costuming, which lends him an aura of idealized unreality and allows him to integrate into the animated mise-en-scène. However, this harmonious integration belied the historical context of an era in which African American bodies were strongly marked by the lack of integration in the American South, where the film was set and where it premiered. Even though he starred in the film, Baskett was not present at its premiere in Atlanta owing to the southern city's segregation laws—a fact that some southern journalists tried to justify or gloss over. In an unusually laudatory review for the *Atlanta Constitution* from October 15, 1946, titled "*Song of the South* Wins High Praise," reporter Harold Martin wrote, "It is a shame, though, that Baskett cannot come [to the premiere]. The reason, of course, is that he is a Negro, and . . . to bring him here would cause him many embarrassments, for his feelings are the same as any man's."[36] This rhetorical move at once naturalizes segregation ("the reason, *of course*, is that he is a Negro") and displaces the negative affects of shame and embarrassment onto Baskett himself, rather than placing blame on the segregated theater or the systemic racism that created the situation. Martin attempts to soften the blow by praising Baskett's performance and saying that "his feelings are the same as any man's," but he is then content to put those unpleasant feelings aside and continue on with praising the film, writing, "Laying aside the embarrassing sociological problem [of] premiering the picture here and returning to the picture itself—it is a masterpiece."[37] It may seem that Baskett got his due when the Academy of Motion Pictures (spurred by lobbying from Disney) awarded Baskett an Honorary Academy Award in 1948, making him the first Black man ever to receive an Oscar. But even Baskett's Oscar was a source of ambivalence in the African American community, as it was an "accomplishment that often existed in tension with unhappiness about the film itself."[38] Indeed, some theaters that catered to African American audiences refused to screen *Song of the South* at all.[39]

The ambivalent ugly feelings the film conjures up are evident not only in its production and premiere but also in its early reception. Martin was one of very few journalists to award *Song of the South* "high praise." It was a box-office failure upon its initial release in 1946 and was poorly received by most critics of the period, both on social and aesthetic grounds. White critics of the time generally appreciated the skillful animation but disliked the live-action sequences. For instance, Bosley Crowther of the *New York Times* wrote a review titled "Spanking Disney" in which he chastised Walt for using cartoon sequences "with all their fantastic joie de vivre, in a hackneyed and smug 'live action' story."[40] African American reviewers were even more openly critical of the "Uncle Tom" image perpetuated by the Uncle Remus character, with strong protests coming from African American newspapers like the *Chicago Defender* and from the NAACP.[41] Calls for pickets and boycotts were eventually scaled back or canceled when the film performed too poorly at the box office to merit protest. However, as Jason Sperb proves in his book *Disney's Most Notorious Film,* these critical reactions provide strong evidence that "*Song of the South* was *always* considered a racist film" even upon its first release and cannot be excused as a product of its times.[42] The film was rereleased in theaters several times over the decades, and even found commercial success in the Reagan-era climate of the 1970s and 1980s. However, Disney has increasingly marketed only the most lucrative parts of the film to newer generations of children, for instance, by including the song "Zip-a-Dee-Doo-Dah" in compilation music albums, while downplaying or erasing the film's racist imagery, both live action and animated. Tellingly, in 1989, the Tar Baby was replaced with a more generic jar of honey in the Splash Mountain ride based on *Song of the South*—a tacit recognition of the ugly feelings it might arouse.

Song of the South may have generated more controversy than any other Disney film. As such, it has been permanently locked in the "Disney vault." At the time of this writing, it remains unreleased in theaters since 1986 and is unavailable on (official) home video or on the Disney+ streaming service. It is widely available in pirated versions on YouTube and on the Internet Archive digital library, which is how I was able to watch it. Still, the lack of an official release has been the cause of much debate among fans over the decades. Indeed, the debate sprang up again in 2020 when HBO Max removed *Gone with the Wind* (dir. Victor Fleming, George Cukor, and Sam Wood, 1939) (one of Disney's inspirations for *Song of the South*) from its offerings due to its racist imagery.[43] While some fans have rallied in favor of rereleasing the film, others have levied renewed criticisms in the wake of the 2020 Black Lives Matter protests, lashing out at Disney on social media for its slow progress in retheming the Splash Mountain ride into a new ride based on Disney's 2009 film *The Princess and the Frog* (dir. Ron Clements and John Musker).[44]

Still, despite all the controversy, *Song of the South* has become incorporated into American popular culture. As Sperb ably demonstrates, Disney's idyllic vision of the South retains a powerful nostalgic appeal for some viewers. Third-party DVDs are available for purchase in the South, often positioned alongside *Gone with the Wind* memorabilia and Confederate flags. I noticed unofficial DVDs of *Song of the South* for sale in an antiques shop in Athens, Georgia, in October 2017, as part of a star-spangled display of retro Americana. The website SongoftheSouth.org offers its own DVD for sale online, along with a spirited defense of the film's artistic and social value. There is an active fan community for the film online, born of Disney's media convergence strategy which for decades has seen the studio continually repackage deracinated clips, songs, and individual stories from *Song of the South* in books, records, CDs, and video games to promote the nostalgic Disney brand and its legacy of classic, feel-good family films. Some fans commenting on the film on websites like the IMDb genuinely cannot perceive the racism inherent in the film. As Sperb points out, they "operate from a real position of pleasure—as in, the feeling is real."[45] They defend it because they enjoy it or have a nostalgic connection to it from childhood. For some BIPOC viewers, however, the impact of watching *Song of the South* may be more akin to Franz Fanon's famous description in *Black Skin, White Masks* of the racializing moment that struck him bodily with the knowledge that he was Black and therefore Other in the eyes of white American society, as the words "Look, a Negro!" shouted by white children replaced his own "corporeal schema" or tactile, kinesthetic lived experiences of Blackness with "a racial epidermal schema" imposed from the outside.[46] As Willett writes, the film has had an enduring negative effect on how the Brer Rabbit folktales—in particular, the Tar Baby story—are viewed in African American communities. Its attempts at a seamless hybridization of cinematic animation and live-action film in fact result in a form of disjunctive animatedness that reflects and perpetuates the lack of racial integration in American society of the 1940s and reveals a failure to appreciate and respectfully incorporate different bodies into the larger body politic that persists even today.

"Bad Taste" in Adult Hybrid Films

Though racial representation is the main focus of Ngai's chapter on animatedness, not every hybrid film that displays animatedness is based on negative racial stereotyping. The sensation of disconnect, disjunction, or disturbance of the objective and subjective can be evoked in many ways. Consider, for instance, hypersexualized female cartoon characters, such as the sequin-spangled femme fatale Jessica Rabbit or the aggressively sexual Holli Would from Ralph Bakshi's 1996 hybrid film *Cool World*. In these cases, exaggeration is used to evoke desire. In both of these films, however, there is a moment when the exaggeration goes too far and tips into disgust. In *Who Framed Roger Rabbit*, Eddie Valiant ventures into Toon Town looking for Jessica and instead encounters Rita Hyena: a woman who looks identical to Jessica from behind but turns around to reveal a distorted face with enormous lips stretching obscenely toward Eddie. Likewise, in *Cool World*, the "doodle" (or cartoon) character Holli Would, with her curvaceous body and sinuous gestures rotoscoped from the performance of voice actress Kim Basinger, is extremely attractive when attempting to seduce the live-action comics artist Jack Deebs (Gabriel Byrne) and make love to him to become "real." However, once she makes it to the real world, she begins to "blip" into a grotesque clown version of herself as her unstable cartoon nature intrudes on reality. In these cases, as in hybrid films dating back at least to *The Three Caballeros,* there is an oscillation from desire to disgust. In discussing these affects, Ngai writes that

> there is always a certain asymmetry in the pairing of disgust and desire, since disgust is a structured and agnostic emotion carrying a strong and unmistakable signal, while desire is often noisy or amorphous. Like animatedness, desire almost seems pre- or subaffective. There is thus a sense in which disgust is the ugliest of "ugly feelings," yet an interesting exception. For disgust is never ambivalent about its object. More specifically, it is never prone to producing the confusions between subject and object that are integral [to animatedness]. Whereas the obscuring of the subjective-objective boundary becomes internal to the nature of feelings like animatedness and paranoia, disgust strengthens and polices this boundary.[47]

Here, as Ngai explains, disgust is focused on an object: it says "*that,*" pointing to the thing which is the ostensible cause of one's disgust. There is a shift from an abstract and amorphous desire (for instance, for an idealized representation of attractiveness with no concrete body to grasp onto) into a concrete rejection of a specific thing. Disney's family films, like *Song of the South,* tend to operate mostly along lines of representation and animatedness, even in scenes that might be considered to have a potentially disgusting object, like the sticky, malformed Tar Baby. By contrast, independent, adult-oriented hybrid feature films of the late 1980s and 1990s often delve into the dialectic of desire and disgust. This is particularly apparent in a pair of films that deal with sex, food, and cockroaches: Yoshida Hiroaki's 1987 release *Twilight of the Cockroaches* and John Payson's 1996 retread of the same topic, *Joe's Apartment.* The basic premise of these two films can be summed up with the same one-line plot description

FIGURE 9. Cockroach character design in *Twilight of the Cockroaches* (1987).

from the IMDb: "A colony of cockroaches lives peacefully in a messy bachelor's apartment until his new girlfriend moves in."[48] However, the two films are quite different in tone and technique.

Twilight of the Cockroaches can best be described as a melodrama with war film undertones. It begins in medias res with a violent encounter between Naomi, a nineteen-year-old cockroach with a sweet anime-style girl's face on a curvaceous six-legged body (Figure 9), and a horrified live-action woman who has just arrived home to find a cockroach in the kitchen. Though Naomi begins to politely introduce herself and inquire after her friend Hans, the human woman immediately tries to stomp on her, an action visualized frighteningly from Naomi's point of view as a massive live-action shoe coming down directly at the camera. Naomi flees the woman's blows and escapes underneath a refrigerator. This instigates a long, placid opening credits sequence that explores the space underneath the fridge. Melancholy piano music plays over a live-action tracking shot that moves slowly through shadowed dust and debris. Everything is shown in extremely shallow focus so that textures take priority over objects, as with the haptic visuality found in the stop-motion films of the Brothers Quay. The textural environment and slightly shaky camerawork mimic a tiny body's movement through a comparatively vast world. This direct appeal to the senses of sight, touch, hearing, and motion through space invites identification with the cockroach character, immersing us in her embodied experience of the domestic space. However, the opening sequence as a whole also establishes a sense of disgust modeled by the woman, whose reactions of fright and horror at finding a cockroach in the kitchen are likely to be more familiar to many viewers than the imagined sensation of crawling around the dirty floor under a fridge.

Following this opening scene, the film returns to an earlier point in time to set up the anime-style cockroach characters in their "city," an environment that mixes naturalistic background animation with still photography of common household objects and foods. The narrative soon develops into a romance featuring a love triangle between Naomi, her loyal but bland fiancé Ichiro, and the noble, mysterious war hero Hans, who arrives in the night from another house where the cockroaches face daily attacks by humans wielding swatters and aerosol poison. In contrast to Hans's tales of total war, Naomi and her friends live in peace with their apartment's resident human, Saito, an apathetic bachelor who is celebrated by the cockroaches for his lack of housecleaning and tolerance of the cockroaches' noisy nightlife. Naomi's growing feelings for Hans lead her to follow him from this paradise into the apartment where he lives, that of the woman featured in the opening scene. Through Naomi's point of view, the audience is privileged with a double foreshadowing of the violent destruction that will occur when Saito begins to date the roach-hating "Office Lady" and is inspired to clean up his place. The conclusion of the film is melodramatically tragic, as both male cockroaches sacrifice themselves to save the pregnant Naomi, whose immunity to poison and ability to lay hundreds of eggs hold the key to the survival of the cockroach community.

In contrast to the mournful tone of *Twilight of the Cockroaches, Joe's Apartment* is a satirical gross-out comedy that invests the audience's point of view in the human characters rather than the cockroaches. The film opens with an aerial tracking shot of a singing cockroach that flies from the tip of the Statue of Liberty to the streets of New York. In a way, this is similar to the earlier Japanese film, which also starts with a long tracking shot through a seemingly vast environment. However, *Joe*'s cockroach is always visible in the shot, as the camera tracks its flight in an omniscient point of view that holds the roaches at a distance as amusing performers rather than incorporating them as embodied beings whose world we experience intimately through subjective camerawork. The narrative proper begins when the live-action human character Joe arrives by passenger bus in New York City. He begins by mentally composing lyrical letters about his arrival in the big city to his mother in voice-over, giving the audience access to his thoughts and establishing him as the film's protagonist and a locus of identification.

Upon disembarking from the bus, Joe is promptly mugged three times in a row, setting him up as a classic "country rube in the big city" character. Through dumb luck, Joe manages to take over an affordable but absolutely filthy apartment by claiming to be the son of an old lady tenant who has just died. (In fact, it is later revealed that she was murdered by hitmen hired by a corrupt senator, who is planning to raze the rent-controlled apartment complex and build a maximum-security prison in its place.) As a careless bachelor, Joe makes no attempt to clean up the squalor in the old woman's apartment. In fact, he eats an old piece of toast he finds lying around even after seeing that a cockroach has been sitting on it, in one of the film's first big gross-out moments. His complete lack of disgust and ignorance of basic hygiene earn the respect of the horde of cockroaches inhabiting the space: a wise-cracking, pop culture–referencing, singing-and-dancing ensemble cast rendered in CGI. Unlike the human characters in *Twilight of the Cockroaches,* Joe can understand the roaches' speech, so he is aware that they are magically sentient and also extremely annoying. However, he is content to live (more or less) in peace with the roaches until he falls in love with a beautiful and idealistic young woman named Lily, who dreams of reforming his run-down East Village neighborhood by starting a community garden. Her good-hearted attempts to improve the environment shine out visually in the colorful flowers that she plants in the filthy urban alleys. Her purity also contrasts with the designs of her father, the aforementioned corrupt senator who wants to raze Joe's apartment and build a prison on the site. Joe woos Lily by helping her in a variety of secretly revolting ways, such as collecting manure from horse-drawn buggies and an elephant parade with his hands to provide rich soil for her garden. Just as things seem to be going well, however, he quarrels with the cockroaches and Lily after the insect horde ends up literally falling all over her in an attempt to help Joe "get lucky." As a comedy, the film has a happy resolution in which an all-powerful wave of cockroaches builds the community garden, unites the quarreling lovers, and provides Joe with the deed to the entire apartment building, thwarting the scheming senator's plans to raze the insect paradise.

As these brief plot summaries would suggest, the generic tropes and animation techniques in these two cockroach films are quite different. *Twilight of the Cockroaches,* with its melancholic tone and tale of interspecies warfare, fits into what Susan J. Napier describes as the "elegiac mode" of Japanese anime, which inspires "a mood of mournfulness and melancholy, perhaps mixed with nostalgia."[49] The film is comparable to other 1980s elegies dealing with the material and spiritual effects of war on the "little people" *(shomin),* such as *Grave of the Fireflies* (dir. Isao Takahata, 1988) and *Barefoot Gen* (dir. Mori Masaki, 1983). This is no coincidence, because *Twilight*'s animation director, Hirata Toshio, codirected the first *Barefoot Gen* film and directed the sequel *Barefoot Gen 2* (1986). In a more allegorical way, *Twilight* can be read through the "representation" discourse as yet another anime that comments on Japan's wartime experiences and on racist or Orientalist perspectives of the Japanese held by Westerners. Indeed, according to a 1989 review of the film in the *Washington Post,* "director Yoshida has said that *Twilight* is about Japan, [and] that the concept of a 'hated' species is not unlike the racial and cultural enmity with which Japan is perceived."[50] Given that the late 1980s were the peak of the techno-Orientalist discourse based in alarmist Western responses to Japan's economic advancement,[51] it is perhaps not surprising that American reviewers were quick to pick up on and amplify commentary that made the film into a clear-cut representation of Japan as a nation and figured the cockroaches as Japanese Others.

Looking beyond the "national representation" discourse, however, it can also be argued that war-themed anime films are based on bodily engagement with the hardships faced by their innocent, identifiable characters, drawing on shared human experiences that have the potential to create empathy across differing national, cultural, and historical experiences. Takahata's *Grave of the Fireflies,* which depicts two war orphans struggling with hunger, exposure, and illness, is difficult to watch without crying sympathetic tears, even for non-Japanese viewers. Likewise, Masaki and Yoshida's *Barefoot Gen* is designed to provoke universal horror at the graphic depiction of flesh being stripped from the skeletons of Hiroshima's citizens by the atomic bomb. *Twilight* aims for similar major affects as other animated war elegies, especially in its violent, melodramatic climax in which all the cockroaches except Naomi are massacred. However, whether one finds the allegorical use of cockroaches touching or bathetic is a more subjective matter. Some scenes I found quietly moving, particularly the slow-tracking subjective camera shots showing the bug's-eye view of a vast world seen in shallow focus, which touched me with a sense of intimate vulnerability. However, I was not moved to tears by the tragic conclusion; in fact, I felt the urge to laugh at the earnestness of it all. Seeing such a serious narrative played out by 1980s-anime-styled cockroaches struck me as campy, as in Susan Sontag's description of "naïve, or pure, Camp [in which] the essential element is seriousness, a seriousness that fails."[52] Rather than invoking pure major affects, there is a kind of minor ambivalence or low-key abjection about the film that stems in part from its uneasy mixture of "giant" live-action humans and quasi-human animated insects.

Joe's Apartment also creates abject embodied affects, but from a completely different generic and national context. The feature was based on an MTV station-identifier short created by director John Payson, who was at that time the television network's director of on-air promotion and animated identifiers.[53] Payson was inspired to create his short film in part by *Twilight of the Cockroaches,* which was aired on television in the United States with an English dub starting in 1989 and played throughout the 1990s. However, like the network that aired it, Payson's film is much more grounded in the American youth culture of Generation X, which embraced satirical, body humor–based cult films like Kevin Smith's *Clerks* (1994) and crude animated television series like MTV's *Beavis and Butt-Head* (1993–2011). Following this trend, *Joe's Apartment* best fits into the subgenre of the gross-out comedy. Like Bakhtin's carnivalesque, gross-out comedy depends on "the lowering of all that is high, spiritual, ideal, abstract; it is a transfer to the material level, to the sphere of earth and body in their indissoluble unity."[54] In particular, gross-out films focus on bodily parts and functions that are embarrassingly out of the mind's control, such as vomiting, farting, and fluid emissions. These are cases in which corporeality asserts itself and provokes abject physical reactions of gagging, looking away, exclamations like "ew!" or, in the case of more pornographic imagery, sexual arousal. The first time I saw *Joe's Apartment* on television, I recall being almost unable to watch it. I was so irritated and disgusted that my body went into revolt. I kept impulsively standing up, pacing toward the television to turn it off, then returning to my seat to see what would happen next. Both *Joe's Apartment* and *Twilight of the Cockroaches* draw on narrative tropes and generic expectations of the body genres in the physical reactions they can provoke. Their modes of engagement are radically different, from the aesthetic valences of elegy to the low-brow appeal of gross-out comedy. However, the counterintuitive physical reactions they can provoke—ironic laughter at an elegy, restless irritation at a comedy—also hint at a deeper ambivalence of minor affect shared by the two films.

The affective dimensions of these two films are mediated by the techniques of hybrid animation used in each. On the surface, the two films take a very different technical approach to hybridization. *Twilight of the Cockroaches* juxtaposes live-action footage with the flat, simplified, animetic style of television anime, using both crosscutting (type 1 hybridization) and cel-animated cockroaches overlaid on live-action backgrounds (type 2 hybridization). There is little interaction between the humans and cockroaches besides a human foot or a swung newspaper crushing a roach—an easy effect to create compared to Disney's hybrid films, given that it requires simply the animated cockroaches to disappear rather than to have a reciprocal effect on the live-action actors. In addition, the character designs of the cockroaches are antinaturalistic to the point of being almost surreal, as the cockroaches have fully humanized faces on quasi-insect bodies. They stand on two humanlike back legs at many points, but they do not have any hands and crawl on all sixes with their legs bent and heads held up at humanly impossible angles at other points. With minimal shading, cycled mouth movements, and simplified features, the 2D character animation is markedly different from both the lush background paintings and the live-action footage. In contrast to the Disney tradition, there is almost no attempt to blend the hybrid elements of this film into a seamless whole.

Joe's Apartment, on the other hand, represents an early successful effort by New York's Blue Sky Productions at seamlessly integrating stop-motion and CGI with live-action footage of insects and humans (type 0 hybridization). The cockroaches are somewhat anthropomorphized in their bodily gestures to facilitate riding surfboards and performing Busby Berkeley dance routines, and so they have a certain quality of "animatedness" to them that stands out. However, they also have naturalistic anatomical features complete with mandibles, compound eyes, and a convincingly chitinous texture. They are further integrated into the live-action mise-en-scène using dynamic lighting, whereby the direction and color of light falling on the set are replicated on the cockroaches' oily carapaces. In this way, the animated images are able to convincingly interact with live-action actors in a more traditional Disney fashion.

Despite these differences, there are some striking similarities in the ways that animation and live-action are incorporated in these films, particularly as they evoke and disrupt desire with disgust. In both films, shots coded as sexually voyeuristic are rendered uncomfortable or even disgusting through animated excess. In *Twilight*, the frequent use of roach's-eye views also subjects the Office Lady to one of the most common shots in Japanese soft-core pornography: the panty shot. She is often shown from below in "upskirt" shots, and in one scene, she is also shown taking off her work clothes and putting on a short, tight party dress and red stiletto heels. The theme of voyeurism is even touched on narratively in a scene in which the Office Lady sits in her open window to cool off and is spied upon by Saito. The scene opens with a close-up of the Office Lady's full, glossed lips and her hand, with red-polished nails, holding a crystal glass with a few ounces of liquor and tinkling ice. Her fingers toy with her hair, stroke her throat, and set her glass down on her round, bare knee, all shown in extreme close-up in the fetishistic style of camerawork famously identified by Laura Mulvey in her work on the male gaze.[55] The sequence of close-ups and overhead shots of her body lasts around thirty seconds, allowing the viewer's gaze to linger on her. Finally, she gets up, showing the laced-up, corset-like back of her form-fitting top, and opens the window to sit outside. After a beat, there is a cut to a topless man standing on his balcony across the way, watching her. A cut back to the Office Lady shows her falling off the window ledge in a comically frantic attempt to get back inside. Placed significantly to the center left of this shot is a laundry rack with a bright blue bra and matching pair of lacy panties, which seem to glow as they are backlit by the light from her apartment. The woman tries to fetch her embarrassingly visible underwear, but the lace panties get caught on a clothespin, leaving her tugging at them in vain. This kind of encounter, which in a pornographic film would lead to a hook up, does in fact lead the Office Lady to begin dating Saito, the bachelor from across the way. Given that most of this film is about the elegiac tragedy of the cockroaches who die at the hands of the Office Lady, such sexualized depictions of her seem bizarrely out of place, even exploitative. They are scenes in remarkably bad taste, just as likely to evoke derision as desire. The sense of disgust is furthered by the fact

FIGURE 10. Cockroaches fall onto Lily's body to create a scene evocative of desire and disgust in *Joe's Apartment* (1996).

that every time we see the Office Lady after this, she is depicted as a giantess with massive, clunky footsteps, egging Saito on to mass murder via cleaning chemicals and insecticides. We may see up her skirt, but we also see up her nose. In this way, the Office Lady becomes a figure who both expresses and evokes disgust.

Such ambivalent affects are even easier to come by in *Joe's Apartment,* which, as a gross-out film, takes disgust as its primary affect. However, there are moments when desire intrudes inappropriately, in bad taste, and in the same exploitative manner that relies on displaying women's bodies. The scene in which Joe brings Lily home to his apartment is a case in point. The climactic moment comes just as Joe and Lily are becoming intimate. As the two get closer, the cockroaches that have been swinging on the lamp above their heads lose their balance and come pouring out of the shade onto Lily. A tilt down from her shocked face emphasizes that they fall not just on her head but also into her cleavage, which is highlighted by a strappy black tank top (Figure 10). The composition of the shot, in which Lily's face is cut off and her breasts are emphasized by the plunging angled lines of her necklaces and the spray pattern of the cockroaches, suggests an element of titillation in this gross-out moment, which ambivalently evokes both disgust and desire. But once again, it is a moment of bad taste, as it is used purely for shock value in an exploitative way.

Toward "Good Effects"

There are cases in which the blending of disgust and desire in animation can be used in good taste. Consider, for instance, the stop-motion films of the Brothers Quay, such as *Street of Crocodiles* (1986), which viscerally evoke such gut-churning yet sensually intriguing experiences as stroking raw meat. Or take the live-action and stop-motion hybrids of Jan Švankmajer, which depict people being aroused by such typically distasteful sensations as stuffing balls of rolled-up bread into their nostrils and ears or having their toes nibbled by fish in *Conspirators of Pleasure* (1996). These auteur works are generally recognized as having artistic merit because the affects of desire and disgust are used within a restrained, patterned, and (especially in the case of Švankmajer) socially critical way, reflecting the aesthetic traditions of European surrealism.[56] Hybrid live-action and animation films like *Song of the South, Twilight of the Cockroaches,* and *Joe's Apartment,* on the other hand, are generally considered ethically problematic, or just bad films made in bad taste. That said, even "bad" hybrid films can effectively evoke embodied sensations and complex affects like animatedness, desire, and disgust, as there is something clearly disjunctive about the ways in which they (mis)match live action and animated bodies. Animation's lively characters attract us with their haptic visuality, their affective power, and their apparent spirit, even as we may recognize them as inaccurate and possibly harmful representations of the lived bodies and experiences of humans who have been depicted in exaggerated or stereotypical ways. Likewise, the actual bodies of actors and actresses become animated in hybrid films, imbuing them with the attractional power of animation even as they are stripped of their lived dimension for all but the sharpest-eyed observers. For those who watch James Baskett as a skilled, dignified actor in *Song of the South* rather than the stereotypical character of Uncle Remus, it may be possible catch the photochemical traces of the actor's body at work. At the same time, for those who watch the Tar Baby for its uncanny transformation or the cockroaches in *Twilight* for their moments of intimate vulnerability, it is possible to perceive the traces of another kind of laboring life: a liveliness brought about by the incorporation of image, technics, and experience that takes place between the animator, the anime machine, and the audience. This kind of liveliness is powerful in itself, but it is also subject to the manipulations of larger disciplinary powers operating in society that aim to shape perception and embodiment along particular lines that support dominant ideologies.

The power dynamics of embodiment in animation are the topic of the next chapter, which examines CGI and special effects in films of the 2010s and early 2020s. Contemporary digital cinema extends the techniques of hybridization begun in films like *Song of the South* and *Joe's Apartment* by perfecting the seamless blending of CGI animated effects into live action. Although digital films are technically "hybrid" in terms of their production techniques, the animation is no longer highlighted through metalepsis as a distinct space or way of being but is rendered in such a perceptually realistic fashion that it becomes difficult or impossible to distinguish CGI from live-action footage. This drive toward seamlessness and perceptual realism is particularly evident in the so-called live-action remakes of classic cel-style films by Disney studios, as well as in Hollywood remakes of Japanese manga and anime. So, in the next chapter, I discuss how seamless compositing is used to incorporate and reshape CGI animation, live-action footage, actors' motion-captured bodies, and the sensory perceptions of those watching live-action remakes of animated films.

CHAPTER 3

Phenopower in Live-Action Remakes

Just after the title card for *The Lion King,* there is a short scene in which an adorable four-striped grass mouse almost becomes a snack for the villainous lion, Scar. In the 1994 cel-animated version, this scene is narrative driven: it establishes character motivation through Scar's dialogue ("Life's not fair, is it? You see I, well, I shall never be king") and foreshadows events in the film through the escape of the big-eyed, chubby-cheeked mouse, which slips through Scar's claws as the equally innocent, neotenous lion cub Simba will do later. In the 2019 version of *The Lion King,* however, this sequence serves another purpose. First and foremost, it establishes the film's aesthetic as the latest (at that time) in a series of "live-action remakes" released by Disney. Expanding on a shot of the mouse that lasts only eight seconds in the cel-animated version, director John Favreau and his team of digital animators and virtual reality cinematographers create what is to all appearances a two-minute nature documentary short that tracks the mouse's journey through a lushly detailed natural environment.

The sequence begins with a view across a small, shallow pond, in which we briefly see the reflection of a mouse flash by in the gently rippling water. The mouse runs down a log toward the camera to take a drink from the pond. As it sips, the camera tilts down very slightly, as if a wildlife filmmaker has adjusted the camera's position in real time to make sure the mouse stays in frame. When the mouse takes off suddenly to the left, the camera tracks it, moving fast as it scurries, pausing when it pauses, and performing an L-shaped maneuver as the mouse runs down a curving fallen trunk. When the mouse emerges into the foreground, a quick change of focus brings its face into clear view as it pauses to clean its whiskers, as the cel-animated mouse in the 1994 version did (Figure 11). Then it is off and running again, engaging physically with a rocky terrain that takes visible effort to traverse. It spirals around a stalk of grass as it climbs and slips

FIGURE 11. Selective focus highlights the face of a CGI mouse in the live-action remake of *The Lion King* (2019).

back, trying to scale a vertical rise. The clearest visual referent to the nature documentary genre comes as the mouse climbs a tall stalk of grain that bows down under its weight. In this delicate moment, the mouse waves its tail for balance as the stalk bends and the image shifts in and out of focus as the camera operator (seemingly) struggles to keep a lock on a small, moving subject shot at close range. The mouse's balancing act is so accurate and the camerawork so attuned to the difficulties of capturing a small animal in action that it is easy to imagine that this scene is purely live action, perhaps even wild nature captured directly from life.

Favreau has been a vocal supporter of the idea that his remake of *The Lion King* is a novel kind of live-action filmmaking despite being entirely computer animated. In interviews and making-of featurettes, he insists that he was "trying to pursue an approach that made this film feel less like an animated movie and more like a live-action film. And not just a live-action film, but a live-action film in the way that I'm used to photographing it."[1] His motives were not only aesthetic but overtly commercial. In another interview quoted in *Cinefex* magazine, he bluntly stated, "We felt if we made a movie that *appeared* to be animated, people wouldn't have a reason to see it. . . . But if we could make it appear to be live-action, that would warrant a whole new production of *The Lion King*."[2] The appearance of live action that Favreau stresses here was created using the latest in digital animation and special effects technologies. For instance, an interactive 3D model of the savanna setting was created in a VR volume that could be recorded live by a team of cinematographers. This allowed voice actors to shoot their scenes together on a soundstage "in" the VR environment, rather than recording lines individually in a sound booth. The VR world's designers made extensive use of video reference material shot on-location in Kenya with live animals and even programmed virtual grass to grow to different heights in a kind of controlled experiment in artificial life. In these ways, this film goes beyond what is traditionally considered animation. And yet, it also falls short of what is traditionally considered live action. In entertainment journalism and online fan forums, debates have raged over whether the 2019 *Lion King* should be considered animation, live action, a hybrid film, or some other, brand-new medium representing a dramatic technological advance. Not surprisingly, Favreau has actively promoted the "new technological medium" side.

My concern in this chapter, however, is less with the ontology of live action versus animation and more with the phenomenological experience of so-called live-action remakes. For these films to *appear* as live action, the animatic or "an-ontological"[3] aspects of animation—that is, the fact that animation is not indexical but is created frame by frame and has its own mode of existence—must be downplayed or recast within a discourse that sees CGI as a supplementary special effect used to enhance (but not replace) 35mm or digital film footage. Ontologically speaking, these films do not present an entirely novel challenge to either animation or cinema. *The Lion King* is technically a fully animated film created frame by frame with digital animation software, whereas the majority of Disney's remakes that combine live-action footage with digitally animated effects, such as *Mulan*, can be seen as extensions of the hybrid films discussed in chapter 2 into the digital era. Indeed, the majority of the "live-action" Hollywood blockbuster films released in the 2010s and into the 2020s are a composited blend of photographic footage (either celluloid or digital) and animated characters, objects, or environments. What has changed is the way in which these films are classified as genres and how they generate new audience expectations and responses.

I consider the rhetoric of photorealism and "live-action-ness" surrounding Disney's recent remakes to be an effort at distinguishing the computer-animated films created at Walt Disney Animation

Studios in the twenty-first century (say, *Tangled* [dir. Nathan Greno and Byron Howard, 2010] or *Frozen* [dir. Chris Buck and Jennifer Lee, 2013]) from the live-action fantasy and adventure films with computer-animated effects produced by Walt Disney Pictures, such as the Pirates of the Caribbean franchise (2003–17). In contrast to the computer-animated film proper, with its careful balance of 3D realism and stylized exaggeration drawn from the history of cel animation, live-action remakes are positioned as a subgenre within Hollywood's larger "special effects blockbuster" tradition and, in particular, the digital cinema blockbusters of the early twenty-first century. Favreau may insist that his *Lion King* is "an entirely new medium,"[4] but in fact Disney's live-action remakes follow the basic template described by Manovich in the year 2001 for mainstream digital cinema as a kind of filmmaking based on compositing various graphic and photographic digital assets. Today, these assets include things like texture maps, lighting setups, algorithms for particle motion and fluid dynamics, VR environments, character models, and motion- or performance-captured data, with the goal of creating a seamless photorealistic effect. Though they are supported by digital compositing, however, live-action remakes do not actually stake their claim to generic difference based only on the ontology of the medium itself. They are no more grounded in the ontology of the photographic image than computer-animated films, which are also an assemblage of various digital assets. *The Lion King* remake; the 2019 Oscar winner for Best Animated Feature, *Spider-Man: Into the Spider-Verse* (dir. Bob Persichetti, Peter Ramsey, and Rodney Rothman, 2018); and a live-action special effects blockbuster like *Avatar: The Way of Water* (dir. James Cameron, 2022) are all "animated" films in that the majority of their imagery was created through frame-by-frame animation techniques like CGI and motion capture, composited with other video assets. What matters in categorizing these films as "live-action" or "animated" is an aesthetic and discursive difference in which live-action remakes are identified as such based on their promotion of the photorealistic visual style common to mainstream digital cinema, especially in Hollywood blockbusters. As such, they are distinguished phenomenologically, as the audience is meant to experience the live-action remake as something different from the cel-animated original by perceiving it through the lens of digital cinema or "postcinema" and not through the tradition of hand-drawn animation. Favreau recognizes this (perhaps inadvertently?) when he claims, "To say [*The Lion King*, 2019] is animated I think is misleading as far as what the expectations might be. And it also changes the way you sit and watch it."[5] Hybrid films may be old news, but the public's expectations for live-action remakes, as well as "the way the audience sits and watches" them, have changed materially and perceptually.

In this chapter, then, I argue that live-action remakes can be grasped not solely through their digital ontology but also through a particular set of discursive, stylistic, and narrative conventions that direct or train the audience's sensory experience of the film. These qualities include a valorization of perceptual realism and seamless compositing in the films' production and advertising, as well as a mode of nostalgic remediation in their reception. These discourses and practices together promote a media ecology based on what I call *phenopower*: a form of biopower that is specifically concerned with shaping the audience's perceptions of sensory or embodied experiences in accordance with dominant ways of seeing, hearing, and feeling. In the case of live-action remakes, this means training audiences to accept a form of "realism" or haptic visuality based on the dominant conventions of photographic lenses and recorded motion. Of course, cinematic movement into depth and ballistic vision can be found in many earlier animated works, notably in the expressive hyperrealism and technical superiority that have defined "Disney-Formalism" since the 1930s.[6] However, I show that the live-action remake subgenre is part of an intensification and increasing pervasiveness of phenopower in the twenty-first century. In many respects, live-action remakes are part of a much broader trend in mainstream digital cinema of the 2010s and early 2020s. This is evident not just in Disney's remakes of its own works, such as *The Lion King* and *Mulan*, but also in Hollywood adaptations of Japanese anime, such as Rob Letterman's *Pokémon: Detective Pikachu*, in which we can see how the ideology of seamlessness affects depictions of racialized, disabled, gendered, and nationally coded bodies. Following on the considerations of cinematic anime and hybrid films in chapters 1 and 2, this chapter considers live-action remakes and adaptations of cel-animated works as examples of the ways in which haptic visuality and sensorimotor experiences have been reterritorialized within global late-capitalist societies of control to manage audience expectations and expand the "training of the senses" that has long been a part of mainstream cinema.[7]

Defining Phenopower

To define phenopower, I would first like to unpack the concepts mentioned earlier that underpin it, namely, perceptual realism, seamlessness, and the training of the senses. In his 2010 article "Through the Looking Glass: Philosophical Toys and Digital Visual Effects," digital effects scholar Stephen Prince revisits his earlier conception of perceptual realism, defined as "the replication via digital means of contextual cues designating a three-dimensional world," such as "information source about the size and positioning of objects in space, their texturing and apparent density of detail, the behavior of light as it interacts with the physical world, principles of motion and anatomy, and the physics involved in dynamic systems such as water, clouds, and fire."[8] Along with imitating life itself, perceptual realism is based on imitating the effects of the camera recording that world, such as lens flares or shaky-cam effects, which generate a sense of photorealism: the visually coded type of realism associated with photography and with indexical live-action film's ability to capture reality directly and objectively. Importantly, Prince argues in his 2010 article that perceptual realism does *not* depend on the photochemical capture of reality on celluloid film. Instead, he believes that "digital tools give filmmakers an unprecedented ability to replicate and emphasize these [contextual] cues [for photorealism]" and that "the referential status of the representation does not matter in this conception of realism."[9] Just as I have argued of live-action remakes, the ontology or origin of the image is not what is at stake here. The key factor is maintaining the *appearance* of reality, no matter the source of the image. As an example, Prince contrasts contemporary digital special effects with the practical effects in early films like *The Lost World* (dir. Harry O. Hoyt, 1925) and *King Kong* (dir. Merian C. Cooper and Ernest B. Schoedsack, 1933), in which "the compositing of live action, matte paintings and miniatures . . . was visibly false, compromised by overt matte lines between the elements and by the planar rendition of space that prevented the matted creature from interacting with the live actors."[10] In digital special effects, by contrast, elements can be composited without the artificial "seaminess" of visible lines or separated planes of action, which break the illusion of reality. Paradoxically, "real" (indexical) practical special effects can appear more "fake" to the average viewer today than "artificial" (anontological) digital images, which are considered "realistic." This complex play of realism and illusion is an effect of perceptual realism.

To give a concrete example, perceptual realism in the live-action remake of *The Lion King* is grounded in the densely textural, spacious, and naturally lit world of the savanna, with its plains of waving grass and rough, rocky gorge. The naturalism of the mise-en-scène is further enhanced by the dimensionality of the VR volume soundstage, which cinematographers could physically move through and record using digital sensors attached to the dollies and Steadicam rigs that would traditionally hold a film camera. *Photo*-realism is enhanced by shots that mimic the effects of lens-based photographic equipment, such as the inclusion of shallow depth of field and focusing problems in the mouse scene. The lions, too, appear much more photorealistic than the 1994 film's "cartoon" lions in terms of their textured fur, bodily proportions, and behavioral gestures, such as pacing and ear flicking, which match what might be called our "natural perception" of lions—that is, the perception we would have if we were to see a living lion in a zoo or in the wild. We are more likely to accept the digital lions we see on-screen as animals that could exist in our material world than we are the Simba and Nala of the 1994 film. We might even say that they really do exist in the form of the lions living in Disney's Animal Kingdom and in the Maasai Mara game reserve in Kenya that were used as models for the characters. At the same time, however, we know that they are not *really* real, because real lions can't talk, much less sing and dance. And so, when watching animated films, we are also more critical of "unnatural" or "unrealistic" animal motions and expressions that might break the suspension of disbelief and reveal the mediated nature of our perceptions. For instance, I find the "lip flaps" of talking animals weird and distracting in photorealistic films because they do not match my natural perception of the motions that animals can perform, whereas I easily accept lip-synced mouths in cel-style animation because such stylization is a naturalized part of the genre and medium. Therefore live-action remakes create a certain tension between the expressive, animatic potentials of digital imaging and the gesture toward indexical referents ("based on real lions!") created by the photorealistic style. The special effects and animation in live-action remakes like *The Lion King* are judged "good" by mainstream audiences to the extent that they are consistent with the photographic conventions of perceptual realism and as "bad" or "weird" to the extent that they break the illusion by revealing the seams between the various sources or planes of the image.

The seamless integration of elements from many sources is crucial not just in live-action remakes but in Hollywood's digital cinema blockbusters more broadly. In *The Language of New Media,* Manovich holds up seamless compositing as the primary goal of mainstream, commercial digital cinema as it was developing at the turn of the millennium. In a prescient passage, he writes, "In principle, given enough time and money, one can create what will be the ultimate digital film: 129,000 frames (ninety minutes) completely painted by hand from scratch, but indistinguishable in appearance from live photography."[11] This description of the "ultimate digital film" matches closely with Favreau's stated goal of creating a film entirely using digital tools that appears exactly like the other live-action films he has made and with the seamless perceptual realism evident in *The Lion King.* It should come as no surprise that Disney would take this approach, given that Manovich views seamless compositing as a common technique in Hollywood blockbusters like *Forrest Gump* (dir. Robert Zemeckis, 1994). However, seamlessness is also associated in Manovich's work with other forms of illusion created for social and political control, such as carefully planned routes that were traveled by motorcades of visiting officials in the former Soviet Union or the facades of the "Potemkin Villages" used to convince Catherine the Great of her subjects' (nonexistent) prosperity. Seamlessness, in Manovich's view, is also a form of elision, papering over the cracks in the foundations of the image.

Given that live-action remakes, as a subgenre of Manovich's digital cinema, use seamless compositing to create perceptually realistic worlds and bodies full of texture and dimension, it may seem that they are better equipped to evoke embodiment through haptic visuality than are cel-animated films or traditional cel and live-action hybrid films. *The Lion King* places a great deal of stock in depicting weight, balance, and movement into the depths of a highly tactile world. From the mouse slipping back as it tries to scale a cliff face to the dramatic difficulties that Mufasa faces while climbing the gorge walls in the stampede scene, *The Lion King* consistently displays the kind of "musculature" described by Jennifer Barker in her phenomenological account of embodiment in cinema.[12] When I saw the 3D release of this film in the theater, I was struck by how the scene of Mufasa trying to climb the crumbling rock walls made me *feel* the muscular effort of interacting with the physical world to the point of tensing up and holding my breath, even though I knew very well that both the world of the savanna and the lion's sinewy bodies were digital creations. Christopher Holliday likewise argues that "by confronting head-on the seduction and spectacle of convincing computer graphics, certain phenomenological accounts citing the computer-animated films [such as Barker's analysis of *Toy Story*] counter any critical assumption that the boundaries of film sensorium and embodied spectatorship are policed solely by experimental and avant-garde film practices, or that they operate chiefly outside Hollywood within international art cinemas."[13] As Holliday suggests, embodied spectatorship is frequently found in mainstream films, including digitally animated ones. I do not dispute this claim; in fact, it is essential to the arguments in this chapter.

However, if critical reaction to *The Lion King* remake is anything to go by, there is still something crucial missing in these highly tactile, seamlessly composited, perceptually realistic digital films. A quick, unscientific survey of reviews on the aggregator website Rotten Tomatoes reveals a recurrent complaint among professional film critics: *The Lion King* remake lacks something like heart or spirit or the magic of animation. These objections are not just technological conservatism or a rose-tinted preference for the "original"; rather, they point to a lack of what I have termed the "liveliness" of animation, born from the balance of stylized representation, self-reflexive mediation, and affective incorporation that has always characterized animated works. It is my contention that just because live-action remakes *can* depict more perceptually realistic 3D environments, textures, and bodily movements than cel animation does not mean that they must automatically convey a strong phenomenological sense of embodiment as an experience *felt from within* or perceived subjectively from an embodied perspective, rather than viewed from an abstract or instrumental outside position. Most live-action remakes work within a photorealistic paradigm that emphasizes adherence to the laws of physics, lens-based perception, naturalized or given appearances, and the seamless compositing of live-action and animated images. In some of these cases, the body can become nothing more than another asset: a digitized commodity, a manipulable object, a conduit for biopower or even ontopower—the power to determine what exists and how it does so. As shorthand, I call such an occurrence the *body-as-asset*. It is this type of body that is crucial to the development of phenopower.

Much like perceptual realism, phenopower may be seen as a form of what feminist film scholar Elizabeth Stephens has termed the "training of the senses" through cinema.[14] Stephens points out that no sensory experience, be it sight or touch, is purely natural. All of our senses are trained by cultural tradition, and more often than not this training is shaped by hegemonic forces within a given society at a given time. While many feminist film phenomenologists, such as Sobchack, Marks, and Walton, and, to some extent, my own work, tend to hold up tactility as resistant or counterhegemonic within an optical regime that privileges vision, Stephens points out that touch, too, is part of its own discourse, often related to gendered concepts of sensuality and sexuality. Drawing on Foucault's concept of biopower, she argues that the "cinema of sensation" is also a "technology of the self" that can become a disciplinary "technology of power."[15] In the end, Stephens is trying not to criticize or dismantle the project of feminist film phenomenology or to deny the power of the tactile but to point out that "while the heightening of the senses experienced by film-goers can provide the means by which to cultivate different modes of subjectification and new kinds of sensation, it can also serve as form of disciplinary training."[16]

This disciplinary training can take place through many avenues. Stephens draws primarily on Foucault's concepts of biopower as a structural feature of society that governs the bodies and behaviors of subjects. In a complementary but different way, Lamarre focuses on platformativity and ontopower, defined as an infraindividual interconnection between screen, platform, and viewing subject, or a form of power that "strives to capture the relation between the human life-form and the signalectic life-form"[17] without becoming mired in the personal psychology of individual viewers. However, to consider how films engage the senses on intimate and personal levels, as in queer and feminist phenomenology, there needs to be a way to explain how media exercise power over the individual's sensory perception, both in its prerational moment and in its moment of transition into reflection or cognition. This is the process that I define as *phenopower*: a training of the senses in which perception is modulated and bodily experience is evoked for the purposes of discipline or social control.

To put it simply, if ontopower is control over what *is*, then phenopower is control over what *appears*. It is a means of subtly training audience expectations, perceptions, and experiences of films. One example is the use of lens-based photographic cues in perceptually realistic special effects, such as rack focus, shaky cam, and lens flares, which are repeated until the majority of viewers agree that the photographic style is "realistic" (and therefore serious, mature, and prestigious) while the animetic style is "cartoony" (and therefore frivolous, immature, and gimmicky), despite that digital live-action and animated images are both made up of pixels with no indexical connection to reality.

Phenopower concerns both what is screened for us and what is screened from us, that is, what is made to appear and what is kept out of our fields of perception. This is not simply a matter of hiding coded or subliminal messages in media works, as theories of film as representation would have it. Neither is it based on conceptions of mind and consciousness that come from idealism or Cartesian dualism, which would separate biological life (bio-) or being (onto-) from abstract mental appearances. Instead, phenopower takes place throughout our entire field of perception as it occurs in embodiment and enworldedness. This is because phenopower acts on us not only through rational recognition of an object for what it is (its ontological dimension) but also in the prerational stage of perception that provides instantaneous sensations of empathetic pleasure or pain, adrenaline release and motor reactions, and other physical effects born of the action of mirror neurons. However, this does not mean that the viewer is merely a biological automaton deprived of agency and individuality under the operations of phenopower, as film critics like Baudry argue when they describe film as a manipulation of the unconscious.[18] I do not believe that phenopower, and the digital media that promote it in live-action remakes, has such a totalizing, deterministic effect. It rather addresses each viewer individually, evoking fleeting memories, sensory associations, embodied traumas, and neurological pathways built up along many different frameworks. We cannot say that certain viewers are more susceptible to phenopower because they have a given physical or mental "disorder." As Lamarre rightly says, this kind of approach among media scholars has led to some "highly abusive accounts of consumers,"[19] such as those found in physiological and psychological typologies of otaku. Phenopower affects individuals in different ways not as a function of fixed types but through the fluctuations in sensory and perceptual processing that each of us experience throughout our lives. If all viewers perceive differently, however, we must all still perceive *something* in order to interact with it, or at least become aware of a momentary lack of perception, as in Lamarre's "stuff of blink."[20] Therefore phenopower does not target any one type of viewer or create disordered behaviors like addiction. It simply affects us on the level of perception, a process we all must necessarily go through if we are to engage with media at all. It is something we are both empowered and entrained by, sometimes simultaneously.

This is where a phenomenological account of media spectatorship becomes useful for watching live-action remakes and digital cinema in general. Recent postphenomenological scholars, such as Shane Denson in his work on discorrelated images, have argued that phenomenology is no longer quite so useful as an analytic tool because digital imaging today supersedes the capacities of our senses and perception.[21] Indeed, discorrelation is evident in some examples I consider throughout this chapter. On the other hand, however, James J. Hodge argues in his book *Sensations of History* that even though "a certain opacity shapes any human encounter with digital media because they largely operate at scales and speeds beyond human cognition and perception," it can still be argued that "phenomenology furnishes an especially pertinent critical vocabulary for encountering the experiential opacity of digital media" because it allows us to consider how we perceive the experience of the imperceptible or the opacity of digital media itself.[22] He further states that "in the digital age, *animation* emerges as a newly significant field of moving images forms for grasping, understanding, and encountering historical experience."[23] Hodge's focus is on animation used in experimental video installations, but phenomenological approaches can also be applied to the seamlessly composited digital animation of live-action remakes and to the flows and blockages in perception that they present.

The most basic exercise of phenomenology is to release the mind into prerational perception and to then reflect on that perception, rather than taking our preconceived notions of the world as natural, given, and inevitable. To respond to the operations of phenopower, it is necessary to throw oneself bodily into a film as if being thrown into the world, as Heidegger says—to embrace the "thrownness" of that experience and *feel* the film as much as possible, without criticizing or judging beforehand. Only then can we reflect on what was perceived and begin to notice the ways in which our senses were trained, even if the exact mechanisms of that training remain opaque. For instance, you might contemplate what it is like to be made to identify with a form of embodiment that is uncomfortable or alien to your own lived body. This is a feeling cisgender women might have to deal with in a male-oriented mediascape where women are viewed from the outside as sex objects rather than felt from the inside as subjects. (I suspect that it is also something that BIPOC viewers may experience in a white-dominated society, though as a white person, I cannot speak to that from my own situated knowledge.) Or then again, you might consider what it is like to feel very strongly identified with a body that is unlike your own, or is maybe even impossible for you to achieve: an animal, an alien, an object—in short, a Body without Organs (BwO) that acts as a virtual plane of desire (about which, more in chapter 5). All of these experiences may be subject to phenopower in different ways. Like Foucault's biopower, phenopower can operate either in the directly controlling fashion of punishment, by forcing one to adhere to a perception of embodiment that does not fit but is socially regulated, or in the more subtle fashion of discipline, operating through desire and the self-work required to reach the perceived fantastic body, as when fans emulate their favorite movie stars or dress in cosplay as anime characters. However, if you notice and reflect on these phenomenal experiences, it is possible to alter or intervene in the operation of phenopower. In terms of live-action remakes, this means accepting the appeal to perceptual realism that the films make, yet feeling them over carefully for both their seamlessness and their seamy, uncanny, or disturbing moments. It also means reflecting on the impact these films are having in the world in which we are entangled and on the bodies that are incorporated in and by animation.

Live-Action Remakes and the Digital Body

To understand how live-action remakes shape the senses through phenopower, it is important to consider how digital cinema has (re)animated the body. While I have argued in the previous two chapters that cel animation can evoke haptic visuality and liveliness, live-action remakes differ from cel-based works in raising the issue of digital media and embodiment, which has been a major point of debate in film phenomenology. In this section, then, I distinguish between the kinds of embodiment found in computer-animated film proper and in digital animation used for special effects within a live-action context and show how live-action remakes relate to both.

In the field of animation studies, it is widely asserted that animation is not a genre but a medium in itself, encompassing many forms of frame-by-frame image creation from the most orthodox cel-style cartoons to the most experimental new imaging techniques.[24] Within this larger medium, individual genres and subgenres may emerge. For instance, in *The Computer-Animated Film,* Holliday argues that the purely computer-animated film, of the sort produced by Pixar and Disney Animation Studios, can be considered a unique genre within the medium of animation. Computer-animated films share common narrative and thematic tropes, such as parodies of other genres and narrative structures focused around the journey. They also share a "heightened three-dimensional aesthetic style," though the exact look may vary from studio to studio or film to film.[25] Finally, they are characterized by their "creative bargains with the real, adopting a compromise position that checks the received teleological narrative of realism with the expressive possibilities of the cartoon."[26] In this way, the "textual legibility of the computer-animated film as a genre is primarily informed by the distinctiveness and creativity of animation as both a medium and a set of formal histories."[27] Computer-animated films are thus a distinct new genre but one that still continues the legacy of (largely American) cel animation in their mix of naturalism (for instance, in the lighting, texture, detail, and volumetric modeling of backgrounds) and stylization, as when the facial structures and bodily proportions of human or animal characters are exaggerated for expressivity. As such, the style of embodiment found in computer-animated characters retains a measure of the plasmatic, transformative, and lively qualities of the cel-animated characters discussed in the previous chapters of this book.

By contrast, live-action remakes, along with other digital effects blockbusters, tend to draw more on tools that enhance the perceptual realism of character bodies, such as motion and performance capture. The major goal of this stream of filmmaking has been to eliminate the disruptive "uncanny valley" effect that was evident in early attempts at animating human or animal bodies in perceptually realistic ways. As Nicholas Bestor summarized, the term *uncanny valley* was originally coined by Japanese robotics researcher Mori Masahiro in 1970 to describe the unsettling effect of an "*almost* perfect human representation."[28] Computer-animated films, such as *Final Fantasy: The Spirits Within* (dir. Hironobu Sakaguchi and Motonori Sakakibara, 2000), and films that relied heavily on performance capture, such as *The Polar Express* (dir. Robert Zemeckis, 2004), can be seen as prime examples of the uncanny valley effect. In the latter case, Bestor notes that senior visual effects editor Jerome Chen developed the style of performance capture used in *The Polar Express,* in which both bodily movements and facial expressions are captured at once rather than in separate passes, specifically because "it was too difficult to get the performance to be seamless" when bodily motion was separated from facial performance, as in earlier motion capture techniques.[29]

Despite aiming for seamless integration, however, a new kind of split arises in these films: the cognitive dissonance caused by perceptual reflexes in the human brain when it recognizes natural, lifelike movement in artificial, inhuman forms. Quoting special effects scholar Dan North, Bestor argues that when "the balance between the visibly false and the partially realistic has been upset," we perceive the "seams" between the human and the inhuman.[30] Other critics of performance capture, such as Scott Balcerzak, have seen this split as evidence of the disembodiment that results when human actors are transformed into virtual characters. Writing on Andy Serkis, Balcerzak argues that in performance capture, "the actor is literally stripped of his physical body to exist as pure kinesis."[31] However, Serkis himself has tried to mitigate the uncanny valley effect in interviews and in his performance style by redefining performance capture as a highly physical, humanized, and expressive new form of acting. As Bestor shows, Serkis's efforts are considered successful when they can be figured as seamless by reviewers like Roger Ebert, who claimed, "One never knows exactly where the human ends and the effects begin, but Serkis and/or Caesar gives the best performance in the movie [*Rise of the Planet of the Apes* (dir. Rupert Wyatt, 2011)]."[32] In this regard, we can see the seamless integration of body and digital image in performance capture as a way of overcoming both the uncanny valley effect and the anxieties around disembodiment that haunted early digital cinema.

That said, critics from within the field of animation studies have also expressed qualms about the use and representation of the body in performance capture. In her article "Collaboration without Representation: Labor Issues in Motion and Performance Capture," Mihaela Mihailova traces two seemingly opposed but in fact interrelated trends in the discourse on performance capture. The first, evident in promotional material for digital films and video games, is to elide the labor of animators and place all the creative value in the work of actors, like Serkis, who perform the roles, despite all the work that animators must do to transform the raw data received from performance capture into fully rendered, expressive characters. The second, and diametrically opposed, is a historical tendency stemming from Disney Studios to downplay the female actors who performed roles for rotoscoping and reference footage, along with the labor of women in the ink-and-paint department, and instead place all the emphasis on the creative work of male key animators. In both cases, the result is a system in which masculine visions are privileged and female characters are often represented in highly sexualized ways as erotic spectacles, suggesting that the "gendered body is still being performed in virtual realms, in spite of some significant advances . . . negating the idea of a postcorporeal male or female identity. As a consequence, social norms of beauty, fitness, and health continue to inform these bodies."[33] In this way, we can see how motion and performance capture have become a force of biopolitical control by positioning the labor of both animators and female actors as supplemental to the "real" creative forces, namely, those which are most in line with the class and gender of studio heads or production controllers. As I show in the coming pages, live-action remakes are becoming major contributors to this aspect of the media ecology today.

A similar argument (though one less grounded in feminist labor studies) is made by Drew Ayres in his book *Spectacular Posthumanism: The Digital Vernacular of Visual Effects*. In this work, Ayres identifies a constitutive duality in discourses of posthumanism, namely, a tension between digital disembodiment, or the transhumanist discourses that emphasize transcending the body or "uploading the consciousness" into an immaterial virtual form, and a return to embodiment in posthumanist approaches that value the materialities of bodies and technologies that connect with each other. According to Ayres, this duality is evident in performance capture, because the images are at once uncannily inhuman and convincingly embodied. He goes so far as to argue that

> in performance capture, the actor's body both touches and is touched by their digital avatar in a recursive feedback loop. Through the process of viewing the digital avatar in real time, the actor can adjust their movements based on the screen image, and the screen image itself adjusts to the actor's movements. . . . In other words, the "actor" and the "avatar," as categories of being, emerge only out of their interaction as an assemblage, and their relationship constitutes their unique subjectivity and embodied presence. . . . Regardless of these spatial gaps and shifts in temporal scale, the human body, in a very real and material way, phenomenologically persists within its digital avatar, and the digital avatar persists within the human actor.[34]

Although this sounds positive in theory, Ayres notes that in practice, the bodies of characters represented through motion capture often fall into highly standardized and gendered forms: the sexualized and objectified woman and the hard-body male action hero. These figures can be assembled from parts (one actress's face mapped onto another's nude body) or presented through the "spornosexual" discourses of physical training and digital enhancement (an actor's muscles being "popped" using digital and practical effects). This is what Ayres terms, in the title's chapter, "The Body's Digital (Dis)Honesty."

While I accept Ayres's critique of the misogyny of both Hollywood creators and online fans who consume digitally manipulated celebrity nudes, I find that this discourse is not countered in Ayres's work by any alternative ways of seeing gendered digital bodies or by a recognition of the work of female animators, as in Mihailova's research. As such, there is a risk here of reinforcing the instrumental vision that informs the creation of such object-bodies. In his analysis, bodies are viewed as parts: nipples, merkins (false pubic hair), pecs, and glutes, as they are visibly displayed on the screen. To read performance capture this way is to read it through the optical paradigm of corporeal representation rather than through haptic visuality. While Ayres invokes phenomenology to describe the persistence of the body in a digital avatar, the *lived experience* of the body is not explored in his chapter. There is little focus on what these films make the audience feel about what it is like to inhabit the bodies depicted. One would think they are not meant to be inhabited at all but only to be seen as objects of voyeuristic, scopophilic pleasure, as Laura Mulvey famously observed of Hollywood cinema in the 1970s.[35] I argue, however, that contemporary live-action remakes (as well as other films that use digital animation for special effects) operating under a regime of phenopower oscillate between the lived experience of the body and the externally perceived objectified body or the body-as-asset. Where the emphasis falls strongly affects how audiences may engage with the characters on both phenomenological and ethical levels. To explain how this dialectic of embodiment and scopophilic spectatorship plays out in live-action remakes, I now outline some of the formal qualities that define live-action remakes and explain how they reflect certain trends in the contemporary film industry.

Formal Characteristics and Origins of Live-Action Remakes

Although animation and live action can be defined as separate media, live-action remakes draw on aspects of computer animation, digital cinema, special effects blockbusters, and performance capture that strive to seamlessly blend the two media, generating a work that combines and exceeds its source materials. In this case, animation acts as a supplement to the live-action image in the sense that Jacques Derrida discusses in *Of Grammatology*, where he states that the supplement is not simply an external addition to a completed work but rather a constitutive element without which the work cannot be complete.[36] Likewise, the special effects blockbuster would not be complete without its special effects, making digitally animated images constitutive of today's "live-action" films.

Still, as I argued in the introduction to this chapter, we do not perceive live-action remakes and (computer-)animated films as identical in today's media industry landscape. They are discursively separated by their positioning as distinctive genres and by "the way the audience sits and watches" them, creating different phenomenological effects. As a result, live-action remakes are distinct from both computer-animated films and standard live-action films that use digital animation as a supplement—though not, as Favreau would have it, because of the remake's unique technical capacities or their ontological distinction from either animation or live action. Rather, remakes work more like a genre, or at least a subgenre within the larger genre of digitally driven special effects blockbusters. As such, live-action remakes of the digital era share a number of characteristics, which can be enumerated as follows:

1. They are remakes or adaptations based on existing works of animation (which may themselves be original works or adaptations of stories in other media, ranging from oral folktales to print media such as novels and manga to digital media such as video games).
2. They are most often perceptually realistic in style, as defined by Prince, and imitate the effects of lens-based photochemical cinema while eschewing the graphic and gestural stylization of the animated film.
3. They are a form of digital cinema, as defined by Manovich, that relies on the seamless compositing of various digital assets, including photographic footage (either analog or digital), frame-by-frame animation, motion and performance capture, VR environments, and other forms of digital imagery.
4. They are promoted to audiences through the interplay between a popular work of animation from decades past and the novelty of updated digital special effects, generating nostalgic remediation.

As Holliday says, the qualities of any given genre are neither prescriptive nor totalizing, which means that not every film in a given genre needs to neatly check off all the genre's definitive qualities. While we can see recurring themes in computer-animated films, such as the "journey" narrative, especially across the serials, sequels, franchises, and remakes that make up today's feature film release strategy,[37] the characteristics of a genre act more as identifying signposts that aid audiences in forming expectations. When it comes to live-action remakes, audiences can expect to see familiar characters, plot points, settings, and even particular shot sequences, songs, lines of dialogue, or jokes repeated again, but in a photorealistic digital cinema style.

Remaking classic films is a well-established strategy in Hollywood. It forms an especially important part of Disney's modus operandi now that it is in charge of several major franchises characterized by remakes and reboots, including the Marvel and Star Wars cinematic universes. Retelling and revising existing material has been a Disney specialty since well before the twenty-first century. As Bérénice Bonhomme writes, the "recovery strategy" of reusing particular character types, musical styles, shot patterns, and narrative structures "has always been a constitutive element of the Disney world. Disney draws its strength, in part, from the constitution of a memorial palimpsest, according to a system of internal references" that create a recognizable Disney brand.[38] The remake is part of Disney's palimpsestic quality, both as a way of encouraging repetition in viewing and recollections of childhood experience and as a form of "memory wealth [that] is consciously exploited by Disney, in a commercial logic" of fan-based consumerism.[39] However, while Bonhomme is keen to emphasize the continuity of Disney's style and corporate logic in the recent trend of live-action remakes, we may also see them as responding to a new media ecology, as they strengthen the established Disney brand while engaging with emerging trends in expansive serialization, platformativity, and postcinematic filmmaking in the 2010s and early 2020s.

While some lists of Disney live-action remakes found online (for instance, on the Disney Fan Wiki at http://disney.fandom.com/) place the start of the "live-action remake" trend in the 1990s with films like *Rudyard Kipling's "The Jungle Book"* (dir. Stephen Sommers, 1994) and *101 Dalmatians* (dir. Stephen Herek, 1996), I would argue that these isolated forerunners were not yet established as part of a live-action remake subgenre as we see it operating in later decades. Contemporary entertainment journalists like Adam B. Vary of *Variety* and Pamela McClintock of the *Hollywood Reporter* more often cite Tim Burton's 2010 adaptation of *Alice in Wonderland* as the start of the live-action remake as a deliberate serial strategy, which was hailed as "a new approach" for the studio.[40] In January 2020, Vary summarized the success of the remake strategy by writing that "since 2010's 'Alice in Wonderland,' Disney's strategy of remaking its animated classics as (presumptively) live-action films has been highly lucrative, grossing over $8.2 billion worldwide, and the studio shows no signs of slowing down."[41] It goes without saying that profits are a prime motivator and often the measure of success in business-based assessments of Disney's performance. Along with securing profits, however, remakes also help to secure Disney's interpretations of its branded properties and even to defend its versions against other studios or creators who may wish to encroach on its territory, as happened in the mid-2010s when Disney released its live-action version of *The Jungle Book,* directed by Favreau in 2016, just ahead of Andy Serkis's adaptation of Kipling for Warner Bros., *Mowgli: Legend of the Jungle,* which was also set to release theatrically in 2016 and had to delay its release to 2018 on Netflix.[42]

In the face of such competition, Warner Bros. and other studios have since adopted Disney's strategy of remaking classic works from their own catalogs (or the catalogs of corporate partners and co-producers) to secure their legal and cultural hold on lucrative brand properties. The live-action remake, as Favreau has made very clear in interviews, provides a handy justification for the remakes, as each new version is touted as an update to both the visuals and the cultural content for newer generations. Visually, the seamless perceptual realism of digital special effects provides a more contemporary aesthetic, in keeping with the dominant strategies of live-action blockbusters. In terms of the content, remakes are often used to remove material from the original films that is no longer considered politically correct and to provide more positive representations of BIPOC and LGBTQ+ characters (if sometimes in a tokenistic manner). In this way, live-action remakes shape audience perceptions of these properties and the forms of embodiment they promote.

As examples, I now consider two Hollywood live-action remakes that draw on East Asian hypotexts: Disney's 2020 remake of *Mulan,* directed by Niki Caro, and the 2019 Legendary Pictures and Warner Bros. release of *Pokémon: Detective Pikachu,* directed by Rob Letterman. In these examples, I hope to show how live-action remakes tend, as a genre, to depict bodies and evoke embodiment both through appeals to the viewer's various senses and, more problematically, through preconceived or fixed representations of bodies-as-assets viewed from the outside, thus imposing phenopower.

Remaking *Mulan*

The tale of Hua Mulan has had a long and varied history of adaptation, reinterpretation, and controversy. So, to set up the cultural politics behind the live-action remake, I would first like to examine the reception of the 1998 film and its status as a transcultural adaptation. When Disney first released its cel-animated version of the film in 1998, scholars critiqued it as a bastardization of the cherished legend that "trivializes a people's cultural heritage by forcing the elements of the story into a Hollywood formula."[43] For instance, Mingwu Xu and Chuanmao Tian have examined how the 1998 adaptation of *Mulan* follows the classic Disney formula by focusing the narrative around individualism and success through effort, a dualistic good versus evil approach to conflict, young romance, and cute or funny animal sidekicks. "As a result," Xu and Tian argue, "the original Chinese culture loses its authenticity, and cultural deformation arises in the film."[44] In focusing on issues of authenticity, these scholars follow a cultural studies approach of critiquing cultural imperialism and Disneyfication, of the sort most clearly laid out in Ariel Dorfman and Armand Mattelart's seminal 1971 postcolonial text *How to Read Donald Duck*.[45]

Even in the work of Xu and Tian, however, there is a recognition that Disney's power is not total, because adaptation takes place in a complex field where distributors and receivers can alter the text in material and discursive ways. Xu and Tian point out that if the Mulan story was "culturally deformed" by Disney, it was also re-formed for its release in East Asia. Local voices were restored in the Chinese VCD and DVD releases, which were dubbed over by famous actors like Jackie Chan and Qing Xu in the standard Mandarin version, as well as pop stars like CoCo Lee in the Taiwan Mandarin version and Kelly Chen for the Hong Kong Cantonese market. The changes also extended to linguistic nuances, such as rendering Americanized names for characters like Mushu the dragon and Cri-Kee the cricket in amusingly appropriate Chinese characters, restoring correct forms of address and titles for the Emperor and Matchmaker, and translating Mushu's American slang into local idioms (for instance, replacing the slang term "black and white" for a newspaper with the phrase *te shu kuai di* or "special express" delivery). Xu and Tian thus argue that authenticity can be reclaimed through a dynamic process of cultural mutation, transfer, and reformulation.[46]

Other scholars have further questioned whether "authenticity" should be used as a yardstick in determining the worth of an adapted text at all. As Zhuoyi Wang has pointed out, there is no single, fixed, original version of the "Ballad of Mulan." The text that is commonly reprinted today has been undergoing a continuous evolution for more than a thousand years, during which time it has been used to promote various nationalist ideologies and to create an illusory unity based on the needs of the ruling dynasty or government in each era.[47] Even the identification of the ballad as a "Chinese" text, in a monolithic and fixed sense, is a discursive construct, because "the Northern Wei Dynasty, in which 'Ballad' emerged, was not a Confucian state of the native population of China proper, or the so-called Han Chinese, but ruled by the Xianbei, a nomadic people who conquered Northern China. It is highly possible that "Ballad" derived from a nomadic people's oral folklore in their language."[48] Wang traces the various usages of the ballad, from Qing Dynasty (1644–1912 C.E.) operas like *A Tale of Two Rabbits* and novels like *The Legend of an Extraordinary Girl Who Is Loyal, Filial, Courageous, and Heroic* through to the 1939 film *Mulan Joins the Army,* released in Shanghai by the Xinhua Film Company. Each version contains differing accounts of the story of Mulan, altering in each account her physical abilities and sexual attributes (such as whether she has bound feet and what parts of her body are revealed to her male comrades-in-arms), her relations to core philosophical concepts like filial piety, and her links to national identity. As a result, Wang argues that "similar to the previous layers of conflicting adaptations constituting the enormous hypotext, Disney's *Mulan* is simply another hypertext continuing Mulan's metamorphosis, and it by no means contains the most dramatic intertextual change."[49]

Wang's critique of the authenticity discourse draws on Joseph M. Chan's earlier argument that Disney's *Mulan* is an example of adaptation as transculturation. In his 2002 book chapter, Chan writes that

> *Mulan* is not genuinely Chinese, nor is it all American. It has become a transcultural text: a combination of old and new, traditional and modern, East and West, collectivism and individualism, female submissiveness and women's liberation, filial piety and reciprocal love between father and daughter. This represents an important way by which the world's cultures are being hybridized to form what can be called a global culture. Not only is it hybrid in content, but also in visual style.[50]

Part of the credit for this hybridity could be given to Chinese American screenwriter Rita Hsiao, who has been cited by journalists like Jingan Young as someone who "no doubt helped to create the film's sense of the second- and third-generation immigrant experience."[51] In this light, *Mulan* can be read as a sign of "Disney's growing consciousness of changing culture in the United States and other parts of the world" and the ways Disney has become "more sensitive to the contribution of foreign culture in its business of cultural globalization."[52] However, that does not mean Disney's influence is entirely positive. As Chan also notes, "transculturation is a form of cultural borrowing in which one culture reconfigures another for its own purpose. This is an extension of the observation that cultural borrowing, as a rule, serves self-aggrandizement despite the fact that the best intentions may be involved."[53] In a capitalist society in which profit is the main motivator, the cultural exchange may result in inequalities, even as transculturation acts as "a form of boundary-crossing between the global and the local and between the foreign and the indigenous."[54]

The 2020 live-action remake is situated within this context. As in Xu and Tian's examples, Disney's latest version of *Mulan* attempts to restore an impression of cultural authenticity. In terms of narrative, it subverts the Disney formula by removing the talking-animal sidekicks, the romance subplot, and the musical numbers. Thematically, it deemphasizes Mulan's individual rags-to-riches journey in favor of an emphasis on filial piety. Visually, it dispenses with animetic caricatures and instead foregrounds the kind of wirework stunts and stylized fantasy action sequences found in *wuxia* (historical fantasy) films from mainland China and Hong Kong. And intertextually, it draws direct connections with "Ballad of Mulan" by having the protagonist paraphrase the famous line "Two hares running side by side close to the ground / How can they tell if I am he or she?"[55] All of these elements show an awareness of historical Chinese literature and contemporary cinema styles. That said, the discursive promotion of "authenticity" is not without a purpose. After all, transculturation is a mode "in which one culture reconfigures another *for its own purpose*."[56] For Disney, remaking *Mulan* serves the purpose of promoting the live-action remake genre and training audiences to accept their depictions as more realistic, authentic, and culturally sensitive than previous adaptations. However, if *Mulan* can be said to promote boundary crossing and hybridity, it does so by integrating its representation of Chinese legend into the material production practices of seamless compositing that generate its impressive imagery. This can be seen from the first moments of the film, which, like the mouse sequence in *The Lion King,* serve as a visual introduction to the film's aesthetic approach, as well as its transcultural aspirations.

This film opens with an overt recognition of the many existing versions of "Ballad of Mulan." It begins with an aerial shot moving toward a sunrise over dramatically silhouetted mountains, accompanied by a Chinese-accented male voice telling the audience in English, "There have been many tales of the great warrior Mulan. But, Ancestors, this one is mine." As in Wang's account, this opening line addresses the issue of plurality in the Mulan tale and claims to provide a new perspective: that of the father who has come to embrace his daughter's athletic prowess. The voice-over continues as the camera cuts to a fluid tracking shot that spirals around Mulan as she practices fighting with a bamboo staff in a field of tall, vivid-green shoots of grass. Mulan is poetically compared to the vital landscape around her as the narrator calls her a "young shoot all green," newly coming into the powerful abilities of her "*qi*," or "the boundless energy of life itself." Just as Favreau set up his 2019 *Lion King* in the style of a photorealistic nature documentary, so *Mulan* begins with a smooth tracking shot that highlights the (digitally enhanced) natural beauty of China, composited seamlessly with footage of actress Liu Yifei performing her choreography on a bluescreen stage.

Along with demonstrating Disney's technical prowess, however, there is also a more explicit moral being introduced. The father directly asks the audience, "If you had such a daughter . . . could you tell her that only a son could wield *qi*?" This establishes the feminist message of the film, namely, that a girl can carry on cultural traditions just as well as a boy. Viewers familiar with *Mulan*'s director, Niki Caro, will recognize this theme immediately from her award-winning film *Whale Rider* (2002), which depicts a Māori girl named Pai who wants to learn how to fight with a *taiaha* staff and ultimately proves she is fit to take on the leadership of her traditionally male-dominated community. In the first minute of *Mulan,* then, we see several appeals being made at once. First, there is an appeal to recognize multiple versions of the Mulan tale paired with an equally strong desire to establish a fixed sense of cultural authenticity (basically, "there is no singular 'Chinese,' but this movie is definitely authentic Chinese"). This sets up the film's national and ethnic dimensions. Second, there is a feminist stance grounded in Caro's credentials as an established female director of girls' coming-of-age stories. Finally, there is Disney's overarching imperative to stake its claim on adapting the legend of Mulan for Western audiences using the most technologically advanced new special effects.

A similar tension between hybridity, authenticity, and credibility arises when it comes to depicting the body in this film, particularly the body in action. Although many action sequences were shot on-location and executed by actors and stunt performers using wirework in the "wire fu" style of East Asian *wuxia* films, they still use the intensified continuity editing style, which David Bordwell has described as a prominent approach in contemporary Hollywood cinema. In *Mulan,* as in Bordwell's examples, the camera moves about restlessly, performing arcs and cranes even during relatively calm conversation sequences. During action sequences, the camera sharply turns ninety degrees on its axis, altering the frame orientation mid-stunt, on three occasions: when the Huns scale the walls in their first attack scene; when the witch Xianniang fights the guards of a Northern garrison in a diversionary attack to draw out Mulan's regiment; and finally, when Mulan battles the Hun leader Bori Khan in their climatic showdown in a palace under construction. These kinds of kinetic camera movements might have been considered disruptive or "bravura" moments in the past, but in the age of intensified continuity, as Bordwell points out, "gestures which earlier filmmakers would have considered flagrantly self-conscious—arcing cameras, big close-ups, the flourishes of a Welles or Hitchcock—have become default values in ordinary scenes and minor movies."[57] While this could be seen as a case of mere style over substance, Bruce Isaacs has countered that such shocks to the camera help to generate the "experiential logic underpinning the mainstream action genre" in which "continuity is more than a matter of the spaces and times contained within a film image. [Rather,] continuity is also contingent on processes of perception and reflection" in audiences.[58] In short, intensified continuity editing and digital effects can be used to enhance the audience's haptic engagement in the action, even as such scenes depict actions that are physically impossible for humans to perform.

That said, intensified continuity editing is not always used to such engaging effect. Even shocks to the camera become part of a spectacle that places the emphasis more on Disney's technical mastery of the image than on Liu's embodied performance or her affective connection with the audience. Although Liu went to great lengths to perform many of her own stunts, the way they are framed through a seamlessly integrated intensified continuity style often undercuts the impression of her exertion in the film. Like the film's lackluster digitally animated phoenix, which is often seen at a distance, fleetingly, or out of focus, Mulan's body in action is rendered strangely abstract and uninhabitable despite Liu's physical performance. This can be demonstrated by comparing the depiction of Mulan in the 1998 cel-animated film to her 2020 remake.

Take, for instance, the scene in which Mulan proves that she is finally ready to become a soldier after training long and hard among her fellow conscripts in the imperial army. In the 1998 film, Mulan uses the heavy weights tied to her wrists as leverage to climb to the top of a post and fetch down an arrow, fulfilling a challenge set by Captain Shang. This scene, set to the final chorus of the ironically playful song "I'll Make a Man Out of You," invites the audience to participate in Mulan's negotiation with the physical forces of weight and balance. The scene begins with Mulan contemplating the post in the cool, blue-toned dimness of the predawn camp. She first tries to climb the post by jumping up and wrapping her arms and legs around it, but the weights drag her down, and she falls off onto her back. Then, after looking at the weights for a moment, she swings them out with her arms and lets them twist together by their ties behind the post to form a brace. Mulan then plants one foot on the post and hauls herself up, pulling against the wide cloth bands anchored by the weights for support. Close to the top, she slips, and there is a cut to a close-up of her alarmed and then determined face as it emerges into the light of the rising sun. Through this close-up, the audience identifies with Mulan emotionally as well as physically. Her actual leap up to the top of the post is hidden by elliptical cuts to her comrades on the ground and Shang emerging from his tent to see the arrow strike the ground. The next shots show Mulan perched on top of the post smiling as the men cheer for her under the warming glow of a yellow dawn sky. The audience does not need to see how she actually got onto the top; they have already climbed the pole in their own minds, based on their haptic engagement with the physical experiences of weight and leverage. Crucially, however, the audience members themselves do not need to be physically strong or trained in martial arts to identify with Mulan in this moment, because she uses leverage and wits more than strength or special skill to succeed.

In the 2020 film, by contrast, Mulan must prove herself by carrying two buckets of water up to the top of a mountain, a feat that she accomplishes with the power of *qi*. In an earlier scene from her childhood, Mulan was established as a girl gifted with strong *qi* that allowed her to jump onto the village rooftops while chasing a chicken and fall from the eaves unharmed. Now, having accepted that she no longer needs to hide her abilities, Mulan simply picks the buckets up and carries them to the top with no evident effort at all. She does not shake, quiver, or stumble on her way up. She steps smoothly past one of her fellow conscripts who is blocking the way on the stairs. Though the audience knows logically that the buckets must be heavy because the men cannot hold them up, she carries them as if they weigh nothing, her arms bobbing gently as she walks rather than appearing weighted down by her load. She is often shot from a low angle and from behind, hiding the insides of the buckets so that the audience cannot see the water in them. This creates the impression (for me, at least) that the buckets might as well be empty because there is no visible negotiation with the movement of water inside them. The camera also rises with unnatural smoothness in a subjective point-of-view shot of the stairs from her vantage, suggesting Mulan's unflagging progress up the steps. Once she reaches the top, there is a brief extreme long shot of Mulan on the mountaintop, followed by a cut to a close-up with an intensified continuity-style tracking shot that arcs 180 degrees around her face. On the soundtrack, a flute plays the final chorus riff from the 1998 film's most famous song, "Reflections." The song is nostalgically evocative of the original film, but Mulan's expression is remote as she gazes off into the distance, leaving the music to create all the emotional lift. The impact of the scene overall is muted in comparison to the cel-style version. Because Mulan's feat appears so effortless, so seamlessly and smoothly performed, it fails to engage in the phenomenological dilemmas of weight, balance, and proprioception as *felt* experiences, from an internal, muscular perspective. Instead, it positions the audience as external viewers witnessing a miraculous demonstration of *qi* power that they cannot hope to accomplish or even haptically engage with on an imaginative level. Here Mulan becomes a body-as-asset: a memorial palimpsest of Disney's brand power signaled through the iconic theme song, enhanced with seamless compositing and intensified continuity editing but devoid of inhabitability or somatic connection. This is in line with what Denson describes as the "discorrelation" of image from embodied perception in contemporary digital cinema.[59]

The problem here is not just that the remake uses contemporary digital editing styles and special effects. Intensified continuity editing and CGI special effects can be used in artful and impactful ways, both in mainstream blockbusters and in indie or art films. In this case, however, the remake version of Mulan's training scene fails due to a somaesthetic disconnect. In his article "Martial Somaesthetics," Eric C. Mullis draws on Richard Shusterman's definition of *somaesthetics* as "a field of investigation that centers on examining philosophical approaches to human embodiment such as phenomenology, existentialism, and pragmatism."[60] Mullis's concern first and foremost is to account for the inner lived experience of performing martial arts from a practitioner's perspective, drawing on both traditional Chinese concepts like *qi* and sciences that focus on the body, such as physiology and neuroscience, particularly in studies of dance.[61] Following scholars of dance, he notes that an observer of martial arts performances can appreciate the performance even from the outside due to the action of mirror neurons that fire in the observer's brain in imitation of the observed action (also examined by Sylvie Bissonnette in her work on the evocation of embodiment in animated film). He extends this schema into an analysis of East Asian martial arts, noting that "the phenomenology of movement reveals that, when performers appreciate movement quality, they often are attuned to the flow of *somatic energy*,"[62] which can be felt in both accomplished dance performances and experiences of martial grace that embody *wuwei* or "effortless action."[63] Mullis ultimately argues, however, that martial arts demonstrations or films created for entertainment purposes are "at odds with the end of martial practice"[64] because demonstrations are disconnected from the entire somatic process of gaining competence and coming to experience wuwei internally. What we see instead is someone performing an action that merely *looks* easy. Likewise, while we may appreciate seeing Mulan's skillful manipulation of the staff in sweeping crane shots, or rock with the camera as it vaults through ninety-degree turns, we are also kept at a distance from her actions and sealed off from her embodied experience. In the revised training scene especially, the live-action remake of *Mulan* turns the somaesthetic experience of wuwei into a spectatorial entertainment that is at odds with the embodied practice of martial arts.

Issues of embodiment and biopower are evident not only in the text of the film itself but also in the political controversies surrounding its release. In the years leading up to the film's planned summer 2020 release (which was delayed until September and moved to Disney+ because of the Covid-19 pandemic), some media coverage of the film was concerned with its connections to two major political issues: the questionable ethics of director Niki Caro shooting location footage in the Xinjiang Uygher Autonomous Region during an alleged cultural genocide and star Liu Yifei's support of police actions against pro-democracy protests in Hong Kong. On September 28, 2017, Caro posted a location scouting photo of sand dunes to Instagram with a location tag for Urumqi, the capital of the Xinjiang Uyghur Autonomous Region in the northwest of China. As the BBC and other major world news outlets have widely reported, this area has been the site of alleged human rights abuses by the Chinese government against the Uyghurs (a Turkic ethnic minority group) and other Muslim minority groups since mass detentions of up to one million people in "reeducation camps" began in April 2017. Several countries, including the United States, Canada, and the Netherlands, have accused China of committing crimes against humanity in these camps, including forced labor and involuntary sterilizations of women, amounting to cultural genocide under international conventions. The Chinese government has denied these accusations, asserting that the purpose of the reeducation camps is to control terrorism and Islamic extremism. In light of this situation, many Instagram users left comments on Caro's picture of Urumqi condemning her and Disney more generally for supporting this possible genocide (or, at least, not actively opposing it). Once the film was released in 2020, social media users were also quick to point out that the end credits for *Mulan* offer legally obligated special thanks to the Publicity Department of the CPC Xinjiang Uyghur Autonomous Region Committee as well as the Publicity Department and Bureau of Public Security for the city of Turpan, which is northeast of Urumqi in Xinjiang. As a result, Disney has been accused of complicity with the Chinese government's attempts to "spin" reporting on events in the region in its own favor.

The second controversy arose in August 2019, when Liu posted a message to Chinese social media platform Weibo in support of the Hong Kong police's suppression of pro-democracy protests. The text, reading "What a shame for Hong Kong," was accompanied by the hashtag #IAlsoSupportTheHongKongPolice, followed by a heart and a strong-arm-flexing emoji. Her original post in Mandarin was quickly screen-capped and retweeted with an English translation on Twitter and other English-language social media platforms. In response, a #BanMulan hashtag began trending on Twitter. It was often grouped with other hashtags in support of various activist groups or individuals, including the pan-Asian #MilkTeaAlliance, a tag "used by protesters to voice support for democratic movements and concern over China's power in the region,"[65] and #FreeAgnesChow, used to rally support for politician Agnes Chow after she and two other activist leaders were arrested on illegal assembly charges during pro-democracy protests. Memes circulating around the time of the film's release even depicted Chow as the "real Mulan," in opposition to both the live-action and cel-animated Disney versions (Figure 12).

Such reactions to the film, both in the mainstream press and on social media, suggest that Disney's bid for greater Chinese cultural authenticity and ethnic inclusion in the *Mulan* live-action remake was rejected by at least a portion of the audience, namely, those who were familiar with contemporary East Asian politics and critical of China's role in the region. Disney has been subject to critiques of Americanization and cultural imperialism for decades, but America is clearly not the only determining center of global power in this situation. As Koichi Iwabuchi explained, globalization has been "re-centred" in multiple regional powers throughout East Asia, and any film adaptation that attempts to engage with these powers is subject to complex cross-currents of reaction.[66] This dynamic becomes even clearer when Western studios adapt and remake contemporary animated media from East Asia, such as Japanese anime films, TV series, and video games.

FIGURE 12. A meme that calls for the "real" Mulan by showing and rejecting Liu's Mulan and Disney's animated Mulan before approving activist Agnes Chow.

Live-Action Remakes and Adaptations of Japanese Anime

Live-action remakes may be a relatively new trend for Disney, but in Japan, adapting and remaking popular works multiple times across a variety of media has been a standard practice for decades. As Marc Steinberg describes, the Japanese entertainment industry has long been characterized by the "media mix" or the "system of interconnected media and commodity forms" that began in the 1960s and intensified in the following decades.[67] This is especially apparent in what is today termed the "contents industry," which encompasses a wide range of media productions and platforms where complex practices of adapting, rebooting, and remaking can be observed.[68] While manga, anime, and gaming have made up the three pillars of this industry (at least in terms of scholarly attention and media coverage), live-action cinematic adaptations have also played a role in establishing major mainstream franchises. In this way, the media mix expands the classical, linear concept of cinematic adaptations that move from "one text to one film" to include multiple versions and modes of production in a more lateral and rhizomatic structure.

Since the intensification of the media mix in the 1980s and 1990s, it has become commonplace for popular manga to be adapted into multiple animated features, anime series, live-action films, television dramas, video games, light novels, 2.5D stage plays, and so on. Film and television producers throughout Asia have recognized the lucrative potential of the live-action remake, as evidenced by the transcultural phenomenon spawned by Kamio Yoko's manga *Hana Yori Dango* (*Boys over Flowers,* 1992–2008), which has been made into more than a dozen separate live-action films and television dramas created and set in South Korea, China, Taiwan, Indonesia, and India, as well as Japan and the United States, since the mid-1990s and early 2000s.[69] Some Asian media mix franchises may be serialized in that they present original content in each release to continue the narrative or delve deeper into the world and characters introduced in previous versions. However, the majority of them are remakes that tread the same narrative territory over again in another medium or another national or cultural context. In each case, the act of remaking involves its own unique cultural politics. Since Ien Ang's foundational 1982 study of the worldwide reception of the American television show *Dallas,*[70] cultural critics have either celebrated localized versions of globally circulating texts as acts of resistance to hegemony or read them as instances of complicity that pull attention and funding away from "genuine" local production.

The situation is differently inflected, however, when it comes to American attempts to remake canonical Japanese manga and anime. Hollywood has long been critiqued by cultural theorists as a globally hegemonic force bent on appropriating the most popular works from other cultures for its own profit. In practice, not many major Hollywood studios have actively scouted for Japanese anime to remake, at least not initially or consistently. American adaptations of anime in the late 2000s and 2010s were just as likely to be driven by directors or producers seeking to adapt their favorite anime as passion projects, as Northrop Davis has described in his 2015 book *Anime and Manga Go to Hollywood.*[71] Some examples of adaptations by creators with a documented interest in anime include the Wachowskis'

2008 *Speed Racer,* an adaptation of the 1966 manga and 1967 anime *Mach GoGoGo,* and Robert Rodriguez and James Cameron's 2019 *Battle Angel Alita,* based on the manga *Gunnm* by Kishiro Yukito (1990–95). However, since the early 2010s, there have also been more cases of Hollywood studios or producers securing the rights to canonical Japanese works and hiring directors with little preexisting knowledge of the texts or the fanbase. This was the situation with Paramount's 2017 live-action remake of *Ghost in the Shell,* directed by Rupert Sanders, who admitted in an interview with *Vice* magazine that he was not an anime fan and "knew very little" about it before taking on the project.[72]

As a result, English-language remakes of manga and anime continue to be viewed with distrust by anime fans in the West, particularly older fans who protested the Americanization that resulted from the egregious editing and inaccurate dubbing of anime in the late twentieth century, such as Miyazaki's *Nausicaä of the Valley of the Wind* and television series like Ikuhara Kunihiko's *Sailor Moon* (1992–97). Compounding the issue in live-action adaptations is the racial dimension of casting particular stars to play famous anime characters. Concerns about whitewashing are raised every time a white American actor is attached to a project in development or given a starring role as an originally Japanese character, such as Scarlett Johansson's casting as Major Motoko Kusanagi in *Ghost in the Shell,* which was roundly mocked by fans online in memes that parodied Paramount's #IamMajor viral marketing campaign.[73] Of course, transcultural anime fandom itself is not without its own internal politics, as I have detailed in my previous work.[74] By critiquing the Hollywood treatment of anime, Anglophone anime fans not only draw attention to the power dynamics of global media but also uphold the legitimacy of their own subculture, in which fans' credibility or "cultural capital" is maintained by displaying their specialist knowledge of the original anime and signaling their commitment to "authentic" Japanese pop culture. In an article on fan subtitling or fansubbing in the Anglophone anime community, Matt Hills likewise notes how fans can act within an individualistic and competitive neoliberal framework of their own despite their "cult" status in opposition to the "mainstream."[75] As a result, Hollywood live-action remakes of anime are often caught in the crossfire between competing agents of global phenopower, such as animation and live-action film studios, and transcultural anime fandom's own subcultural politics.

The many forces at play in anime remakes are too complex and diverse to be captured in one subsection of a single chapter. So, for the purposes of this study, I narrow my focus to a study of embodiment in one recent American–Japanese coproduction that has found surprising success: the 2019 film *Pokémon: Detective Pikachu* (hereafter referred to as *Detective Pikachu*). This film was adapted from the 2016 *Detective Pikachu* video game released on the Nintendo 360 platform. It was produced by Legendary Entertainment, known for its strong investment in graphic novel and video game adaptations and its MonsterVerse series of Godzilla and King Kong remakes (2014–). The film was directed by Rob Letterman, an established director of both computer-animated films (e.g., 2004's *Shark Tale*) and live-action genre films (e.g., *Goosebumps* in 2010). Although he is not a notable anime fan, he claimed in an interview leading up to the film's release that he "went after hardcore fans first" as a target audience by "work[ing] really closely with the Pokémon Company and the original creators" to ensure that the film followed the "rules" of the Japanese franchise in every detail.[76]

The digital animation of major Pokémon characters like Pikachu was carried out at the British visual effects production company MPC under VFX supervisor Peter Dionne, who also worked on Disney's *The Jungle Book* and *The Lion King*. Warner Bros. ensured the film's widespread distribution and secured its status as a blockbuster aimed at families and general audiences, with a suitably blockbuster-sized budget of $150 million. It premiered on May 2, 2019, in New York and then went into theaters in Japan on May 3, a week before its May 10 wide release in the United States. At the time of its release, it was the top-grossing video game adaptation of all time. It premiered at number one in the United States with a $20.5 million opening night and garnered an international opening weekend debut of $103 million. At the Japanese box office, it premiered in the top three films and went on to beat out both of its major competitors, *Avengers: Endgame* (dir. Anthony Russo and Joe Russo) and *Detective Conan: The Fist of Blue Sapphire* (dir. Tomoka Nagaoka), during its second and third weeks of release.[77] Despite its popularity among both American and Japanese audiences, however, this film still demonstrates how the rhizomatic and participatory qualities of the Japanese media mix and its attendant fan culture were lost during the process of remaking an animatic, anontological media text into a seamless, perceptually realistic work of mainstream digital cinema following the conventions of Disney's live-action remakes.

Pokémon's Place in the Media Ecology

Before jumping into the plot or style of the film, it is important to establish the crucial role that Pokémon has played not only in the media mix—with its multiple video games, trading card games, manga, anime, and film series—but also in the embodied shaping of the senses that is part of the media ecology. In *The Anime Ecology,* Thomas Lamarre explores the ramifications of the infamous "Pokémon incident," during which thousands of children in Japan experienced photo-sensitive epileptiform seizures after watching a sequence of red and blue flickering lights used as a special effect in the 1997 episode "Dennō senshi Porigon." The children's susceptibility was attributed by some journalists to the way they sat too close to the screen and watched the flickering effects with a passive, wide-eyed, unblinking stare. However, Lamarre argues that this famous incident does not simply represent a binary relation of active controlling technology and passive child victim, as depicted in the media panic surrounding it. Rather, he says, "The evidence of seizures demonstrate that blinking (or not) constitutes the ground (or more precisely the plane or fabric) for the experience of animation (and cinema), not an external limit or a passive material."[78] Drawing on William James's philosophical approach of "radical empiricism," Lamarre argues that in the "stuff of blink" or moment of flicker, we get down to the most basic level of pure experience: the impersonal, yet mutually constitutive and entangled, relationship between screens, eyes, and brains. In this nonbinary relation, no one force controls or embeds all the others. For instance, television is not a totalizing force that causes the same effects in every viewer in the same way. Still, the acute physiological reaction experienced by some children with photosensitivity who suffered "Pokémon Shock" syndrome reveals the tangible effects that images can have, in the right (or wrong) circumstances, on the entire physiological system of the eyes, the brain, and, in this case, the muscular tension of the body. Indeed, Lamarre prefers the term *blink* to *flicker* because it evokes the haptic, which is "neither visual nor tactile; it is touch in sight, or sighted touch," and so is "multisensory" in its expression.[79]

While Lamarre's concern in *The Anime Ecology* is primarily the "brain–screen interface," which draws on and critiques neuroscientific discourse, his example of Pokémon shock suggests how the entire body is brought into play in animation viewing, in its muscular and visceral dimensions as well as in its neuronal and cognitive ones. Likewise, Lamarre's take on the radical empiricist concept of "pure experience" is compatible with my interpretation of phenomenology in their common emphases on the entangled, the planar, and the multisensory—though the empiricist pure experience differs from the phenomenological *perception* of experience, in that perception for Merleau-Ponty and the queer feminist phenomenologists who follow him is not prepersonal or impersonal (that is, never ideal or transcendent) but grounded in a particular human or inhuman subject that perceives from a given material instantiation or viewing position.

Another important contextual factor that Lamarre brings up regarding Pokémon is the cultural dimension of techno-Orientalism that accompanied its reception overseas. As many scholars of East Asian pop culture have demonstrated, the global distribution of this Japanese anime (and its accompanying manga, video games, trading cards, and other merchandise) in the late 1990s gave rise to a moral panic among journalists and parents in the West, who perceived the franchise as an alien invading force out to capture the attention and pocket money of their children.[80] Lamarre summarizes Christine Yano's chapter "Panic Attacks: Anti-Pokémon Voices in Global Markets" by writing that "panicked responses to Pokémon projected localized anxieties over capitalism onto this global Japanese franchise, thus disavowing their own capitalist excesses."[81] The moral panic around Pokémon generated yet another set of binaries (audience–television, the West–Japan) that Lamarre argues need to be disrupted through a more multiple, complex model of media distribution and reception.

The proliferation of media industries, distribution platforms, and global audiences for animation through coproductions, streaming media, and the widespread acceptance of niche fan cultures that has arisen throughout the 2010s may have quelled the moral panic around Pokémon somewhat, but it has done nothing to mitigate the "capitalist excesses" of the 1990s. Instead, we have seen only a further commodification of the sensory shifts occasioned by the embrace of haptics in mainstream globalized film and media—an embrace that is strongly evident in the tactile visuality of MPC's work on both Disney live-action remakes and *Detective Pikachu*. As Stephens has argued, the evocation of haptic and multisensory experience is not *in itself* resistant or liberatory but is, like the bodies of subjects under biopower, prone to management from without and complicity from within. We can see how the planes of cultural production, distribution, and reception have shifted toward the condition that Lamarre later calls *ontopower*—and the elaboration of it that I have termed *phenopower*—by examining live-action remakes of Japanese anime in Hollywood, particularly the case of *Detective Pikachu*.

Detecting Bodies in *Detective Pikachu*

Detective Pikachu combines the Japanese media mix megahit Pokémon with the Hollywood genres of mystery and film noir. It follows a disaffected twenty-one-year-old biracial man named Tim Goodman (Justice Smith) who is summoned to Ryme City, where Pokémon and humans live side by side, after his police officer father is killed in a car accident. Tim is immediately drawn into a mystery involving a talking Pikachu that only he can understand (voiced and performed via facial capture by Ryan Reynolds). Together, they investigate a mysterious drug in the form of a purple gas labeled "R" that makes Pokémon run wild and attack humans. The drug is eventually traced to Clifford Industries founder Howard Clifford (Bill Nighy), who initially claims to be promoting harmony between humans and Pokémon but is in fact seeking to harness the latter's evolutionary abilities to overcome a physical disability that leaves him unable to walk. The climax of the film sees the villainous corporate founder transfer his consciousness, and the minds of many innocent human victims, into Pokémon bodies via a "neural link," a recurring trope of posthuman film and literature that I examine in more detail later.

In terms of visual style, this film may seem more "cartoony" than either *The Lion King* or *Mulan*—that is, closer to the blend of stylization and realism that characterize the computer-animated film according to Holliday. This is partly because the Pokémon Company stipulated that "no matter what situation [the Pokémon] are in, they always have to be cute," following the animetic Japanese style of *kawaii* imagery.[82] This meant that the animators were obligated to retain some of the eye-catching colors and animetic body constructions that define their original characters, such as Pikachu's bright yellow body, red cheek spots, and lightning-bolt-shaped tail. In addition to the animetic style, the film draws on the expressionist mise-en-scène of film noir, which emphasizes planar shadows that create dramatic geometrical patterns and chiaroscuro compositions. In *Detective Pikachu,* we can see multiple instances of the flattening effect of chiaroscuro lighting, for instance, in the diagonal patterning of the shadows of blinds across Tim's face when he first meets his father's boss on the Ryme City police force, Lieutenant Yoshida, played by Ken Watanabe. The stylization also extends to the use of color in the mise-en-scène, for instance, in the saturation of blue tones punctuated by bright neon signage reflecting on wet pavement in nighttime views of Ryme City, evoking another Japanese-inflected tech noir classic, *Blade Runner* (dir. Ridley Scott, 1982).

That said, the animetic elements of this film sit in uneasy juxtaposition with the 3D depth, naturalistic movement, and textural detail demanded by the seamlessly composited style of the live-action remake. To blend 2D anime characters with live actors and photographed sets shot on 35mm film, those characters had to be given bodies conducive to the creation of perceptual realism. Pikachu is thus given fur modeled after the follicle patterns of rabbits, along with proportions and behaviors drawn from bush babies and lemurs.[83] Like the human teeth given to Sonic the Hedgehog for the 2020 remake of that video game franchise, Pikachu's fur initially caused consternation among fans, who tweeted reactions such as "I don't like this at all, the hyper-realism is just too creepy."[84] Here we see an instance of CGI evoking the uncanny valley effect due to the dissonance between the established animetic style of the Pokémon franchise and the style of American live-action remakes, especially Disney's stock-in-trade hyperrealism. Unlike Sonic's teeth, which were deemphasized to avoid unsettling audiences, Pikachu's fur was naturalized by the subtly animallike movements of his body and by simple repeated exposure to audiences through many promotional teasers, trailers, ads, and commercials. This made the furry-bodied Pikachu believable and familiar enough to audiences that by the time of the film's release, it was more common to find him described as "cute" once again, as intended by the Pokémon Company and Dionne.[85] In this way, seamlessness and perceptual realism were upheld as core features of the live-action remake, bringing the animetic and gamic style of Pokémon in line with the photorealistic style that Favreau and Dionne have both worked to promote for Disney's live-action remakes. Audiences soon came to accept the shift in character representation, despite some initial reluctance, owing to both the technical skill involved in creating the rendering and the promotional strategies used to present it to the public.

If the visual style of the film aims to smooth over the seams between animetic and cinematic styles, however, the narrative contains some striking discontinuities when it comes to handling bodies and consciousness. Throughout the film, we are presented with a Pikachu that speaks in the voice of Ryan Reynolds, who, at the time of the film's release, was most recently known for his recurring role as the foul-mouthed, R-rated antihero Deadpool. Although most animated films aim to create harmony between voice and visible form, *Detective Pikachu* creates an unavoidable—and unavoidably self-reflexive—contrast between the kawaii character of Pikachu and the mature, sarcastic voice of Reynolds. The self-reflexivity of Deadpool, who frequently breaks the fourth wall and makes pop culture references, spills over into Reynolds's performance as Pikachu, allowing him to allude to the Pokémon media franchise in ways that logically should not be possible in a diegetic world where Pokémon are real. For instance, in one parodic scene, a heartbroken Pikachu tearfully sings the English-language theme song for the 1998 *Pokémon* anime series to himself as he walks alone down a country road, a moment calculated to draw nostalgic laughs. Although pop culture references and "Easter eggs" are common in what Kristen Daly has termed "Cinema 3.0" or the "interactive-image" of cinema of digital culture and video gaming,[86] this reference is a bit seamy in that it is both highly recognizable and narratively implausible (why would there be an anime theme song with lyrics like "gotta catch 'em all" in a world where Pokémon are intelligent living creatures, not collector's cards?).

Easter eggs may serve a positive function in allowing fans to engage actively with a text and with each other, but some of the film's other narrative "seams" are more problematic, particularly when it comes to depicting bodies. In the climactic scene of the film, the villain, Howard Clifford, reveals the true purpose of his plot, which has driven the action of the film up to that point: using a neural link, he

FIGURE 13. Mewtwo's powerful, athletic body is contrasted with Clifford's unconscious, immobile human body.

will transfer his consciousness into the body of Mewtwo, a powerful, genetically modified Pokémon characterized by its feline face and large, sinewy, kangaroo-like legs balanced by a flexible tail. Throughout the film, Clifford is shown to have paraplegia and uses a wheelchair for mobility. Although it is not stated outright that he is seeking to overcome his disability through the neural link, his thin, immobile body is visibly contrasted with the strong, athletic legs and tail in Mewtwo's character design, suggesting that the transfer will act as both wish fulfillment and overcompensation for Clifford's disability (Figure 13). The villain motivated by a disability to commit heinous misdeeds, either in revenge or while seeking a cure, is a long-standing and socially harmful ableist stereotype in theater, literature, and film. In *Detective Pikachu,* however, this trope is also overlaid with the transhumanist aspiration of transferring the mind into another body, as if consciousness is a form of pure information that can be uploaded into any container, with empowering or evolutionary effects. In this film, the "neural link" stands in for the triadic mind–tech–body connection. However, the core concept of transferring consciousness originates in the Cartesian dualist separation of mind and body, and finds parallels in Hans Moravec's 1988 fantasy of liquefying the brain layer by layer and uploading the consciousness into a computer, which N. Katherine Hayles cites as one of the ur-fantasies of the posthuman discourse in which the mind is equated to disembodied, container-neutral information.[87]

The neural upload trope is so often used in digital-age science fiction blockbusters, from *The Matrix* to *Avatar* (dir. James Cameron,

2009) to *Transformers: Age of Extinction* (dir. Michael Bay, 2014), that it would barely raise an eyebrow on its own. As Ayres says, the play of embodiment and disembodiment is central to the digital vernacular of (post)cinema. However, in *Detective Pikachu,* the premise is extended in ways that actively disembody not only the information/mind but also the material form. This happens when Clifford's neural link technology is applied to all the citizens of Ryme City, who have gathered to watch a Pokémon-themed parade. Hidden inside the parade floats are clouds of the purple gas that drives Pokémon "out of their minds" to make room for a human consciousness. Once the gas is released, however, something very strange happens. Even though Clifford's human body is shown to remain intact but "asleep" while his mind soars the skies in Mewtwo's form, all of the citizens whose minds are melded with their Pokémon companions do not fall to the ground in comas. Instead, human and Pokémon bodies are "merged into one," as the Clifford-controlled Mewtwo says, through a digital metamorphosis effect. The transformation of the entire crowd is somewhat masked with brilliant white flares of light, ambient smoke, and handheld shaky-cam effects. However, the end result is a crowd of Pokémon wandering the empty streets, confused and unable to speak, but clearly inhabited by human minds. Here Letterman avoids the uncanny, disturbing image of thousands of "dead" bodies lying around and instead turns the frightening scene into a potentially alluring fantasy: the chance to become a Pokémon, a beloved animation character. Inhabiting animated bodies is part of what viewers do psychosomatically when watching animation, according to phenomenological scholars like Jennifer Barker and Sylvie Bissonnette. Even more significantly, merging CGI and live action "into one" is at the heart of the seamless compositing in live-action remakes. However, the complete transformation of the able-bodied humans into Pokémon, when compared with the persistence of the villain's disabled body in the wheelchair, can also be seen as a strongly ableist narrative in which normative bodies—bodies that can act as assets—become transparent vehicles of the mind that are easily transformed and restored, whereas a disabled body is a permanent liability that leads to the villain's downfall.

In the end, Tim defeats Clifford by pulling off the neural link headband that connects him to Mewtwo, causing Clifford to fall out of his wheelchair and onto the floor, helpless once again. Mewtwo also falls from the air and drops Pikachu from a great height, but Mewtwo is able to recover and catch Pikachu with an invisible force field that floats the smaller Pokémon gently to the ground. Floating is a key sensation in the embodied cinema of haptic visuality, as discussed in chapter 1, but in this case, those sensations are limited only to the bodies that the filmmakers wish to make "present" and are denied to those who are nonnormatively embodied or made "absent" within the visual field of the film. In this way, *Detective Pikachu* promotes the mainstream Hollywood visual style of the live-action remake (and digital cinema at large) through its attempt at seamlessly compositing 2D animetic characters into a 3D cinematic mise-en-scène. However, it also inadvertently reveals the problematic side of the live-action remake through its normative ableist assumptions and its underlying Cartesian dualism, which splits the mind and the body even as it tries to merge filmed and digitally animated images into a single, seamless style of perceptual realism. In short, it promotes phenopower, which manages both what appears and—crucially, in this scene—what does *not* appear as a viable form of embodiment through the cinematic shaping of the senses.

Why should scholars care about live-action remakes like *Mulan* or *Detective Pikachu*? On one hand, remakes can be seen as nothing more than cash grabs, even more unoriginal than sequels or franchises because they do not generate any new narrative content but simply repackage market-tested material in new forms. And yet, if film is a perceptual motion machine that helps to shape our views of embodiment and the world, then we must ask, what forms of perception are live-action remakes creating among audiences? On the basis of the preceding examples, it seems that while these films still have the potential to awaken the imagination to different, even posthuman, forms of embodiment, they also risk reterritorializing embodiment within an instrumental schema in which the body is seen as an asset to be controlled through phenopower. This happens when the evocation of embodied experience is embedded in a form of seamless perceptual realism based on preconceived notions of both perception via the camera lens and realism based on the mimetic imitation of live action.

In this chapter, I have argued that live-action remakes and adaptations have trained us to accept actors' and digitally animated characters' bodies as assets, like wire-frame models that can be manipulated, dissolved, and reinstated at will. While hybrid cel and live-action films and computer-animated films hold with the traditions of animation in which stylization and realism are balanced, creating gestural characters whose liveliness jumps off the screen, live-action remakes by definition aim for the mimetic or simulationist aesthetic, reinforcing an instrumental view of the body that must be rendered perceptually realistic in both its optical and tactile dimensions according to received schemas of perception and realism. Here we see the operation of phenopower that entrains individual perception to the exercise of biopower on a larger political and cultural level. However, this is not the only route that digital media can take. Even in Hollywood blockbusters, moments of somaesthetic connection can emerge, generating a sense of lived experience that is grounded in human embodiment and sometimes even goes beyond what is humanly possible to generate an imaginative immersion in different ways of moving and sensing, such as animal perception or posthuman cyborg perception. As Daniel Yacavone points out, when it comes to "emotional, imaginative, and conceptual" experiences like these, "here any phenomenology of film experience reaches its outermost descriptive and explanatory boundaries and must cede part of the stage to semiotic, narratological, cognitive, and Deleuzian insights, for instance."[88] To this end, I turn in the next two chapters to works that require an understanding of body and world not only in their spatial or material aspects but also in terms of time, duration, and the virtual dimensions of experience, such as those found in Deleuze's theory of the time-image and Deleuze and Guattari's conception of the BwO.

CHAPTER 4

Time and Reanimation in Electro Swing Music Videos

"Give me a body, then": this is the formula of philosophical reversal.

—Gilles Deleuze, "Cinema, Body, Brain, Thought," *Cinema 2*

In *Cinema 2: The Time-Image,* Gilles Deleuze traces a shift in cinema between the movement-image found in Classical Hollywood cinema and the time-image characteristic of post–World War II cinema, particularly New Wave art films made in Europe and Japan. Though his argument is often understood to apply to cinema as a whole in the abstract, Deleuze's conception of cinema is in fact profoundly embodied. The movement-image is first and foremost a sensorimotor phenomenon: a linkage between the perception-image, the affection-image, and the action-image, in which a film character who sees something and feels strongly about it will then act directly in response to the stimulus. For instance, characters in Classical Hollywood films typically have a clear motivation and act upon it in physical ways that forward a linear narrative. However, Deleuze says that this straightforward sensorimotor link between perception and action was broken in postwar art films, where "the purely optical and sound situation takes the place of the faltering sensory-motor situation."[1] Characters no longer act immediately in relation to what they see but are more often placed in passive positions of viewing, listening, and reflecting on their observations, more like members of the film audience themselves.

In looking back on Deleuze's oft-rehashed schema of film history, I would like to highlight that the shift from action to vision, or from a sensorimotor schema to pure optical and sound situations, does not mean that the body itself is dissolved or abandoned, as in the postmodern discourse of digital disembodiment. Rather, the body is seen in a new light, as something multilayered and dedicated to exploring haptic sensations, rather than following set patterns of stimulus and response. In terms of acting, Deleuze speaks of how characters in the films of Godard enact the "*gest*": the gesture that moves between two attitudes or postures and also between different times; between different sensory modes, such as sound and vision; and between the physical and the metaphysical or aesthetic. In this conception of movement, "the attitude of the body is like a time-image, . . . which puts the before and the after in the body, the series of time."[2] Likewise, along with the eye (as symbol of vision) and the brain (as symbol of thought), the *hand* still forms an important part of the cinematic body in postwar cinema, as the embodied organ of tactile apprehension and self-figuration—as it has been in animation from the silent era's visible "hand of the artist"[3] to the mobile "manicule" of online gaming.[4] In the era of the time-image, the hand "relinquishes its prehensile and motor functions to content itself with pure touching,"[5] emphasizing the role of haptic visuality in postwar cinema. In this way, according to Deleuze, "the body is no longer the obstacle that separates thought from itself, that which it has to overcome to reach thinking. It is on the contrary that which it plunges into or must plunge into in order to reach the unthought, that is life."[6] This sensation of plunging into unthought life, as well as plunging into time, echoes phenomenological concepts of "thrownness" and enworlding. Indeed, Deleuze relies on Henri Bergson's phenomenological description of time as duration or experiential time, rather than the quantifiable time of the clock, in articulating his own concept of the time-image. As a result, the time-image brings about, not a lack of embodiment, but a layering of multiple embodiments across gestures, haptic sensations, times, and forms of perception. So, in this chapter of my phenomenological study of animation, I use Deleuze's concepts of the gest and the time-image to address a temporally layered form of animated embodiment that has arisen in the twenty-first century: the electro swing music video and its associated dance culture.

At first glance, it may seem counterintuitive to use Deleuze's concept of the time-image, which is grounded in post–World War II art cinema, to discuss an electronic dance music genre of the 2000s based on a nostalgic image of the 1920s. However, even Deleuze recognized that the postwar era was not the end of his story when it came to film. The conclusion to *Cinema 2* looks forward to another major shift in cinematic history: the coming of electronic media. The tone in this conclusion is neither celebratory nor immediately dismissive. Deleuze does write about data "replacing" nature but admits that the electronic image could have both positive and negative effects. For instance, he writes that "the electronic image, that is, the tele and video image, the numerical image coming into being, either had *to transform cinema or to replace it,* to mark its death."[7] Later, building on this either/or sentence structure, he writes, "The fact is that the new spiritual automatism and the new psychological automata [of electronic images] depend on an aesthetic before depending on technology. It is the time-image which calls on an original regime of images and signs, before *electronics spoils it or, in contrast, relaunches it.*"[8] The ordering of positive and negative terms in the phrases I have highlighted here is reversed from one statement to the next, as if to avoid privileging one possible outcome or the other. For better or worse, then, Deleuze anticipated the coming of a third kind of image, a new aesthetic that would transform or replace, spoil or relaunch, that of cinema: the time of the electronic image.

Many scholars in the decades since *Cinema 2*'s publication have tried to capture the shape of this shift as it has happened, experiencing it no longer in the imminent future but as the recent past of the 2000s and 2010s. Some scholars of digital cinema and new media have built upon Deleuze's historical continuity of *Cinema 1* and *Cinema 2* by identifying the next stage in the progression, as Kristin Daly does in her article "Cinema 3.0: The Interactive-Image."[9] Others have built upon individual concepts from Deleuze's Cinema books to theorize a new form of postcinema. For instance, Steven Shaviro draws on the concept of the "disconnected line" in Deleuze's analysis of Mizoguchi's films to analyze the postcontinuity editing style in contemporary cinema as reflective of "the 'space of flows,' and the time of micro-intervals and speed-of light transformations, that are characteristic of globalized, high-tech financial capital."[10] Others look beyond Deleuze's reliance on Bergsonian duration to posit "a new image that is already beyond the time-image"[11] or even a complete postphenomenological discorrelation of the image, which is now said to outstrip the human capacity for perception.[12] In this chapter, however, I follow Hodge's work on digital media, animation, and temporal experience in his book *Sensations of History.* Refuting the primacy of conscious thought or perception, Hodge admits that digital media have outstripped not only our sensorimotor capacities but also our cognitive and perceptual abilities, as the bulk of machine communication that takes place in the average computer or smartphone is "not for us,"[13] as human users, but rather for machines to communicate within themselves and with each other in ways imperceptible to us. However, he also argues that "animation allows for phenomenal encounters with the experiential opacity of digital media precisely without dispelling that opacity."[14] Phenomenological explorations of perception and sensation thus remain an important tool for understanding digital media, especially in their relation to the traces of history and our lived relation with the past. Embodied encounters with animated media remain central to this exploration, even in an age of electronic images that seem to surpass both the sensorimotor schema of traditional Hollywood film and the Bergsonian experience of duration in the time-image. And so I repeat: "give me a body, then," because the body, in its relations to time and dimensionality (space), will be essential to understanding the new temporal and virtual media ecologies examined in this chapter and the next.

In chapter 3, I examined how live-action remakes, which depend heavily on CGI animation and motion capture special effects, can fail to evoke somaesthetic experience and instead promote phenopower, casting the actor's motion-captured body as one asset among many other digital assets to be manipulated. As a counterexample to how the "flesh of animation" is evolving in the digital age, this chapter considers a more niche phenomenon in the realm of digital media: electro swing music videos and the complex relations to time that they evoke, especially among dancers. Electro swing is a genre of electronic dance music (EDM) that uses samples from American swing jazz standards of the 1920s–1940s remixed with the regular 4/4 beat and heavy bass lines of techno and house music popular in the 1990s–2000s. Despite using American popular music as its base, electro swing is mainly European in origin. It became recognized as a distinct genre between 2004 and 2010, a period that saw the rise of electro swing albums, music festivals, clubs, and dance events across Europe, along with international tours by popular performers, such as the Austrian DJ Parov Stelar and the French seven-piece band Caravan Palace. Along with live performances and recorded albums, electro swing is consumed through music videos on streaming platforms. Visually, these videos often evoke the cinema of the 1920s and 1930s, either by mimicking historical film and animation styles or by including clips from actual historical footage, for instance, by using heavily looped and remixed dance scenes from early Classical Hollywood cartoons like Disney's *The Skeleton Dance* and the Fleischer Brothers' Betty Boop in *Snow-White* (1933).

In this chapter, I analyze electro swing music videos as encompassing another kind of image that retains the qualities of the movement- and time-images but also extends beyond them to reflect the new social and historical conditions of the 2000s–2020s. First, like the movement-image, electro swing music videos link perception, affection, and action through bodily mimicry as human viewers attempt to dance along with animated or digitally reedited images of human and inhuman dancers, both past and present. Second, like the time-image, this genre demonstrates the "incompossible" interrelations between different times[15] as the history of swing music is enfolded into the futuristic genre of EDM. Beyond these two aspects of movement- and time-image, however, electro swing also demonstrates a particularly self-reflexive and nostalgic relation to the past born of the new media cultures of the twenty-first century. For instance, electro swing relies heavily on the trend in digital culture for *nostalgic remediation,* which I have defined elsewhere as "a form of adaptation that does not just bring an old text into a new form, but reveals the shifting frames, contexts and transferences through which memory and media jointly function."[16] It also reflects in new ways on the older affect known in German as *Sehnsucht* or "life longings" for a situation or era that can never be attained and perhaps never existed in the first place.[17] In the case of electro swing, both nostalgic remediation and Sehnsucht manifest in videos that depict idealized, utopian visions of 1920s America, causing some fans to express hope for an equally glamorous return to the Jazz Age in the 2020s. As such, I argue that electro swing music videos act as a *reanimation* of the movement-image of Classical Hollywood film, inflected by the layered temporalities of the time-image and the perceptions and affects that have arisen around twenty-first-century digital media.

Along with formally classifying and analyzing animated electro swing music videos, I show how electro swing music videos connect with the embodied somaesthetic practices of dancers. Electro swing is a form of dance that crosses back and forth between physical spaces and virtual ones as dancers post videos of themselves on YouTube and

TikTok, which in turn inspire other dancers to perform the moves in houses, clubs, dance studios, and public spaces around the world. When dancers perform to electro swing music, they may enact the gest that Deleuze described in that they "put the before and the after in the body" by mixing old jazz moves with the looped, mechanical rhythms of EDM. Electro swing dancers reanimate themselves in much the same way as Betty Boop is reanimated in fan-made music videos, where her dances are looped and recut to techno beats. That said, I will qualify my generally positive assessment of electro swing by noting how the fan culture surrounding this genre has changed in the first few years of the 2020s as fans' celebratory calls for a revival of an idealized 1920s jazz culture in the "new twenties" were complicated by the Covid-19 pandemic. As Deleuze has noted, "the gest is necessarily social and political" as well as philosophical and aesthetic.[18]

To demonstrate how electro swing functions in contemporary digital culture, I first consider its history and formal properties, following the work of philosopher Nick Wiltsher on EDM. In subsequent sections, I provide a close analysis of some electro swing music videos and their audience reception through the gest of dance. I conclude with a section on the philosophical implications of contemporary digital media like these, drawing on the related concepts of nostalgic remediation, Sehnsucht, and reanimation.

The History and Aesthetics of Electro Swing

The ceiling was dripping with the condensed heat of the crowd. That is one of the things I remember most clearly about going to see a live show by the preeminent electro swing band Caravan Palace at the Mod Club in Toronto on June 29, 2013. The club had been decorated for the event in a playfully parodic vintage French style. A scale model of the Eiffel Tower was lit up with silvery blue light. Vases filled with luxurious white plumes were set against sheer-draped walls. Hostesses in French maid costumes offered miniature chocolate-filled croissants on platters to members of the audience, who had gathered an hour or more before the show's opening to chat and lounge in white leather booths. The "Frenchness" of the whole affair was played like a burlesque, with a knowing wink. In fact, a burlesque performer was employed to perform a striptease, along with several other performers doing acrobatics and fire performance, as an added attraction to the show. Once the band came on, however, a different set of influences came to the fore. The performance mixed DJ beats and sampled riffs with live, improvised keyboard, brass, and woodwind solos in the classic American swing jazz style. At one point, two of the musicians took center stage to dance, launching into a series of lightning-fast "swing-outs," the circular, eight-count pattern that lies at the heart of the Lindy Hop, as pioneered in Harlem's Savoy Ballroom by the famed Black dancer Frankie Manning. By the end of that set, the metallic beams of the ceiling were literally dripping: the music, the energy, and the atmosphere made physically manifest.

Though this was my first Caravan Palace show, I did not come into it as a complete novice to electro swing or to swing jazz more generally. Throughout the 2010s, I was heavily involved in the local swing dance scene in my hometown as a performance team dancer, musician, and board member for the Hepcat Swing dance studio (formerly Hepcat Hoppers) in Waterloo, Ontario. I played clarinet in a semiprofessional swing jazz band, the Hepcat Seven, and performed historical dance routines like the Shim Sham and the Black Bottom at street festivals and community arts events. I also organized and promoted local electro swing dance nights, and performed newly created electro swing group dance choreographies. The Caravan Palace show at the Mod Club, however, was the one event that made me ask, what's really happening here? The Toronto club presented the event as a burlesque of Frenchness, but the band that came from France to play there was bringing us a hybridized electronic version of an originally American sound: the *swing* of *electro swing*. Along with the sensation of transatlantic travel, the entire event was wrapped in an aura out of time, trying to bring the audience back to a diffuse, imaginary historical setting in which the decor, dress, and dance choreography wavered, mirage-like, between 1920 and 1940.

This double displacement in space and time is characteristic of electro swing, if not exclusive to it. Nostalgia, more generally, is a quality that can be identified in many postmodern, remediated works of digital culture, from popular cinema to new media installation art. For instance, Jason Sperb has analyzed the phenomenon of twenty-first-century cinematic nostalgia in his book *Flickers of Film: Nostalgia in the Time of Digital Cinema*. There Sperb looks at live-action nostalgia films like Baz Luhrmann's 2013 adaptation of *The Great Gatsby* through a critical materialist lens, demonstrating the ways in which nostalgia is commodified in mainstream cinema.[19] This is very much in line with the marketing of nostalgic remediation in Disney's live-action remakes discussed in chapter 3. By contrast, many electro swing events and music videos remain a bottom-up effort, driven by small or mid-sized independent record labels, local volunteer organizers, and experimental directors and animators whose efforts are funded through arts subsidies or grants. Even Caravan Palace, one of the most successful and popular electro swing groups, relies in part on French government subsidies to make professional-quality videos.[20] As such, electro swing allows us to examine how nostalgic remediation functions on the margins of the late capitalist paradigm driven by profit motives and personalized mass distribution (though of course, electro swing is not entirely free from that paradigm altogether). To do this, however, we must first consider its origins and formal properties.

In his two-part article "The Aesthetics of Electronic Dance Music," Wiltsher draws on the philosophical tradition of analytic aesthetics to explore what EDM can tell us about "definition and evaluation, the natures of experiences, and the natures of entities such as works."[21] Setting aside the question of whether works of popular music can be considered works of art in a classical (or classist) sense, Wiltsher rather considers such questions as, How is a given work of EDM classified as belonging to that genre? How does a work of EDM come to be considered "authentic," rather than fake, appropriated, or derivative? How is EDM seen to be part of particular cultures or ethnic identities, such as Black musical cultures, which have been the basis of much popular American music from jazz to hip-hop? and What effects do the formal qualities of EDM, such as samples, loops, breaks, and repetition, have on embodied engagement with the music in dance? Many of these questions are especially relevant for electro swing, and so it is worth engaging with Wiltsher's work in depth to compare the larger history and aesthetics of EDM with the specific aesthetic and phenomenal qualities of the electro swing subgenre.

According to Wiltsher, a genre of music can be defined not only by its formal properties but also by its cultural and historical positioning. For example, two punk bands may perform songs that are virtually identical to the casual listener, but fans will distinguish strongly between them, calling one a "real" punk band and the other a "fake" or derivative punk band. This is due in part to the fans' understanding of the genre's historical trajectory, in which a band that pioneered a particular style is considered "more authentic" than a newcomer that imitates the original band because the sound has become popular or profitable. This also applies to EDM. Wiltsher describes the history of EDM as follows:

> dance music began when producers in 1980s Chicago and Detroit, influenced by disco, krautrock, synthpop, and industrial music, carved out two genres: house and techno. House is a descendant of disco, with a melodic, organic and soulful feel, typically running at around 120–130 beats per minute (BPM), with a steady four-four beat (archetypes include InnerCity's "Good Life"). Techno runs at a similar speed or slightly faster, but is artificial, "urgent," and has a more percussive swing overlying a four-beat (archetype: Underground Resistance, "The Seawolf").[22]

Following close on the heels of house and techno were two more related subgenres, hardcore and garage. Wiltsher goes on to describe their evolution, saying that "by the end of the 1990s, these four fundamental genres of dance music—house, techno, hardcore, and garage—were firmly established, along with some significant variants, including drum and bass, trance, and gabba."[23] This history plays an important role in establishing the authenticity of a given work, because "whether a genre fits in the continuum depends on whether its culture is evolved from and similar in kind to the culture of precursors."[24]

The *electro* in *electro swing* indexes its connection to these precursors and places it firmly within the EDM continuum. The influence of both early house and techno can be felt in its use of four-four time, its "four-on-the-floor" rhythmic pattern in which the bass or kick drum is hit on every beat, and its tempos, which generally range from 95 to 135 BPM. It also makes use of digital sound editing techniques, such as sampling existing melodies, lyrics, or bass lines; looping sound elements into repetitive sequences; and digitally manipulating sound waves (sine waves, square waves, saw waves, etc.) to produce distortions in the sound. The *swing* in *electro swing*, by contrast, references the EDM genre's combination with another set of important precursors: the lineage of American and European swing music. Traditional swing music is characterized by its stretchy, syncopated "swung" rhythms and its improvisational solos, with melodies often carried by brass and woodwind instruments. The heyday of swing music spanned the middle of the twentieth century, from the "sweet" and "hot" jazz styles of the 1920s to the big band sounds of the 1940s. Although a full history of swing is beyond the scope of this chapter, suffice it to say that swing music and swing dance also had their own precursors in turn-of-the-century musical genres like ragtime and dances performed by African Americans, such as the cakewalk. Swing also has its own successors in early rock and roll and in the nostalgic swing revival of the 1990s, epitomized by bands like the Big Bad Voodoo Daddies. Electro swing is most clearly characterized by the remediation of old swing melodies and instrumentation through the new rhythms and digital technologies of EDM. When an electro swing composition strays too far from this core combination, fans may question its authenticity or belonging within the genre, as we will see later in some electro swing works from the early 2020s.

Electro swing itself, like many EDM variants, was consolidated as a genre in the early 2000s. In his history of electro swing, Chris Inglis suggests a number of early American forerunners in the 1980s and 1990s, mostly in the area of experimental jazz, such as Herbie Hancock's *Futureshock*, released in 1983, and the late-1980s hybrid subgenre of jazz rap developed in New York. We might also consider the connections (or lack thereof) between electro swing and the Afrofuturist "electro hop" movement pioneered in Los Angeles and promoted by the city's first all-hip-hop radio station, KDAY, in the 1980s.[25] However, Inglis states that "it wasn't until 2004 that 'a new genre as such really began to coalesce.' . . . This year saw the release of Nicolas Repac's *Swing-Swing* (2004), and Parov Stelar's *Rough Cuts* (2004), the first examples of entire albums dedicated to the sound."[26]

From this point on, the innovators of electro swing were primarily based in Europe. The newly consolidated subgenre flourished in France (home of Nicolas Repac, Caravan Palace, and Chinese Man, among others), Italy (Swingrowers), Austria (Parov Stelar), the Netherlands (Caro Emerald), Denmark (Swing Republic), Romania (Alice Francis), and other Western and Northern European nations. That is not to say that all electro swing performers are white: Alice Francis is of African descent, though born in Romania and based in Germany. Likewise, not only Europeans can create electro swing. As Inglis points out, "although most of the genre's development was occurring across mainland Europe, it is worth noting the formation of Goldfish, a South African duo who released their debut album, *Caught in the Loop,* in 2006."[27] Likewise, in 2010, the Australian duo Yolanda Be Cool released the song "We No Speak Americano," which topped the charts across Latin America and became one of the earliest electro swing tracks to break into the Billboard Top 40 in the United Kingdom. However, Goldfish and Yolanda Be Cool are lesser known in comparison to European festival headliners with multiple albums positioned indisputably within the genre, such as Parov Stelar and Caravan Palace, who have continued to release new music into the 2020s.

Why is it that European artists have found such success mixing electro beats with American swing jazz sounds? This is a question that ethnomusicologists are just beginning to address. In the 2019 book *Remixing European Jazz Culture,* Kristine McGee uses ethnographic fieldwork conducted at European electro swing festivals to argue that "while some might dismiss the 'vintage' impulse of such mixes as yet one more example of . . . 'retromania,' I contend that in the context of mixed-arts and aesthetic festivals and participatory culture, electro swing signals a performative engagement via a reworking of twentieth-century crisis-inspired aesthetic movements, especially with the 'Golden Age of Jazz,' as is often referenced in European histories of the 1920s through the 1940s."[28] McGee argues that electro swing performances, both in physical sites such as festivals and in online manifestations, act as a "survival technology" that allows participants to react to the economic and environmental crises of the early twenty-first century through a return to and revision of the upheavals of the early twentieth century.[29] Building on this, I would further suggest that since the Covid-19 pandemic, electro swing and other nostalgia-based EDM and pop genres have increasingly appealed to the affective state described in German as Sehnsucht, a more melancholic form of nostalgia based on a particular relation to historical time and the time-image.

Developmental psychologists Susanne Scheibe, Alexandra M. Freund, and Paul B. Baltes define this term by stating that "the German concept of Sehnsucht captures individual and collective thoughts and feelings about one's optimal or utopian life. Sehnsucht (life longings; LLs) is defined as an intense desire for alternative states and realizations of life."[30] According to Scheibe, Freund, and Baltes, these LLs have six interrelated core characteristics:

(a) utopian conceptions of ideal development;
(b) sense of incompleteness and imperfection of life;
(c) conjoint time focus on the past, present, and future;
(d) ambivalent (bittersweet) emotions;
(e) reflection and evaluation of one's life; and
(f) symbolic richness.[31]

Initially, electro swing might seem to have little in common with the poignant, bittersweet, and reflective qualities of Sehnsucht. As a subgenre of EDM, the best-known electro swing songs tend to be celebratory, parodic, or sensual rather than contemplative or wistful. "Dark electro swing" and "electro blues" are represented in collections from the UK-based indie electro swing label Freshly Squeezed, but they make up a smaller portion of releases than dance-oriented tracks. However, electro swing does share several characteristics in common with Sehnsucht. First, there is a certain utopian or idealized quality of the imagined Jazz Age depicted in its videos, in which actual social problems of the mid-twentieth century, such as racial segregation, genocide, and patriarchal domination, are elided in favor of idealized fantasies. The videos are rife with sexually liberated flappers, science fictional encounters with robots, plasmatic transformations of animated bodies, and even the resurrection of the dead—visions that are clearly unreal and unattainable but nonetheless maintain their attractive power. However, this fantasy is haunted by a sense of incompleteness and imperfection in the formal properties of electro swing music videos, which use glitching effects and scratchy, "lo fi" sound and image quality. This reveals the limitations of sampling and reediting historical film footage and the obscure qualities of new media, which operate according to principles different from cinema and from naturalized human perception more generally.

Most significant for electro swing, however, is the third characteristic of Sehnsucht: its "ontogenetic tritime focus." This term describes how "LLs involve life as a whole and simultaneously include aspects of the past, present, and future. Retrospection, concurrent evaluation, and prospection operate together in creating the experience of LLs."[32] This affect recalls the multilayered gest of Deleuze's time-image, in which time is apprehended through "the simultaneity of its peaks, the coexistence of its sheets," or the folding together of past, present, and future.[33] Electro swing is also strongly evocative of an ontogenetic tritime focus, because it involves a concurrent awareness of historical time periods and media, contemporary culture and musical styles, and a certain sense of the "futuristic" that accompanies the electronic soundscapes of EDM. A similar experience of Sehnsucht can be identified in contemporary online fandoms for other international pop and electronic genres, such as the 1980s Japanese City Pop movement and its contemporary online fandom. In a presentation at the 2021 Mechademia Asian conference, Rhea Vichot explored the utopian qualities and the tritime focus of City Pop, arguing that fans born outside of Japan after the 1980s continue to enjoy the synthesizer-based sounds and carefree youth-oriented imagery of City Pop even while consciously reflecting on their distance from it.[34] Inspired by her presentation, I began to listen to City Pop music (which I also enjoyed in a strange, nostalgic way) and to pay attention to comments that reflect a simultaneous sense of longing, utopianism, and unreachability or temporal distance. On one representative YouTube playlist I enjoyed titled "warm nights in tokyo [city pop/シティポップ]," posters writing in 2019 and 2020 made comments like "This is reminding me of everything that never happened" and "I remember back in the day when I'd drive through the Tokyo streets at night with the window rolled down, neon lights on buildings, everyone having a good time, the 80's were great. Wait a minute, I'm 18 and live in America."[35] As Vichot has argued, nostalgia in general, and the affective state of Sehnsucht in particular, can be seen as a feature in the reception of global (or newly globalized) historical musical genres like City Pop.

The effect of Sehnsucht in popular music is arguably more pronounced in electro swing's remediation of the 1920s. With the passing of centenarians who might remember the Roaring Twenties from their youth, the 1920s are receding from living memory into historical record. As such, the decade is coming to be regarded with a mixture of idealized utopianism and poignant regret at the passing of an era. The painful aspects of longing for an idealized yet unattainable Jazz Age have only intensified since the outbreak of the Covid-19 pandemic, which caused the cancellation of many swing dances and music festivals, curtailing hopes for a "new jazz age" in the 2020s. So, while electro swing was not necessarily created with the intention of evoking

Sehnsucht, it has joined a larger culture of nostalgic remediation in cinema, television, media, and music in which the early twentieth century has become a kind of tritime crystal, refracting elements of desire for a utopian past, concerns about the crises of the present, and longings or fears about the future.

Before I move on to analyze some examples of electro swing music videos, one further issue related to the history and aesthetics of electro swing must be raised, which is the issue of cultural appropriation. American swing jazz is historically associated with African American culture, and swing dancing was pioneered in large part by Black dancers. However, the idealized images of the 1920s found in films like Luhrman's *The Great Gatsby* and in electro swing music videos are generally (though not exclusively) created by white directors and composers and are presented to the public by actors and singers who are mostly (but not entirely) white, able-bodied, and conventionally attractive. Wiltsher has pointed out that cultural appropriation is an issue, not just with electro swing, but with EDM more generally. In considering what makes EDM "authentic," he addresses the criticism that EDM is not "Black enough," in that it does not reflect the Black experiences or lifeworlds that lie at the roots of American popular music. However, Wiltsher problematizes the "not Black enough" discourse surrounding EDM in three ways. First, he quotes from the book *The Conjectural Body: Gender, Race, and the Philosophy of Music* by Robin James, who argues that the shift from "Black music" to "white music" is often framed as a shift from body to mind: "Frere-Jones says 'black' when he means 'body' and physical pleasure (e.g., dancing, rhythm), and 'white' when he means 'mind' (thought, introspection, contemplation, klutziness, and all that is not 'cool')."[36] Wiltsher links this to EDM, saying, "The point generalizes to dance music: the criticism that a certain genre lacks blackness may often be construed as a charge that it's turned from the embodied joys of the dance floor to more contemplative pleasures."[37] In EDM (and electro swing), achieving contemplative abstraction from the body is more difficult than it was in, say, indie rock or free jazz, as dance music is designed for dancers and aims to provoke embodied reactions. That said, Wiltsher also cautions against accepting a reductive view of "Black music" as a singular genre or the simplistic and stereotypical equation of "Black = body." Instead, he suggests that "perhaps we shouldn't expect there to be a single black life-world, instead of a multiplicity of black identities."[38] These multiple identities are expressed through different musical genres, with differing qualities and aesthetic approaches. Third, he argues that "the idea here is that black (dance) musics are defined, implicitly or explicitly, against a white mainstream."[39] This approach risks perpetuating the segregation of musical styles and, by extension, their audiences.

Rather than framing electro swing as a white European appropriation of African American music, it may be more productive to understand it instead as part of a complex transcultural and transhistorical negotiation in which musical influences are exchanged—albeit unequally, and sometimes with friction—to create new genres. Granted, inequality and systemic racism do still operate in digital dance cultures. Even in 2021, it was common to see viral dance moves on TikTok, such the Renegade, created by fourteen-year-old Black TikToker Jalaiah Harmon, reach mainstream popularity only after being imitated by white performers, in this case, Charlie D'Amilio and Addison Rae, the latter of whom reaped the benefits of an increased media presence by demonstrating Harmon's moves on *The Tonight Show Starring Jimmy Fallon*. However, the very same digital platforms also allow original creators to regain the credit for their own work, for instance, when Black creators mobilized to draw attention to their contributions through a TikTok "strike" in July 2021 under the hashtag #BlackTikTokStrike.[40] In the past decade, electro swing has also seen the inclusion of more Black actors, dancers, and singers, for instance, in the global success of Alice Francis and in the all–African American cast of Caravan Palace's single "Midnight" (2016).

Some swing dance communities have also begun to include explicit acknowledgments of the African American roots of swing. These notices appear on the websites of swing dance communities, which may also provide information on the historical origins of the dance in Black culture along with antiracism resources. For instance, the international dance school Swing Patrol's website includes a page on "Acknowledging the Black roots of swing and jazz."[41] In-person dance groups, such as the Hepcat Swing dance school that I attend in Waterloo, Ontario, have also begun to include spoken acknowledgments at the start of formal meetings (for instance, board meetings or annual general meetings), recognizing that white dancers do not share the same lived experiences as racialized dancers, both past and present, and affirming a commitment to promoting equity, diversity, and inclusion within the community. As such, electro swing today can be seen as part of the ongoing remediation of the past through complex transcultural negotiations in the present.

In summary, Sehnsucht may involve idealized longings for a utopian age that never was, but its tritime focus also encourages reflection on how these visions of the past impinge on the present and inflect our aspirations for the future. As Hodge argues of digital artworks, the traces of the past persist in the present, and new media—particularly animation—can help us to reincorporate that trace in a transformative way. To demonstrate how this happens, I now present some case studies of electro swing music videos and the techniques that characterize them, such as reanimation; remixing disparate musical styles, visual styles, and media; and bridging animation and live action with dance.

Case Studies: Electro Swing Music Videos as Reanimation

In this section, I first provide a broad overview of the four main approaches that electro swing video creators take to visualizing the musical genre through animation and digitally edited live-action film clips, using a number of brief examples to illustrate the scope of the genre. I then look in more detail at two live-action–animation hybrid videos by Caravan Palace: one from the early 2010s that established the paradigmatic look and sound of the genre, "Jolie Coquine" (2012), and one that reflects how the genre has evolved in the early 2020s, "Supersonics (Out Come the Freaks Edit)" (2020). Overall, I show that there has been a shift from electro swing based on historical jazz sounds and Classical Hollywood images toward a more hybrid style in which electro swing is merging with hip-hop and contemporary street culture, showing a greater consciousness of the present- and forward-looking aspects of the genre's tritime focus.

As a preface to these case studies, I would like to define a key technique used in electro swing music videos that I call *reanimation.* Reanimation stands at the intersection of animation and remediation. Animation, at its most basic level, involves creating movement frame by frame, whether using objects, drawings on paper or celluloid, computer-generated models, or still photographs. As a principle, animation is also what creates the uncanny quality of "bringing the dead to life" on which so many electro swing videos rely. Animation theorists, such as Alan Cholodenko and Vivian Sobchack, have long argued that animation is fundamentally concerned with life and death. In a summation of his "First Principles of Animation," Cholodenko argues that to understand what cinema is as a whole, first "we must posit what animation is, including . . . its two major definitions: the endowing with life and the endowing with motion."[42] Animators from the earliest days of American cinema have played on the notion that frame-by-frame techniques can bring lifeless things to life and resurrect creatures long dead. Winsor McCay's 1914 silent film *Gertie the Dinosaur,* for instance, showed McCay using animation to resurrect a "dinosaurus," who goes on to perform "live" on stage with her creator. Gertie dances to bouncy ragtime piano music and appears to give McCay a ride into the silver screen at the end of the show, bringing motion and life to a long-extinct species. Early sound-era animators also created similar connections between dance, the animatic body, and the resurrection of the dead in celebrated shorts like Disney's *The Skeleton Dance,* which shows plasmatic skeletons performing 1920s Charleston moves like the bee's knees, and the Fleischer Brothers' *Snow-White,* which features rotoscoped scenes of jazz superstar Cab Calloway performing his hit "St. James Infirmary" as a loose-limbed ghost. Examples of resurrection and haunting such as these reveal how animation acts as what Jacques Derrida has termed "lifedeath" (variously rendered as "life-death" or "life death").[43] Cholodenko defined this term and applied it to animation studies by stating that "*Lifedeath is animation as the animatic*: both alive and dead, neither alive nor dead, at the same time."[44] The concept of lifedeath helps us to grasp how animation can seem at once "lively," as described in chapter 2, *and* uncannily not-alive or artificial, as discussed in chapter 3. Given animation's self-reflexive and self-figurative properties, the theme of lifedeath reflects the ontology of animation as a medium based on the creation of movement from still images, or the creation of life from death, and the presence of deathly images, such as skeletons, within the liveliness of animation.

In the postmodern era, self-reflexivity has taken on another fold: that of remediation, or "the particular ways in which [new media] refashion older media and the ways in which older media refashion themselves to answer the challenges of new media."[45] Digital new media no longer pretend to bring historic beings like dinosaurs back to life; rather, they bring back the old media *representations* of bygone eras. For instance, the CGI-laden blockbuster *Jurassic World* (dir. Colin Trevorrow, 2015) remediates its digital/analog precursor, *Jurassic Park* (dir. Steven Spielberg, 1993), both in its narrative beats and in its tongue-in-cheek allusions to the first film, such as having characters discuss the ethics of wearing a T-shirt with the original Jurassic Park logo. *Jurassic Park* itself remediated cartoon dinosaurs in a short educational video featuring the cel-animated character "Mr. DNA," who morphs into a lumbering, antiquated, brontosaurus-type creature reminiscent of McCay's Gertie. Here we see both the textual resurrection of dinosaurs and the metatexual remediation of older media representations of them. In contemporary music as well, electro swing is a textbook case of remediation. DJs have taken up the analog style of swing jazz and transformed it into a digital music genre using the new media principles described by Lev Manovich in *The Language of New Media*, such as transcoding vinyl records into digital files, creating modularity by sampling beats and riffs, and generating variability through releasing multiple remixes of the same song. As a result, the "ghosts" or "dinosaurs" of older technologies and popular cultures, such as the film reel, the gramophone, and the Lindy Hop, have been remediated through the new media production techniques of the digital era.

Reanimation, then, is a combination of the generative and uncanny properties of animation-as-lifedeath with the transmedia exchanges of remediation. It is a resurrection of an older medium that makes direct, creative interventions into the imagery of the past by using frame-by-frame changes to generate movements in bodies or bodies in movement that did not previously exist. Electro swing music videos exemplify reanimation in the way they handle visual materials from Classical Hollywood genres, especially musicals and animated shorts. They reanimate images from the past in the same way that an animator gives life to a cartoon character: by imbuing them with new movements.

Remediation and reanimation are found in almost all electro swing music videos. However, these videos do not always function in the same way. After viewing more than a hundred electro swing videos by both professional and amateur creators, I have identified four broad approaches that video creators take in visually representing the musical genre.

1. Original live-action videos. In this category, a brand-new music video is filmed live on-location or on a soundstage, usually featuring the band performing its own original swing-inspired compositions. It is a similar approach to that used in many mainstream popular music videos, though with some stylistic differences. For instance, original live-action electro swing videos will often make visual reference to silent or early sound film by using period costumes and makeup, along with "retro" stylings like title cards, black-and-white or sepia tone, and film grain filters to create a vintage feel. Many have a straightforward "stage performance" narrative, in which the band performs in vintage costumes for a historical audience. For instance, the video for "St. James Ballroom" (2013) depicts singer Alice Francis, dressed in a white beaded-and-fringed flapper dress, performing with her band and a gramophone record-scratching DJ before a black-and-white audience whose members dress and dance like characters from an early Hollywood musical. While most of these performance videos are celebratory or parodic in tone, some pick up on more uncanny themes of resurrection in their content. A stand-out example is the Speakeasies' "Black Swamp Village" (2012). This song opens with an echo of Louis Armstrong's 1928 rendition of "St. James Infirmary"—"I went down to St. James Infirmary / Saw my baby there"—in its own updated first line: "I went to the Black Swamp Village / Where strange people live." The people "living" there are strange because they are actually undead, swing-dancing zombies who perform impressive swing-outs and tandem Charleston moves despite their decaying bodies. The video features performances by world-renowned professional dancers Kevin St. Laurent and Jo Hoffberg, who star as the innocent human characters who stumble into the zombie cabaret. This cinematically styled narrative music video thus plays on the confrontation of life and (un)death. That said, most original live-action videos work through allusion or remediation more so than reanimation, because they evoke the impression of older media through stylistic cues and lyrical references rather than animating or editing footage on a frame-by-frame basis. Animation comes more into focus in the second category.

2. Original animation. Here music videos are fully animated using classical or contemporary animation styles. In keeping with the Jazz Age sound of the music, many animators draw on the 2D cel style of silent- and early sound-era animation to create their own original narrative short films (though the animation itself is often created digitally using Flash or other 2D animation software). Along with early cinema and animation styles, these videos remediate the racial and gendered stereotypes found in classic animation by self-reflexively commenting on them as artifacts of film history.

For instance, the video for the Italian band Jazzbit's "Swingin' Man" (2013) is animated in the style of an American black-and-white "chase" cartoon, complete with monochrome color filters, "rubber-hose" character designs, and a barnyard cast of animals straight out of the 1920s. "Swingin' Man" stars a dark-furred dog with the signature "pie eyes" of silent-era animation and the large lips of an African American stereotype. The short opens with a scene of the "Black" dog evading a cop and sneaking into a cinema to watch a film. On the screen, an animated locomotive speeds toward the audience in dramatic one-point perspective. The other animal audience members flee in terror, recreating film history's apocryphal tale of audience panic at the first screening of the Lumière Brothers' *The Arrival of a Train at La Ciotat Station* (1896). The little dog, however, is paralyzed with fear and does not run away. A title card appears with the word "CRASH" surrounded by clouds of smoke and jagged action lines. The scene then cuts to the dog falling into the train that has "hit" him, in effect entering the screen image (an echo, perhaps, of Buster Keaton's dream-voyage into the cinema screen in the 1924 film *Sherlock, Jr.*). There he is chased by a white pig police officer who is trying to throw him off the train, just as a real pig cop was earlier attempting to throw the dog out of the cinema. The dog evades the pig through a number of slapstick gags, acting as the classic comedy character type that Henry Jenkins calls the "clown," the comic hero who "encapsulat[es] all that is rebellious and spontaneous within the individual, all that strains against the narrow codes of social life."[46] The angry pig is the authority figure or "killjoy" who attempts to enforce those narrow social codes by policing the dog's behavior. However, their conflict is resolved when the chase leads the pair into a cartoon band's performance of the title song, "Swingin' Man." The two bond over their shared surprise and delight at the music in a utopian reversal of the classic chase cartoon's animal antagonisms. So, although this video draws on the visual iconography of racial stereotypes, it refuses the narrative of interspecies competition or hierarchy; instead, it promotes a vision of community based on a shared appreciation for swing music. Canny members of the audience for this music video can also participate, not only in their appreciation for the remixed electro swing music, but also in their shared recognition of the 1920s cartoon styles, film allusions, and comedy tropes that the video reflexively reanimates.

Likewise, in Alice Francis's "Shoot Him Down" (2013), sepia tone and film grain filters lend a vintage appearance to a music video that recalls the racy cartoon shorts made for adult audiences during World War II. Here Francis voices the part of a sexy, white-clad cat singer backed up by a gramophone-scratching DJ, just as in her live-action stage performance for "St. James Ballroom." Rather than remediating live-action musicals, however, this video has more in common with Tex Avery's parodic cartoon *Red Hot Riding Hood* (1943). In Avery's electrified Jazz Age version of Little Red Riding Hood, a lustful wolf pursues an attractive cabaret singer, who leads him on a chase that sees him smashed over the head with a lamp and dropped from an apartment window, among other humiliations. In a similar series of macabre, Averyesque gags, Francis's cat songstress takes revenge on her cheating lover, a mangy, lecherous tomcat who ogles passing women from his seat in the audience, by having his head blown up with dynamite and his teeth chiseled out with a jackhammer, to name just a few of the bizarre tortures he survives through the powers of cartoon resurrection. All the while, she sings in high, cooing tones about how she will "break his neck neck neck neck" and "shoot him down," in a reversal of the more typical stage siren's seductive appeals to male audiences. In this video, as in "Swingin' Man," we can see how electro swing music videos reanimate silent-era and Classical Hollywood short cartoon styles, playing with their visual conventions while remaining within an orthodox narrative animation mode.

That said, animators may also use more experimental modes of animation for electro swing music videos. Some rely on collage techniques, patching together scraps of photographs and vintage magazine illustrations, as is discussed later in this chapter. Others draw, quite literally, on paper, using hand-drawn images in graphite or ink. One example is the official music video for Parov Stelar's "Clap Your Hands" (2014), which remixes samples from Glen Miller's dance-routine song "Doin' the Jive" (1937). This video relies on a nonnarrative montage of hand-drawn and rotoscoped imagery. The animated images are primarily motion studies that recall the early photographic experiments of Edweard Muybridge. The motion studies include a running man created out of horizontal circular scribbles, a heavily crosshatched silhouette of a running greyhound, and rotoscoped outlines or silhouettes of male and female dancers whose fluid, natural gestures are clearly traced from live-action footage. Intercut with these motion studies are numerous still images of cross-sectioned human bodies and body parts entirely filled with intricate gears and clockwork mechanisms, which flicker by in a rapid succession of shots lasting less than a second each. The backgrounds are lent a "retro" air through the use of a vintage typewriter font that types the song's lyrics as they are sung onto what looks like coffee- and ink-splattered paper. As instructional lyrics from the song, such as "clap your hands / and you swing out wide" are repeated multiple times in mechanical succession, so the images of human and animal bodies are also repeated in mechanically looped cycles. As a result, this video comments on the automation of digital music through its rapid, repetitive audio loops and its visual depictions of robotic embodiment. The organic liveliness of the rotoscoped dancers stands in stark visual contrast with the mechanical imagery of gear-filled bodies and the mechanical repetition of identical beats and lyrics. Along with questioning stereotypical images of race and gender, then, some electro swing music videos also question the status of the body itself by recombining and remixing the organic and mechanical, the natural and artificial, the living creature and the automated machine, along the lines of Donna Haraway's "Cyborg Manifesto."[47]

Original live-action and original animation videos make up the first two categories of electro swing videos. However, some electro swing music videos also engage directly with the traces of the past by remixing and reanimating historical visual materials. This brings us to the third category.

3. Reanimated live action. In this category, historical media like analog film clips are encoded as digital video and altered on a frame-by-frame basis to generate new movements or bodies. Almost all these videos work with footage from Classical Hollywood musicals, especially swing dance films like *Hellzapoppin'* (dir. H. C. Potter, 1941) or movies starring 1930s idols like Fred Astaire and Ginger Rogers. In the simplest cases, the footage is simply edited so that the kicks or steps of the original dancers are cut to the beat of the electro swing remix. A simple example can be found in the American band Postmodern Jukebox's "Grandpa Style" cover of Macklemore's 2012 rap/hip-hop song "Thrift Shop," which was remixed with an

EDM beat and looping by Parisian DJs Bart & Baker in 2013. The video for Bart & Baker's remix, which was posted on Postmodern Jukebox's YouTube channel, features footage from two films: the all–African American musical *Hi-De-Ho* (dir. Josh Binney, 1947) starring Cab Calloway and the musical romantic comedy *Pot o' Gold* (dir. George Marshall, 1941) starring James Stewart and Paulette Goddard. Footage from *Pot o' Gold* is used as a framing device to accompany the song's opening melodic piano riff. A seven-second close-up shows Goddard's character staring dreamily off into space, as if suggesting that we, the viewers, are entering into her fantasy world. Then there is a cut to black, followed by the introduction of the EDM bass track along with footage from the climactic tap dance scene in *Hi-De-Ho*. Shots of Cab Calloway energetically conducting his orchestra are crosscut with a tap dance performance by the "class act" Black tap dancer team the Miller Brothers and Lois, who perform, impressively, on a series of raised pedestals that spell out M-I-L-L-E-R. The original dance footage, however, is looped to match the rhythms of the remixed song, particularly in sequences in which the duration of a looped phrase is shortened with each repetition until it becomes an audio stutter. This audio effect is matched visually by a glitch-like kick as Lois's hinged knee flickers between positions at barely perceptible speeds through the power of looped editing.

Overall, this video illustrates how historical film footage is treated as a malleable raw material, with actors as puppets of the digital editor. In this case, the song "Thrift Shop" itself has no historical connection to swing jazz. It is a twenty-first-century creation that was lent a vintage air through Postmodern Jukebox's retro-style cover and then "electrified" by European DJs as if it were a vintage swing song. As a result, the electro afterlife of Postmodern Jukebox's song becomes itself a postmodern pastiche. As Arjun Appadurai describes it, "the past is now not a land to return to in a simple politics of memory. It has become a synchronic warehouse of cultural scenarios, a kind of temporal central casting, to which recourse can be taken as appropriate, depending on the movie to be made, the scene to be enacted, the hostages to be rescued."[48] Electro swing music video editors literally use cinema history as "a kind of temporal central casting," because digitized historical footage acts as a repository of performances out of which new performances can be reanimated on a frame-by-frame basis. In some cases, pastiche can grant contemporary digital artists greater flexibility and agency to reimagine the world. Appadurai notes that "the imagination is now central to all forms of agency."[49] However, it is important not to erase the traces of the past in the exercise of imagination or to overwrite the history of Black dancers and musicians with dreamy white-oriented fantasies, as in the framing shots at the start and end of this video.

Some artists have proven themselves creative and self-aware in their use of historical animation styles and film footage. But that does not mean electro swing videos are entirely free from the frictions that arise when two (or more) cultures collide. This is evident in the final category.

4. Reanimated animation. In this category, clips of historical animation are resurrected and reedited to create new dances or plots. Electro swing filmmakers especially like to exploit the limited animation technique of using "cycles," whereby a single set of sequential drawings—say, a series of frames depicting a cartoon character taking two steps, one with the right foot and the other with the left, while swinging each arm once—was rephotographed multiple times to create the impression of a continuous motion like walking or dancing. These rhythmic movements are perfect for digital looping and for matching to a regular techno beat. Although this technique is not often found in official music videos, it is favored by electro swing fans and semiprofessional creators who do not have the skills or financial resources to create original animation videos. Indeed, several semipro or professional musician YouTubers, such as Phil Doza and Davide Di Bello, specialize in creating their own original electro swing songs with videos based on animated short film series from Classical Hollywood, such as Disney's Merrie Melodies and the Fleischer's Betty Boop, or famous feature films ranging from *Dumbo* (dir. Samuel Armstrong, Norman Ferguson, and Wilfred Jackson, 1941) to *Aladdin* (dir. Ron Clements and John Musker, 1992). In many of these videos, entire scenes from the original films can play out with relatively little reediting, as the creators are making music that matches the tempos of the original songs well enough that the characters appear to dance to the newly added beat in a kind of "auditory Kuleshov effect."[50]

An example that demonstrates a more creative approach to reanimating historical cartoon clips is the French trip-hop band Chinese Man's "I've Got That Tune" (2009). The song is a sped-up, looped, and electrified version of the 1932 song "Hummin' to Myself" by the

Depression-era jazz collective Washboard Rhythm Kings. The video uses footage from several Betty Boop cartoons, including *A Language All My Own* (dir. Dave Fleischer and Myron Waldman, 1935), in which Betty Boop is shown traveling to Japan and performing a song-and-dance number partly in Japanese, in a blatant attempt by the Fleischer Brothers studio to woo the Japanese audience. In Chinese Man's video, the Japanese setting is mostly edited out. Instead, Betty's dancing body has been composited onto a giant turntable, where she performs surrounded by neon pops of color, graffiti-like bubble letters, and doodled symbols (arrows, musical notes, etc.) that spark and vanish around her. The entire video has a surreal quality of ungroundedness: the way her feet do not seem to touch the record, and the way graffitied images appear and disappear around her like smoke, creates a feeling of there-and-not-there, of lively dance and false motion—in short, of lifedeath. Traces remain of the original short film's Orientalist imagery, such as a Japanese paper umbrella that descends from the ceiling holding an enthusiastic audience of tiny Asian figures. However, this already strange image from the 1935 film seems even more absurd when taken out of context and placed in a mise-en-scène in which images appear and disappear with dreamlike transiency. This illustrates how reanimation works as a process that samples, composites, and transforms historical materials. The video takes an American studio's attempt to connect with Japanese audiences using what I have called the "Cute Ethnic Other" figure[51] and updates it with remixed jazz music, reedited footage, and new animation in a twenty-first-century style, in a way that is arguably more self-aware and parodic than the Fleischer Brothers' earnestly Orientalist attempt.

That said, the members of Chinese Man, known professionally as DJ Marseille Zé Mateo, High Ku, and SLY, have faced some pushback for their irreverent approach to Orientalism, not only in this particular video but in the band's name and promotion. In the mid-2010s, their website and the advertising copy for some of their events claimed that their music was disseminated by a character called the "Chinese Man" who was "one-quarter Cantonese, two-thirds Manchou" and "appears to be from the Wu Tang Mountain, not far from Marseilles, France." The fanciful mix of real and imaginary geographies marks the character as fictitious, and indeed it does not reflect the actual backgrounds of the musicians, who are all white men from France. However, not everyone appreciated the tongue-in-cheek nature of the moniker, as the band reportedly faced protests at a 2018 appearance in Vancouver, Canada, over its name, which some Asian Canadians found offensive.[52] In the band's defense, however, the name "Chinese Man" was not chosen as a reference to any real-world person, Chinese or otherwise. It was drawn from a vocal sample in the final track of their first album, *The Groove Sessions* Vol. 1, where two lines from unrelated (and uncredited) English-language films are spliced together to create the emphatic declaration "This is the / Chinese man," in the typical fashion of techno remixing at that time. It is linguistically unrelated to the North American ethnic slur "Chinaman," which some of the band's critics seem to have conflated with "Chinese man." Indeed, the band's claim that they are from the "Wu Tang Mountain" might be seen as a tongue-in-cheek justification of their name, subtly reminding (anti-)fans that the famous hip-hop group Wu-Tang Clan also took their name from a film reference, the 1983 Hong Kong martial arts film *Shaolin and Wu Tang* (dir. Chia-Hui Liu) even though none of the members are Chinese. This is an example of how friction can develop in the process of transcultural exchange, when media elements that were disembedded from their original contexts using techniques of sampling and postmodern pastiche are reembedded and reinterpreted in a new context. Even in the most "virtual" of media, then, we still need to confront the social and political aspects of electro swing, both in its production and in its reception.

Close-Reading the Music Videos of Caravan Palace

So far, I have provided a broad but shallow overview of some common themes and aesthetic strategies used in electro swing music videos. To avoid creating a laundry list effect, however, I would also like to provide an in-depth, comparative, close analysis of two electro swing music videos, following the techniques for formal analysis outlined by Carol Vernallis in *Experiencing Music Video: Aesthetics and Cultural Context*. In the introduction to this work, Vernallis advocates paying close attention to both the music itself, in terms of vocal qualities, lyrics, and instrumentals, and the formal strategies that are used to represent them visually in music videos. The goal of this close analysis, for Vernallis, is to "learn about music video's distinct modes of representing race, class, gender, and sexuality."[53] As this list of topics suggests, Vernallis is particularly concerned with the lived and embodied aspects of music videos as a performative mode of expression. In discussing the role of character and performance in American music videos of the late twentieth century, she argues,

> Music video is ultimately a vaudevillian scheme where the figure is foregrounded against a static background. Compensatory techniques obscure this scheme through partial views, a wandering camera, abrupt editing, postproduction techniques, and so forth. These techniques reaffirm the primacy of the body, however: they encourage the viewer to follow the body and build a complete picture of the performer's form while presenting the background even more schematically, through surprising shifts of context and partial, arbitrary, and slow disclosure. As such, the body seems to mediate our knowledge of the setting and thereby to wield authority over the place.[54]

She further adds that "as the viewer puts together the whole of the song he or she also constructs an imaginary body whose processes seem to *animate* the video—to make it hospitable. . . . Videos can provide suggestions about how to inhabit our bodies—in the bedroom, at a party, in a car, on a city street, or on a suburban lawn."[55] Though Vernallis does not use the term *animate* literally here, electro swing music videos do in fact (re)animate bodies, either by showing band members, singers, and dancers as cartoons or hybrid live-action and animation characters or by editing the gestures of filmed actors frame by frame to create new dance moves that were never, and in some cases never could be, performed in life. In their very form, then, electro swing music videos comment on the body and its relation to historical media and contemporary society, suggesting how we as viewers might also inhabit our bodies in relation to on-screen images.

Of all the major electro swing artists, one of the most committed to animating bodies in their music videos is Caravan Palace. Of the fourteen official music videos listed on their YouTube channel in 2022, nine fall into the "Original Animation" category, as they are either fully animated or hybrid films with a strong focus on the interactions between animated and live characters (Figure 14). While none of these videos fits into the "Reanimated Animation" category, because none uses historical cartoon footage, most do remediate Classical

Original live action	Reanimated live action	Original animation	Reanimated animation
"Plume" (2019)	"Mighty" (2015, sci-fi films)	"Melancolia" (2021, cel shaded)	N/A
"Midnight" (2016)		"Supersonics" (2020, graffiti/ hybrid)	
"Comics" (2015)		"Moonshine" (2020, cel shaded)	
"Dramophone" (2012)		"Miracle" (2019, cel shaded)	
		"Wonderland" (2016, cel shaded)	
		"Lone Digger" (2015, cel shaded)	
		"Rock It for Me" (2012, cel/collage)	
		"Suzy" (2012, 3-D CGI/hybrid)	
		"Jolie Coquine" (2012, stop-motion/collage/ hybrid)	

FIGURE 14. Caravan Palace music video category breakdown.

Hollywood film and animation by using some of the same techniques seen in other animated electro swing videos discussed so far, such as 2D cel-style shading, rubber-hose character design, collages of vintage print materials, and allusions to historical films.

A paradigmatic example of an animated electro swing video is Caravan Palace's first single, "Jolie Coquine." The song was released in October 2008, just as electro swing was being constituted as a coherent musical genre. A video for the song was posted to YouTube in 2012 as the genre began to grow in popularity. As an early example of electro swing, the song musically plays up the "surprise" and "novelty" elements of combining old-fashioned swing music with modern electronic beats. The track starts with a solo violin riff, accompanied after a few bars by an acoustic guitar playing a traditional "gypsy jazz" rhythm known as *la pompe* or "the pump," which stresses beats 2 and 4. This is no coincidence, as one of Caravan Palace's founding members, violinist Hugues Payen, counts Romani guitarist Django Reinhardt, who popularized la pompe, as a major influence.[56] (Indeed, the band's first festival performance was at the 2007 Django Reinhardt Jazz Festival.) Adding to the swing jazz feel is lead vocalist Zoé Colotis's rapid-fire delivery of the opening lyrics "How to do, where to go, what to do without you?" which are not very comprehensible on the track but rather sound like scatting in the style of Ella Fitzgerald owing to her focus on the play of sound and repetition over clarity or meaning. The electronic beat does not drop until thirty-eight seconds into the song. This means that the jaunty, acoustic, gypsy jazz rhythm and scat-style vocals are well established first, and the EDM-style bass line and hi hat are added later as a new development in the song, signaling by extension a new development in the genre of jazz itself. The effect is (or at least, was, in 2008) to provoke surprise and amusement at the combination of old and new musical styles.

The chronological contrast of the music is visually echoed by the video for "Jolie Coquine," which was posted to Caravan Palace's YouTube channel on February 29, 2012. As the opening violin riff plays, there is a close-up of a gramophone needle on a spinning record. When the acoustic guitar enters, there is a cut to a tracking shot moving into the mouth of the gramophone's golden horn, which slowly brings the viewer down into its depths. A brief fade-in from the darkness of the horn reveals a hallway or maze constructed of tatty cardboard plastered with vintage French advertisements and posters. One poster shows a black-and-white line drawing of a woman in a solid black dress listening happily to a gramophone with the words "Caravan Palace" printed above her. As Colotis's vocals enter the soundtrack, the woman becomes animated, tearing herself from the page and springing into the hallways as a jointed, robot-like 3D puppet made of wadded-up brown paper and black cardboard, with live-action black-and-white video footage of Colotis's face superimposed on a flat frame in the head. Brought to life through stop-motion animation, the Colotis-robot sings her opening verses as she walks toward the camera, which tracks back to keep her framed against the other posters on the walls. Another puppet leaps from a picture to join her, suggesting that any of the posters might come alive at any

FIGURE 15. The animated band enters as the beat drops in Caravan Palace's "Jolie Coquine" music video.

moment. Just as the beat drops at thirty-eight seconds in, she turns a corner, and five more members of the band join her from behind the wall (Figure 15). One of them even slides in on his knees precisely as the bass track enters, in a gesture that dramatically plays up the surprising addition of an electro beat to the old swing sound. Thus the opening forty seconds of the video introduce several key visual tropes of Caravan Palace's music videos, and indeed of electro swing more generally, including the gramophone, the robot-body, the collage or pastiche of vintage media and popular culture, and the compositing of live-action and animated footage.

Throughout the video, stop-motion and collage techniques cross the boundaries between print and screen media and also between different eras and nations. Most of the posters in the background are in French and advertise, for instance, the Pâtisserie Breton or Les Petites chorus girls. They are evocative of a generalized impression of "vintage France," broadly spanning the 1890s–1960s. However, there are also several allusions to silent- and early sound-era Hollywood film. At one point, Colotis's robot avatar tears the face off a poster of Boris Karloff as Frankenstein's monster and throws it onto one of her bandmates, whose arms promptly stick straight out in a parody of the monster's walk. Another member is sucked bodily into a machine's cardboard gears in a nod to Chaplin's *Modern Times* (1936). However, just as swing sounds are transformed by EDM beats, so the vintage images are also recontextualized through references to twenty-first-century club culture. The *Modern Times* machine is controlled by a gramophone-playing DJ, who scratches the records on his cardboard turntables and makes the gears reverse directions. The gramophone is featured in many electro swing videos and artworks to link "old timey" musical recording with the DJ's turntables in contemporary nightclubs. Extending the nightclub parallel, a host of 2D paper dolls, having been brought to life from vintage ads, become the crowd at a miniature rave, all dancing under an enormous gramophone record that circles high above them. The final shot of the video withdraws back through the gramophone's horn to frame the device sitting sedately in an office among other ephemera of the past, including an ink blotter, a scattering of handwritten letters, and a deerstalker hat on a hatstand. The audience, however, now knows that the antique appearance of the gramophone harbors a very modern—and, given the robot imagery, even futuristic—musical culture.

Images of robots, gramophones, and dancers are pervasive in other music videos from Caravan Palace's first self-titled album. In the video for "Suzy," a 1920s flapper (played by Colotis in live action) rockets to fame after performing the Charleston on stage with a 3D CGI dancing robot in a collaged city of neon lights and paper buildings. In "Rock It for Me" (2012), a fully animated cel-style version of the band is interrupted mid-performance by a flying saucer invasion, only to be saved by a 3D-modeled "dancing machine" robot that defeats the aliens with the power of its groovy moves. The video for "Lone Digger" (2015) presents a more adult take on the nightclub setting, showing three anthropomorphized black cats dressed in varsity jackets who go to a strip club and end up splattering the venue with the blood of their rivals, a trio of Dobermans in business suits. In all these videos, the dance club setting is saturated with signifiers of past eras, both European and American, along with a dose of science fiction or "retrofuturistic" imagery that speaks to contemporary digital culture. As McGee argues in her analysis of the video for "Rock It for Me," "intertextual knowledge of the musical aesthetics of these two cultures—the architectural spaces of Paris's pre-war culture and of contemporary aesthetics for electronic music—enabled Caravan Palace to connect with participants of both electronic and jazz culture."[57] These videos thus act as time-images, layering multiple temporalities in the mise-en-scène and highlighting the reanimated bodies of cartoon characters through the theatrical and "gest-ural" motions of collaged singers and Charleston-dancing robots.

As a band that draws on contemporary aesthetics as well as historical references, Caravan Palace has continued to evolve along with the changing zeitgeist of the latter 2010s and early 2020s. Increasingly, the group has taken up more influences from late twentieth-century popular culture while retaining prewar imagery and sounds only as subtexts. One example of this evolution is the video "Supersonics (Out Come the Freaks Edit)," which premiered on December 10, 2020, based on a track from the 2019 album *Chronologic*. The video was conceived, designed, and directed by Bechir "Jiwee" Jouini, who had previously worked with the band as an uncredited director for "Suzy." However, despite being created by the same director for the same band, the musical and cultural allusions in "Supersonics" have shifted forward in time by several decades, from the 1920s–1940s to the 1980s to early 2000s. Rather than Classical Hollywood, print ads, and swing jazz, this music video remediates New Hollywood, graffiti, and hip-hop. As in many of the band's previous videos, this is accomplished by combining sounds and images from across media and eras.

The video opens with several quick cuts that show a young man in a puffy reddish-orange vest, a la Marty McFly from *Back to the Future* (dir. Robert Zemeckis, 1985), riding a Onewheel (essentially an electrified, one-wheeled skateboard) into a deserted, graffiti-covered warehouse. As he steps off the Onewheel to look around, he accidentally kicks a can of rainbow spray paint, sending it spinning toward a brick wall. In a classic trick film moment, the can appears to pass through the bricks as the physical object is replaced between the frames by a graffiti-style illustration of a spray can that smoothly continues its trajectory into the wall. The animated spray paint morphs into a can-shaped robot with white, four-fingered Mickey Mouse gloves, which leaps up and splits open to reveal a leaner, mechanical man inside, rendered as if spray-painted in black and white using a stencil. As the robot dances to the beat of the music, the man in the McFly vest begins to bop his head in time, joining in the dance. A match on action cut shows the robot beginning a spin and the young man completing it, suggesting a parallel between the photographic and animated worlds. This parallel soon becomes an outright breakdown between animation and live action as the man encounters several more spray-painted characters who come to life and pull him into their world.

FIGURE 16. The Freaks, the robot, and the protagonist dance between animation and live action in Caravan Palace's "Supersonics" music video.

These include a Mexican-inspired, skull-faced Día de Muertos girl played by Zoé Colotis; a steampunk, voodoo New Orleans man; a zombie styled after John Carpenter's *They Live* (1988); and a tiny, evil-eyed, black alien. The lively graffiti monsters are the "Freaks" of the song's nightlife-oriented lyrics: "Freaks come out until the lights go on." In hybrid-film fashion, all of the characters—monsters, robots, and humans—are able to transform fluidly from animated figures to live-action performers and back again as they jump between the flat, 2D plane of the brick wall and the 3D spaces of the warehouse. Initially, the Freaks chase the protagonist, who escapes using classic Warner Bros. cartoon tactics, such as spray-painting a hole in the floor to trap them or painting a door in the wall to flee from them. However, the end of the video sees the spray-painted robot and the human character perform an irresistibly catchy dance routine that has all the Freaks joining in. As in the video for Jazzbit's "Swingin' Man," the cartoon chase narrative ends with a utopian harmony between pursuers and the pursued brought on by a shared appreciation of music and dance (Figure 16).

As in early Caravan Palace videos, there are still some references to prewar popular culture in "Supersonics," particularly in the dancing and animation. Among the dance moves in the video are a swing-out-like partnered spin performed by the graffiti robot and Día de Muertos girl, created using the time-honored technique of rotoscoping. We also see solo jazz moves, such as skates (raising one foot and shuffling forward on the other while pointing upward with the opposite finger, as shown in Figure 16), in the routine that all the characters perform together. Other dance moves were based on reference material from early animation, such as a bendy legs move performed by the robot and the male character. This is a direct reference to the similarly plasmatic legs of the skeletons in *Skeleton Dance,* as Jouini points out in the making-of video for "Supersonics" by showing a split-screen video comparison of footage from Disney's short film and the dancers for "Supersonics" performing in a studio.[58] This video thus relies on a layering of animetic bodies and live-action performance, not only in its hybrid visual style, but more subtly in the "animated" styles of movement seen across both rotoscoped and live-action bodies. In this way, it also layers multiple temporalities within the body, as in Deleuze's concept of the time-image and, in particular, the gest. While Deleuze does not cover dancing in relation to the gest, he does cover music extensively, describing how, in *First Name: Carmen* (dir. Jean-Luc Godard, 1983), "the curve of the violinist's arm modifies the movement of the bodies which are embracing" and speaking of how "Godard's cinema goes from the attitudes of the body, visual and sound, to the pluri-dimensional, pictorial and musical gest."[59] Likewise, the dancers in this video can also be said to "put the before and after in the body"[60] through the interplay of music and gesture and, more importantly, through the incorporation of animated dance moves from silent-era cartoon shorts into a contemporary, digitally (re)animated performance.

One difference between "Supersonics" and earlier electro swing music videos, such as "Swingin' Man" or "Jolie Coquine," is that swing jazz is no longer the primary musical referent. Though the Freaks carry traditional jazz instruments, such as a double bass and an acoustic guitar, the instruments are not prominently featured in the song itself, and the twenty-first-century techno beat begins almost right away, forming the predominant rhythm track of the entire song. Fans commenting on the track on Reddit have picked up on this shift in instrumentation, noting that "there was like no trumpet/brass in the song so it didn't really even sound like electro swing."[61] As Wiltsher has observed in EDM more generally, the discourse among electro swing fans has shifted from enjoying its novelty to questioning its authenticity and complaining that the music has become (in other commenters' words) "watered down," "generic," or "much more like electro dance" than electro swing. As Wiltsher also says, however, the consideration of EDM's aesthetics should not stop with simple assertions that a track is either authentic or derivative but should include an attention to *how* and *why* these assertions can be made in the first place. In the case of electro swing, as we have seen, the genre originally depended on remediating the popular music of the 1920s–1940s, and its videos were based on imitating or reanimating films from the silent-era and Classical Hollywood periods. Caravan Palace's own early videos were key in establishing these genre conventions, and they continue to some degree even in "Supersonics." However, in their later videos, the musical and visual allusions to the Jazz Age are no longer front and center but are somewhat obscured by a new set of influences coming in from New Hollywood films, street art, and hip-hop music. Thus fans who have followed electro swing since the beginning now find that the "retro" or "vintage" aesthetic they once used to define the genre as authentic is no longer present.

That said, the fact that "retro" is a moving target should not be all that surprising. After all, for those watching "Supersonics" in 2020, 1980 was forty years ago—just as the 1940s were "forty years ago" in the 1980s, when the first musical precursors to electro swing were created. Following the generational pattern of nostalgia, there has been a surge of 1980s references in media of the late 2010s and early 2020s, for instance, in films like *Ready Player One* (dir. Steven Spielberg, 2018) and television shows like *Stranger Things* (2016–). These are used to provoke nostalgia in Generation X viewers and older members of the millennial generation who were raised in that decade and Sehnsucht in younger millennials and Generation Z viewers, who have no lived memories of "the eighties" but have formed an idealized image of the decade as a past era. So this temporal shift in electro swing from early to late twentieth-century references is still fundamentally compatible with the multilayered, tritime structure of electro swing as a genre in which the traces of the past are reanimated according to the imperatives of an ever-changing digital culture. As the 1920s grow ever farther away and our perception of what is "retro" shifts to later decades, references to the Jazz Age are becoming increasingly opaque. That opacity itself is now, as Hodge argues, also a subject for digital art and music. The technologies driving digital culture, from video compositing software to artificial intelligence (AI) text and image generators, make it easier than ever for both human and nonhuman actants to rifle through the "synchronic warehouse of cultural scenarios" and reanimate historical films, artworks, actors, and cartoon characters. The consequences of this contemporary approach to the past may extend beyond electro swing to the future of art itself.

Still, the fact that some electro swing albums, such as Caravan Palace's *Chronologic,* are using fewer obvious "authentic" historical references to the early twentieth century does not mean their swingin' past is entirely erased. Traces of the past persist in the animetic and hybrid quality of many current electro swing music videos, which link the past, present, and future by joining historical animation styles, live-action performances, digital editing, and online distribution. The past also remains present in the gest of the musicians and dancers, whose bodies carry muscle memories of the Charleston and the swing-out. Indeed, dancers have been not only the spectators of videos by Caravan Palace and other artists but also the producers of their own embodied experiences of the music and of animation. As such, I would like to end this chapter with a brief consideration of the somaesthetic experience of electro swing dance. In particular, I look at how the experience of dance has been altered since the Covid-19 pandemic and what impact that has had on electro swing fans' perceptions of the past and the future.

Conclusion: The Phenomenal and Temporal Experience of Electro Swing in the 2020s

In the second part of his philosophical exploration of EDM, Wiltsher argues that while much theory of dance aesthetics focuses on dance as a form of performance for an audience—as seen in music videos—it is also useful to consider the lived experience of dancing as practiced by amateurs in live settings. As he notes, people on the dance floor in a dimly lit club at night do not primarily perform for one another or dance with the expectation of being seen.[62] Quoting Aili Bresnahan's article "Improvisational Artistry in Live Dance Performance as Embodied and Extended Agency," Wiltsher argues that in these cases, we need to consider the ways in which informal dancing acts as a kind of "improvisation performed in order to achieve a movement-based somatic state."[63] A full philosophical consideration of dancing should also involve attention to the muscular, haptic, and kinetic practice of dance as felt from the inside phenomenally and somaesthetically, rather than as seen from outside. Indeed, as in Merleau-Ponty's figure of the reversibility of the flesh, in which hands can both touch and be touched at once,[64] the somaesthetic "inside" and the performance-oriented "outside" of dancing are reversible and mutually influencing.

Personally, I have a strong somaesthetic reaction to electro swing music videos as a dancer with more than ten years of experience in doing the Lindy Hop, the Charleston, and various historical routines incorporating solo jazz and tap moves, such as the Big Apple and the Black Bottom. Put more scientifically, I have "muscle memory" related to these dances due to a strengthening of neuronal connections within the motor cortex from performing them repeatedly—connections that can be activated visually by my brain's "mirror neurons" each time I watch videos featuring them.[65] Much of my solo jazz training is based on the imitation of more experienced dancers in "jam circles" at local dances, as well as on imitating moves from historical film clips and contemporary videos online. Unlike ballet or ballroom, with their formalized postures and strict systems of instruction, swing is an improvisational street dance, so imitation, repetition, and variation are the main ways that swing and jazz dancers have learned their moves since the 1920s.

Electro swing is even more improvisational, as it has fewer existing steps and choreographed routines. Electro swing music, being largely in 4/4 time, does not follow the ideal "swung" rhythm for doing the eight-count Lindy Hop footwork pattern: a "rock step, triple-step, step, step, triple-step," counted "one, two, three-and-four, five, six, seven-and-eight." In addition, the Lindy Hop is a partnered dance, whereas electro swing is largely done solo. Dancers familiar with the Lindy Hop must either speed up their moves—as I witnessed dancers doing at the 2013 Caravan Palace concert in Toronto—or create new patterns based on other dances, such as the Charleston (a 4/4 dance) or solo jazz. For instance, in a popular amateur dance video from 2010 set to Parov Stelar's song "Catgroove," a semiprofessional dancer going by the stage name Forsythe interpreted the music by incorporating a range of movements from across historical periods, including 1920s Charleston footwork, solo jazz "happy feet," a vaudeville-style hat-flipping routine, a fluid shuffle in imitation of Cab Calloway, and a Michael Jackson pose at the first break.[66] I have also done newly choreographed group-based routines based on the 1920s Charleston but set to electro swing music. My phenomenal relation to electro swing music videos thus involves an intertwining of the haptic and the visual, as well as a sense of crossover between technological platforms like YouTube and physical locations like dance studios. This layering of the technological and the corporeal is in fact key to "dance" music in the EDM style. As Wiltsher notes:

> one interesting, unique aesthetic quality of dance music is the almost paradoxical interaction between this technological, mechanical relentlessness and repetition, and the fully embodied, relenting, finite beings who respond to the music by dancing. Dance music is insistently machine-like, lacking a certain sort of humanized meaning. It is, further, machine-like in its repetitions: their relentlessness, their perfection and their infinite duration. And yet the way in which we interact with and experience dance music is embodied, human and meaningful. So dance music involves fluid, fully human engagement with music that flaunts its distance from the human. This, I think, is an aesthetic experience unique to dance.[67]

Electro swing puts another twist on this unique aesthetic experience. EDM, as Wiltsher says, "presents [itself] as potentially infinite: loops of machine music relentlessly stretching into the future."[68] It is a future-oriented genre. By contrast, as I have shown, electro swing requires a multilayered, tritime orientation. The EDM beats and science fictional robot imagery of electro swing music videos do indeed evoke the future. However, the vintage instrumentation and references to historical film and animation styles invite dancers and viewers to participate in a utopian return to the Jazz Age, to reembody those old-time dance moves, even while guiding us in "how to inhabit our bodies" in various settings today.[69]

That said, not all of these settings or bodily engagements with the world have proven to be joyful, celebratory, or liberating, as often depicted in electro swing music videos. In reflecting on the phenomenal experience of dance, it is also possible to find negative affects of exclusion, longing, frustration, and fears about the future, as well as an overall sense of global imbalance or looming crisis. Since 2020, the sense of Sehnsucht in electro swing has been enhanced by a more melancholic awareness of the impossibility of recapturing the utopian past, accompanied by a recognition that the past itself was not so rosy. In the mid- to late 2010s, traditional swing dance and electro swing music groups on social media platforms like Facebook and Twitter regularly circulated a meme featuring a photograph of a flapper woman, or sometimes a group of women, captioned "In a few years it will be the 20s again so I propose we bring back swing music and jazz attire." Variations on this meme featured a screen capture from Luhrman's *The Great Gatsby* in which Leonardo DiCaprio salutes the viewer with a champagne glass, usually captioned something like "364 days to go, old sports, and it's the roaring twenties again." These memes were circulated with updated yearly or daily countdowns for several years, culminating in January 2020 with "Happy New Year" posts optimistically proclaiming it to be the Roaring Twenties or the Jazz Age again. However, after the global outbreak of the Covid-19 pandemic in early 2020, and the high-profile incidents of police brutality, social unrest, armed conflict, and natural disaster felt around the world in the following years, the memes soon became more cynical. Rather than proposing to bring back jazz music and flapper dresses, the cartoon-style memes that circulated during the pandemic pointed increasingly to a resurgence of disease, war, prejudice, and economic instability (Figure 17). The recurrence of times past evoked by animetic digital images has thus become implicated in a return not only to glamour but to crisis as well. As Deleuze has noted, the gest is social and political as well as aesthetic, and this is also reflected in the corpus of electro swing fan interactions online.

Even before 2020, McGee argued that electro swing afforded audiences a way of using crisis-responsive media of the past to cope with current global events. However, after 2020, electro swing–related media have shown an even keener awareness of the bittersweet or painful side of Sehnsucht on the part of its creators and audiences. For instance, while "Supersonics" may be a playful video with a utopian ending, the making-of featurette that accompanied the video reveals a challenging backstory to its creation. Jouini, the director of "Supersonics," describes in this featurette how he attended a live performance of the song in Paris that turned out, regretfully, to be the last Caravan Palace concert before the lockdown in France in 2020. Jouini contracted Covid-19 twice during the production, pushing the video back from a planned Halloween release to later in the fall. More generally, many musicians, dancers, actors, and other artists

FIGURE 17. Comic memes circulating in 2021 put a more critical and pessimistic spin on hopes for a "New Jazz Age" in the 2020s. Image on left reprinted with permission of the original comic artist, Shen Comix.

who depend on performance for their livelihood suffered during the pandemic. Electro swing fans, too, went without festivals to bolster their sense of in-person community, and dancers were deprived of the live events that enable the sensorimotor abandon of improvisational group movement. During the years of rolling lockdowns and in-person gathering restrictions that followed 2020, it became appar-

THINGS WE'RE BRINGING BACK IN THE

anti-semitism

prohibition

Great Depression

daddy <3

ent that seeing something on a screen is not the same as experiencing it in life. Electro swing music videos are not a replacement for festivals and dances, no matter how much they may provoke the impulse to dance alone.

Electro swing fans may be more critical of the genre now and more skeptical of the utopian, retrofuturistic images of the 1920s promoted during its formation. However, that does not mean that they have embraced an entirely apocalyptic or nihilistic worldview. As I have described in this chapter, one trope that recurs across all categories of electro swing music video is bringing the dead back to life. Resurrection and reanimation are often shown through macabre imagery of skeletons and zombies or through more subtly disturbing tactics of making long-deceased stars dance to modern beats. All of these remind us of the inevitability of death. But in presenting those images through animation and frame-by-frame digital editing, they also point to the persistence of lifedeath, or the paradoxical and uncanny coexistence of death in life and ongoing life in death. Every medium builds on the past, but in electro swing music videos, we see a very particular interplay between the digital media environment of the 2020s and the cinematic culture of the 1920s. Reanimation resurrects dead media, gives them a new life-after-death, and reembeds them in the bodily experiences of today's creative movers. While it can encourage a sense of abandon in phenomenal experience, dancing to electro swing music videos can also provoke reflection about the crises of the past and those of today. As media grow increasingly dependent on the digital and the virtual, theorists worry about a loss of indexicality and in-person experience. Reanimation, however, reveals the crucial links between cultural history, visual media, and physical practice among media audiences today. These videos thus incorporate the traces of the past into the gestures of the present and provide a line of flight toward the future. As such, they are a combination of the movement-image that Deleuze describes in *Cinema 1* and the time-image he describes in *Cinema 2*. Perhaps more useful than spotting instances of either movement- or time-images, however, is attending to the connective tissue that holds these types of images together or the plane of immanence in which they circulate. This is the topic of the next chapter, on the Body without Organs in virtual idol concerts and digital avatar performances.

CHAPTER 5

Virtual (Idol) Corporeality and the Posthuman Flesh

When scholars of cinema write about computer-generated animation, it tends to be viewed as a visible manifestation of information. It is virtual, which is to say, it is *not* the indexical trace of a live performance or even the material markings of paint daubed onto celluloid by a human hand. As pure information, digital imagery is a complex pattern of signals that creates the impression of a "photorealistic" image with no grounding in chemical photography or lived reality. To paraphrase N. Katherine Hayles's *How We Became Posthuman,* the history of the digital might be traced by describing "how animation lost its body."[1] In this final chapter, however, I follow Hayles in contesting this discourse of digital disembodiment and calling for a more corporeal form of posthumanism or embodied virtuality. Scholarly approaches to digital media that emphasize disembodiment fail to reflect both the physical practices of artists whose labor goes into producing these works and the audience's bodily experiences of watching animated performances in the world that they inhabit. The "disembodiment discourse" remains caught in an intellectual pattern that has recurred from Descartes to postmodernism and that persisted even among some phenomenological film theorists of the late 1990s and early 2000s. By contrast, I argue that artists and filmmakers who have grown up with digital media as a part of everyday life are now highlighting animation's potential to evoke a posthuman form of embodied experience that incorporates the virtual while remaining grounded in an inextricable entanglement with the living world.

In this chapter, I explore the phenomenology of posthuman embodiment in new media performance arts. In particular, I draw on Gilles Deleuze and Félix Guattari's concept of the Body without Organs (BwO), which addresses the virtual dimensions of the body and desire. I also return to Maurice Merleau-Ponty's concepts of the flesh and orientation as elaborated by twenty-first-century feminist philosophers such as Sara Ahmed, author of *Queer Phenomenology*. While Deleuze and Guattari, Merleau-Ponty, and Ahmed all take different philosophical approaches (and indeed, the later authors are sometimes critical of their predecessors), all three address the topic of the desiring body and how desire moves us or orients us toward the world. As such, their works can be usefully applied to the virtual or "multidimensional" aspects of digital new media, in which 2D animated characters or kyara are brought to life through 3D projection in live event spaces like theater stages, concert stadiums, and art galleries in a phenomenon known across East Asia as 2.5D culture. Of course, mixing live-action footage and animation is nothing new, as my previous chapters on hybrid films and live-action remakes have shown. However, in many of the hybrid and remake films examined so far, from *Song of the South* and *Who Framed Roger Rabbit* to *Pokémon: Detective Pikachu*, animated characters and human actors have remained ontologically distinct, with human actors playing human characters and animation used for inhuman figures like animals, "toons," or Pokémon. In this final chapter, I consider instances in which animated characters seem to enter directly into the lifeworld of the audience, as in concerts performed by virtual idols. I also look at cases in which humans "become animated"[2] through gaming or real-time motion capture performance. In these cases, the relations between the material and the virtual become more chiasmatic and mutually (de)constructive, resulting in a posthuman experience of the body. The works of Deleuze and Guattari, Merleau-Ponty, and Ahmed, as well as those of contemporary scholars of 2.5D culture, such as Akiko Sugawa-Shimada, can provide valuable insights into the experiences of virtual corporeality and queer or nonbinary identities afforded by these new media phenomena.

To illustrate the ways in which embodiment and desire manifest in new media performance, I present two case studies of 2.5D or multidimensional media culture: the Japanese virtual idol Hatsune Miku and the works of Shanghai-based new media artist Lu Yang. These two cases might be called "equal but opposite" in their approaches to virtual embodiment. Hatsune Miku is a virtual idol created to advertise the voice-sampling software program VOCALOID, which performs virtual vocal tracks for original compositions written by amateur and professional musicians. Miku, as fans fondly call her, is the most famous example of the virtual performers known collectively as Vocaloids. As such, Miku provides us with a vision of collective processing in which the iconic figure of the pop idol acts as Deleuze and Guattari's BwO: a plane across which a multitude of agents, both human and inhuman, can express intensity, desire, movement, and uncanny life. As a public figure and a commercial product, Miku is continually moving between states of corporate organization and anarchic disorganization, between material commodity and virtual personhood, between mascot-like kyara and posthuman agency. Vocaloids like Miku are stratified, destratified, and restratified in complex, sometimes complicit ways that reflect the conditions of embodied virtuality inhabited by media fans in the twenty-first century.

Lu Yang's new media artworks, on the other hand, are deeply personal and idiosyncratic. They resist commodification, national identity, fixed gender roles, and stable subject positions. Lu Yang is an artist known for creating digital art installations that combine Western discourses of medicine, diagnostic imaging, and neurosurgical procedures with the iconography of Buddhism and Japanese pop culture. Although Lu Yang's works may allude to Japanese anime and manga, they are stylistically very different, being created through a combination of 3D-modeled CGI figures and motion capture performance. They present a vision of the body subjected to biopolitical control in every aspect, but one that finds its paradoxical liberation in working through such control to overturn assumptions about the nature of corporeal being and conscious perception. Drawing on Ahmed's *Queer Phenomenology,* I demonstrate how Lu Yang creates a form of queer virtual embodiment that crosses lines between multiple dimensions of experience. Together, these case studies reveal the beginning of a new way of being in the world at the start of the twenty-first century, one that operates through the crossing point of the flesh of animation.

The Vocaloid as Body without Organs

Can there really be, as in the title of a fan-published criticism zine, a discourse of "*VocaloCritique*"?[3] After all, the cute characters now identified as Vocaloids began their virtual lives as little more than a marketing ploy, designed to sell a desktop music application that lets users generate vocals by inputting syllables and pitches to produce a reasonable—if somewhat artificial-sounding—facsimile of singing.

The VOCALOID voice synthesizer technology was first developed by the Yamaha Corporation starting around the year 2000. However, related products are now sold by third-party companies, such as Crypton Future Media, a firm that develops and markets databases of professional voice samples performed by anime voice actors like Fujita Saki, whose voice was sampled to create the phonemes and manipulable pitches and tones that would be marketed as the Hatsune Miku database. Crypton Future Media introduced the "Character Vocal Series" in 2007, when it hired the illustrator Kei Garō to create manga-style characters to promote the software. Crypton has since developed ways for pro and amateur musicians to create and distribute Vocaloid material, including KarenT, its own record label; Piapuro, a "consumer-generated media" image site; and Piapuro Studio, its proprietary vocal editing suite. By all accounts, the president of Crypton Future Media, Itō Hiroyuki, never dreamed in 2007 that its mascot, Miku, would become a world-famous icon.[4] Rather, her voice and image proliferated owing to the efforts of fans on the video-sharing website Nico Nico Dōga, where she went viral and took on a life of her own. Since then, the characters have expanded beyond the status of mere musical instruments. Miku and her virtual companions, Luka, Meiko, Kaito, the twins Kagamine Rin and Len, and many others, have attained star status in Japan, where Vocaloid albums have outsold those of established living artists like Tokunaga Hideaki on the Oricon pop charts.[5] The virtual idol's success spread overseas in 2014, the year she opened for pop star Lady Gaga's North American artRAVE: the ARTPOP Ball tour (June 26–July 22, 2014)[6] and appeared on *The Late Show with David Letterman* (October 8, 2014). Along with musical performances, the Vocaloid characters have become prominent in a subgenre of video gaming known as rhythm games, in which players dance with (or against) Miku in competition, such as Sega's *Project DIVA* (2009) and Nintendo's *Hatsune Miku and Future Stars: Project Mirai* (2012).

On a more intimate level, Miku has appeared in interactive apps, such as the *Sleep Together App* (2013), which uses the 3D Oculus Rift VR headset in combination with a body pillow and scented sprays to create the experience of sleeping side by side with the virtual diva.[7] Some fans have even integrated her into their waking lives using a device called Gatebox, which projects an AI-driven image of a character who responds to its owner's questions, comments, and movements in the home environment using a microphone and motion-sensing camera. The Gatebox also connects to the internet, enabling the character to send messages over applications like LINE when the user is away from home. The Gatebox has allowed at least one of Miku's fans, Kondo Akihiko, to proclaim that he is married to the virtual idol. Reportedly, "Kondo spent 2 million yen to throw a wedding for himself and Miku in November 2018. Both of their names stand by the front door to Kondo's apartment."[8] Overall, then, the history of Miku's development illustrates a few of the ways in which Vocaloids have become part of the music industry and new forms of fan sociality and sexuality, both globally and within Japan.

It is not without cause—both corporate and fan driven—that the attractive Vocaloid characters are what propelled an otherwise obscure voice database software program to the forefront of pop music and media culture. Vocaloids have become part of a system of iconic anime-style characters known as kyara: image-beings that fans both idolize and consume. Kyara can be distinguished from both fully rounded literary or cinematic characters *(kyarakutā)* and the simple, 1D brand mascots copyrighted and disseminated by major corporations. As evolving image constructs that thrive on fan adoption and viral videos, kyara cross the planes between psychologically rounded subjects and flattened symbols, between official and unofficial realms of product circulation, between licensed merchandise and free-for-all repurposing on the internet. Because Vocaloid kyara often perform live in concert together with human musicians, they can also be compared to the larger movement known in Japanese as *ni-ten-go jigen* or 2.5D culture. The term *2.5D* "roughly means the space between the two-dimensional (fictional space where our imaginations and fantasy work) and the three-dimensional (reality where we physically exist)."[9] As Akiko Sugawa-Shimada has argued, this movement expresses "virtuality embodied by actual human bodies as well as human bodies that look unreal, which I call 'virtual corporeality' *(kyokō teki shintai).*"[10] Just like Miku herself, however, this raises questions about how power—namely, the power to create and disseminate images and to shape popular cultures—is distributed through kyara. When Vocaloid fans make songs with Miku's voice, or draw pictures of her for a video, does their creative act free them to express their own desires, overcoming all social boundaries? Do they establish an alternative world economy, a new structure of production and consumption based on the free-flowing desires of individuals? Or are the users in fact the ones being used, as their affective labor turns the wheels of the culture industry, like the expressive puppet that is Miku herself?

I would argue that in the Vocaloid phenomenon, we see at once a movement of free creativity, or the destratification of desire, and the ways in which that desire may be controlled or restratified. To support this argument, I explain how Miku works as a kyara by drawing on Deleuze and Guattari's concept of the BwO, a surface for the circulation of desire as intensities that can be blocked or released. I also discuss the problems and benefits of building a kyara-BwO in the current media system. I believe that Miku does offer a potential change in how people create relationships with virtual images and with each other. But to make that potential energy go kinetic, we need to know how to activate it or make it act in the world. We need to ask, what can a Vocaloid do as a program and a mode of collective creation?

To answer this question, I start by looking in detail at a key theory of virtuality, connection, and desire: the BwO. This complex concept, as explained by Deleuze and Guattari in *A Thousand Plateaus*, can be understood at its base as an anti-Freudian, anti-Lacanian theory of desire. Deleuze and Guattari state clearly that "the BwO is desire; it is that which one desires and by which one desires."[11] But it is important to distinguish their use of the word *desire* from its common connotations of sexual attraction and unfulfillable longing. Desire in their work is a more complicated process than wanting an object or body that one does not possess. Indeed, they are explicitly opposed to the models of desire put forward by structuralist psychoanalysts like Jacques Lacan, who argued that we are constituted as subjects by lack or our longing for an unattainable object of desire *(objet petit a)*. This well-worn theorization of "desire as lack" remains significant for the study of kyara, because it underpins a number of major scholarly works on otaku desire for "virtual" anime characters, for instance, by Saitō Tamaki and Azuma Hiroki. For Saitō, the attraction of the "beautiful fighting girl" character for male otaku lies precisely in the fact that she is the "absolutely unattainable object of desire":[12] you can see her image but never have her impossible body. For Azuma, by contrast, otaku do not want an image of a whole, unattainable object but only certain "*moé* elements," cute design elements that create a particular feeling of fond attraction, such as cat ears. Because otaku can easily find these elements by searching databases, they can close their "lack/satisfaction circuit"[13] immediately, in an animalistic fashion. But in both cases, desire depends on either lacking or attaining an object, namely, the anime character's fantasy body or its component moé elements.

For Deleuze and Guattari, on the other hand, desire is not essentially defined by the lack or possession of an object or isolated element. It is not an unattainable ideal like the beautiful fighting girl or an animalistic satisfaction of needs. Instead, desire is a force of creative production in itself. In their words, "desire [is] defined as a process of production without reference to any exterior agency, whether it be a lack that hollows it out or a pleasure that fills it."[14] It is immanent, something created from within, not something transcendent or invoked by an exterior object. We have already in ourselves all we need for desiring-production. We do not need to possess things; we only need to do things, to engage in programs or processes that set desire flowing. This is why Deleuze and Guattari ask not "what is a body?" but "what can a body do?"[15]

To describe a BwO, then, we first have to ask, How is it done? How is it fabricated? and What comes to pass on it? Deleuze and Guattari give many examples of different "programs" or things to do to make a BwO, including sexual masochism and drug use. For sociologist Tim Jordan, social and expressive acts like dancing in raves can also make BwOs by actively setting energy and desire flowing in a collective fashion.[16] In all cases, the key thing is that the BwO causes the circulation of intensity. Intensity may be understood as the degree of strength of a quality or a measure of how much it is present, how faint or vivid it is. In Miyazaki Hayao's *Princess Mononoke* (1997), for example, we might talk about the intense quality of "wolfness" that the main female character, San, has. It is not a matter of her literally being a biological wolf, because San is, biologically speaking, a human raised by wolf spirits. Nor is it a matter of San having a fixed, essential "wolf identity," because she grows aware of (and conflicted about) her multiple heritages. Rather, it is more a matter of her wolfing intensity: the irrepressible quality of wolflike strength and energy that connects San to her adopted mother, Moro, and allows her to fight with ferocity. To draw on another Deleuzian term, this is not a literal being-animal but a *becoming-animal*: a process, a doing. Likewise, the BwO is the process that makes it possible to experience different levels of intensity, whether pain or pleasure, cold or energy, through "becoming" or engaging in activities that generate those experiences. The BwO is the field where intensity can circulate freely without any blocks. So, for Deleuze and Guattari, the programs of desire that constitute the BwO are characterized by the limitless circulation of intensity.

In anime scholarship as well, some academics have proposed that anime and manga, as nonindexical media that go beyond the physical limits of the human body, allow fans to experience the limitless intensity of the BwO. For instance, Patrick Galbraith has argued that when women engage in male homoerotic fantasies by reading or writing *yaoi* or "boy's love" stories based on anime characters, their fantasy "engenders virtual possibilities without limits or control,"[17] because it transcends the women's embodied genders and transforms the characters about which they write. While this is a fascinating approach, I believe we should be careful not to imply that the BwO is completely free from all bounds, as if once you have made yourself a BwO, you can do anything you want. This stance is problematic, because as Jordan argues about Deleuze and Guattari, it depends on an apolitical view of creativity, as if people make texts outside any context. In Jordan's words, "paradoxically, Deleuze and Guattari develop a politics that is unconcerned with differences between political movements except in relation to their ability to produce difference. Difference in Deleuze and Guattari leads to political indifference."[18] This danger always inheres in such "virtual" constructs as poststructuralist philosophy and digital idol singers: the tendency toward disembedding and disembodiment, which all too quickly becomes a kind of transcendent universalism grounded in Western Enlightenment discourses. If we acknowledge and work against such tendencies, however, it is possible to recover a more immanent, embodied social and political concept of the BwO. After all, even in Deleuze and Guattari's original work, there is a tension between the BwO and the structure of organization or stratification in which it is embedded, which can itself be made productive.

This leads us to the third major aspect of the BwO: the intricate process of stratification, destratification, and restratification. When freely circulating desire is organized, it becomes imbricated in a structure of subjects and objects determined by the hierarchical layers or strata in society. In the organization of sexual attraction into compulsory heterosexuality, for instance, men are thought to desire women, and women men, each as their proper object. There is a binary stratification of essentialized gendered bodies such that both are fixed in place. From this point of view, even yaoi fandom can be stratified when it is described simplistically as a "natural" (that is, normatively heterosexual) expression of female desire for male bodies. When a BwO is caught up in such strata, or "stratified," it produces fascist desires—those which restrict and control not just oneself but others—and cancerous cycles of habit. And yet, because the BwO is essentially productive, it is always producing new avenues so that it can destratify the layers that are built up by structuration into subjects and objects. In this way, it can help people escape from entrenched hierarchies and find a new way of desiring. To Galbraith's account of Deleuze and Guattari, then, I would add that the important thing is not to think about the BwO as some kind of formless, essentialized force of desire beyond all limits of power or society. It is never transcendent. It is immanent. To make a full, healthy BwO, you must recognize where your desire is structured; how it is organized in your social, political, embodied, and mediated experience; and then find ways to destratify it.

Anime characters, particularly those that become kyara, may be seen as one example of this process. Kyara clearly illustrate how desire can be stratified into a commodified object possessed by compulsive-consumer subjects and how it can be destratified through multiple practices of access. Typically, moé kyara are pictured as cute, infantilized, or animalized girls, such as the iconic maids and cat-girls that have populated the streets of Akihabara, the male otaku district of Tokyo, since the moé boom of the mid-2000s. Hatsune Miku, with her short, pleated skirt and aquamarine twin tails, is a prime example of a "moéfied" female kyara: sweetly attractive and consummately consumable. If we wished to take Azuma's Lacanian-inflected approach to the kyara phenomenon, we could start here by asking what a kyara is based on these moé elements and analyzing Miku's fans as a function of their database consumption. But instead, let us take Deleuze and Guattari's approach and ask, What can kyara do? How are they fabricated? What comes to pass? How are they stratified and destratified?

In terms of fabrication, it is useful to differentiate kyara from traditional literary characters or kyarakutā. In the nineteenth and early twentieth centuries, the character was the major focus of novels written by single authors by hand (or on typewriters) to express an individual vision. The Japanese genre of the I-novel, or *shishosetsu,* is a good example. Here the main character speaks in the first person and is the singular focus of both expression and identification. The "I" character is a well-rounded, psychologically deep, autonomous subject. In a novel such as Natsume Soseki's *Kokoro,* readers follow this singular character by reading his thoughts and identifying with his plight. Characters thus work through a process of subjectification: they fabricate an ego, a subject, "I." Kyara, on the other hand, are not deep, rounded subjects created to express one vision; instead, they are more akin to surfaces that facilitate the play of desire.

Kohki Watabe has summarized two definitions of the kyara put forward by manga and anime scholars Itō Gō and Iwashita Hōsei. For Itō, the "basic idea is that the kyara is the iconic figure materially depicted by each line-drawing in the manga, whereas kyarakutā is a personality that readers can imagine behind the line-drawings."[19] Iwashita has further elaborated on this model by explaining that "Itō's concept of kyara refers to both 'a relatively simple line-drawing-based icon' and 'something like a personality,'" the former of which can be called the "kyara-image *(kyara-zuzō)*" and the latter the "kyara-personality *(kyara-jinkaku)*."[20] From this comparison, Watabe concludes that both "Itō's and Iwashita's arguments . . . explicitly distinguish between the visual and non-visual aspects of anime and manga characters."[21] This distinction paved the way for a detailed analysis not only of 2.5D culture but also of various other cultural phenomena that incorporate anime and manga into the real world. The autonomous existence of a character's iconography allows fans to use kyara separately from the story and the character's personality. Expanding on Watabe's points, I would argue that a delicate balance of kyara-image and kyara-personality is what allows fans to fabricate, recreate, and engage physically with Vocaloids. In the case of Vocaloids, the kyara-image is strongly foregrounded while the kyara-personality is present but plays a lesser role, allowing fans to flexibly adapt and engage with the characters in multiple situations, both in-person and online. Miku perfectly exemplifies this balance with her exaggerated appearance and minimal personality.

First, Miku has an extremely well-defined kyara-image based on a key moé element that can function autonomously of her actual figure:

her aqua-colored twin-tail hairstyle. As soon as this iconic hairstyle is applied to a physical body, such as that of a cosplayer at an anime convention, or to another kyara, such as the digital sticker character Pusheen the cat in the messaging app LINE, a circuit is created between that body or kyara and the kyara-image of Hatsune Miku, allowing her intensity to manifest in them in a kind of "becoming-Vocaloid." As in the earlier example of San's "becoming-wolf," this "becoming-Vocaloid" does not mean that the human cosplayer or LINE user literally becomes identical to the virtual idol. Rather, it means that the cosplayer or LINE user creates for herself a BwO, a plane of immanence through which she is now expressed by and expressive of the kyara-image of Miku, with all the affective qualities that kyara evokes. This creates a situation similar to Merleau-Ponty's reversible flesh, as the human-becoming-Vocaloid can both see and be seen as the kyara at once. And as the visible and the tangible are conjoined in the flesh, so the becoming-Vocaloid can be felt haptically by the cosplayer who sings, dances, or poses as Miku, or perhaps more subtly as a rising of the pulse accompanying the affect of excitement or amusement felt by someone posting a Miku-Pusheen sticker on LINE.

To transfer from platform to platform, or move from the 2D to the 3D realm, Watabe contends that regular anime and manga kyara are subject to what he terms "character amnesia," or a diegetic erasure of the kyara's memories and previous experiences from its originating narrative world.[22] However, Vocaloids bypass the need for character amnesia, or perhaps exist in a permanent amnesiac state, because they are not based in any narrative world and have little in the way of established kyara-personality. Indeed, there are very few "official" facts about Miku. The first biography released by Crypton Future Media for its pop star in the making deliberately listed only the bare essentials: her age and birth date (a sixteen-year-old born on August 31), her zodiac sign (Virgo), her height and weight, and her suggested musical genres, tempo, and vocal range. Her character design and facial expression in most images suggest a cheerful, *genki* (energetic, spunky) quality, but beyond that, there is nothing—no background, no psychology. It is difficult to see her as a complex subject or "real person" with whom to identify. Instead, her kyara-personality is made up of variable intensities of cuteness, aggressiveness, helplessness, and so on that can be adjusted depending on the scenario one wishes to produce using her image. She is more flexible than a copyrighted brand mascot character (for instance, the Frosted Flakes cereal mascot, Tony the Tiger, or the numerous mascots created for Japanese prefectures), because she is at base a creative tool. Fans are invited to elaborate their own visions of her personality in videos, ranging from a bratty princess in supercell's *The World Is Mine* (2008) to a tormented circus freak in the macabre *Dark Woods Circus Series* by MachigeritaP (2008). In this way, she is less than a realistic 3D kyarakutā but more than a 1D mascot. Miku's plane is the between-space of 2.5D media, which allows her to move between the so-called 2D complex, or the attraction felt by (largely male) fans specifically for 2D animated characters, and the technological and social structures that allow the virtual characters to manifest in 3D physical spaces. This between-space is the virtual, immanent plane through which desire flows: the BwO.

The Vocaloid BwO may be virtual, but the process of creating it is still grounded in the embodied practices of fan production, and so it is affected by the age, gender, and location of the fans in question. For instance, Terazawa Kaoru has recounted how high school–aged female yaoi fans in Japanese classics classrooms will often read Soseki's classic I-novel *Kokoro* (1914) as a romance between the male protagonists, a university student who acts as the *watashi* (I) character and an older, reclusive man known only as Sensei.[23] In this example, the characters become kyara as Soseki's subtle friend relationship is reinterpreted by the female readers through a shared set of yaoi tropes. The watashi/Sensei pairing functions as a BwO not because its readers do anything at all to them without limits (it is not quite to the level of "*Kokoro* in Space with Zombies"!) but because they work within the strata of gendered representations shown in the I-novel and place them on alternative vectors, allowing a new kind of intensity to grow between the men. The pop idol and the I-novel character become kyara, a becoming that carries both a liberatory, destratifying potential and the risk of restratification.

Along with aspects of production like the design of kyara-images, the practice of accessing and distributing kyara is also different from that of traditional kyarakutā. Novel readers like those described by Terazawa typically follow a deep, rounded character in a novel and identify with him as he is portrayed. If that character is then changed entirely for a film version, readers may feel betrayed. Even at an academic level, the attachment to character has resulted in a strain of thought in (mainly older) works of adaptation studies that holds that the book is always better than the film because mass media "dumb down," "reduce," or "flatten" deep, complex characters. However, this need not be the only reaction to the transformation from kyarakutā to kyara. Natsume Fusanosuke, grandson of Natsume Soseki, has argued that kyara appear as they do because they are designed to be mobile across media, time, and space, which allows them to be used for many purposes. A single kyara can appear in light novels, manga, anime, and *dōjinshi* (fan works) and be portrayed quite differently in each. The point is not the kyara's uniqueness; if it were, we would need only one version. The point is the different rates at which audiences can access the kyara: every week on TV, every few months when a new light novel is published, or every day in online fan videos. Natsume says we must consider "what kind of time *[dō iu jikan]*,"[24] or what temporality of access, a kyara grants. Different temporalities create different intensities of experience, sparking the production of desire through the kyara as a BwO.

Just like any other BwO, however, kyara are also stratified on many levels. There are, for instance, the persistent stratifications of gender roles and representations in kyara like Miku. Daniel Black addresses this issue in an article on the Japanese virtual idol in which he argues that virtual idols, through their construction as kawaii, create idealized, unrealistic body images for both living female idol singers and their fans. In his view, the kawaii body is "a diminutive, rounded, passive, tidy body, almost or entirely lacking in orifices and appendages of any kind, implying an inability to exude anything (vomit, excrement) or act upon the world."[25] It is a body without any substance or interiority—a literal body without organs. The transgressive potential of this artificial body is thus restratified within norms of clean, contained, harmless bodies also presented to women in, for instance, advertising for menstrual hygiene products. The result is that,

> as a digital simulation of the female body, the virtual idol can reflect fantasies or idealizations of femininity, but at the same time its status as simulation makes living bodies the benchmarks against which its technical success will be judged. This

> is further complicated by the virtual idol's simulation of a femininity rendered endearing and non-threatening by its lack of exceptionality.[26]

In a similar vein, Deborah Levitt has pointed out the ways in which Miku reflects "long standing traditions of gendered representation in Japanese culture as they have been taken up in manga and anime. She's not only female, but a teenaged female, slender, long-legged, short-skirted and, like many anime characters, has a hybrid of Asian and Caucasian features and an android-like aspect."[27] This long-standing tradition is evident in the trope of the *bishōjo,* or beautiful girl character, as illustrated in manga and anime series like *Sailor Moon* (1992–97). Along with the bishōjo's "hypergendered" appearance, however, Levitt recognizes the "creative potentials" that Miku affords fans.[28] Likewise, I argue that it is important to strategically resist or reformulate those points where the kyara's BwO becomes conflated with its literal appearance as an impossibly slender, pale young woman and so stratified in a commercial media economy that values slim, pale, young, and "pure" bodies above every other. Rather, we must seek ways in which the Miku kyara-image presents other potential uses than those based solely on an anthropomorphic idea of the body.

Along with gendered representations, the kyara may be stratified along more nationalist lines in what has been termed *brand nationalism*. In the late 2000s and 2010s, major Japanese tourist sites have drawn on the kyara boom to produce their own *yuru-kyara* or "soft character" mascot, such as Hikonyan, the official mascot of Hikone Castle in Shiga prefecture. Yuru-kyara owe much to tourism strategies and product mascots in their design and branding, but they also draw on the practices of fan culture and the online circulation of memes in that their images are meant to be taken up by local fans as much as foreign tourists. Some fans, of course, cynically recognize the ways in which kyara are being used to promote Japanese brand nationalism. In one fan-created image, for instance, Hikonyan is shown in a stereotypical samurai battle pose defeating American icon Mickey Mouse, complete with dramatic lighting. This image itself wields a double-edged sword, mocking the Japanese samurai stereotype through a silly cat image while still displaying a measure of national pride in having Hikonyan "win" over Disney's famed mascot. Even kyara that were not originally designed as promotional tools are licensed out to chain stores. Hatsune Miku has appeared in commercials for the FamilyMart convenience store, in which the virtual idol greets supposedly "real" customers and encourages them to shop at FamilyMart. When kyara are stratified along lines of hetero- and cisnormative gender roles, militant nationalism, and rampant commercialism, they can fall into restricted patterns of circulation, which Deleuze and Guattari refer to as cancerous BwOs.

At the same time, however, it is possible for fans to engage with the structures that kyara create and destratify them. They can find ways to experiment with kyara by producing their own programs of desiring. Kyara can become the focus of dōjinshi, songs, videos, and artworks that have very little to do with the organized uses of kyara and more to do with the desires of smaller collectives. They become the province of little packs of fans like dōjinshi circles and eventually of larger groups of audience members who comment on videos, producing archives of response and counterresponse. Hatsune Miku is a key example of a kyara that encourages such collective creation.

So, given this situation, what can a Vocaloid do? How does Miku circulate, and how do fans engage with her? To answer these questions requires us to cut across strata, because Vocaloids, like other kyara, introduce different intensities of experience by crossing between different levels of media and temporality, from official live concerts to fan-led *offu-kai* (offline meeting) events to fan communities on social media.

At the top level of official physical media events are Crypton Future Media's official live 2.5D concerts, which feature the virtual idols performing as 3D-modeled CGI projections on semitransparent screens, appearing together with live musicians. The projections are sometimes described as "holographic," and although they are not, technically speaking, holograms, the effect is very like seeing a digitally animated character performing in the same space as human musicians. Miku's first live solo concert in Japan was 39s Giving Day, also called Miku's Thanksgiving Day, held in 2010 on March 9 (in a pun on the Japanese pronunciation of the numerals 3-9 as both *mi-ku* and *sankyū*, or "thank you," suggesting "Thanksgiving Day"). Throughout the 2010s, Crypton Future Media also promoted its Vocaloid line abroad at international concerts staged in Singapore (2009), Los Angeles (2011), and Toronto (2013), among other cities. This led to the annual Miku Expo, a series of fan conventions featuring live concerts, film screenings, merchandise sales, and other special events. Miku Expo has been held around the world, including in Indonesia (2014), Shanghai (2015), Taiwan (2016), the Americas (a 2016 ten-city tour that spanned Mexico, the United States, and Canada), Malaysia (2017), and Europe (a 2018 tour that spanned France, Germany, and the United Kingdom).[29] In 2020, the Covid-19 pandemic led to the cancellation of major music festivals, such as Coachella, where Miku was slated to perform, as well as a planned twelve-city North American Vocaloid tour. However, Miku's flexibly virtual presence made it possible for her to continue appearing in live-streaming events such as MIKU BREAK, a series of hybrid events, combining in-person and live-streamed elements, held with dance group CODENSE in late 2021 and early 2022, under the joint production of Crypton Future Media and Japanese tech firm Think and Sense. These live-streamed concerts featured Miku dancing along with the CODENSE troupe, all of whom were positioned against white screens with 3D animated light projections playing over their bodies, blurring the perceptual distinctions between animated and human bodies. The MIKU BREAK live streams were promoted as special high-tech events that "blend 2D and 3D boundaries utilizing street culture such as dance and rap."[30] As with electro swing music videos, these events display a mix of transcultural influences and temporalities, combining the high-tech futurism of Japan's digital music scene with the current trendiness of American hip-hop and street culture. Even more so than electro swing, however, they are also overtly playing with dimensionality or the fusion of the 2D and the 3D into a 2.5D media culture.

Enhancing the connection to 2.5D culture is the use of Vocaloids in live theatrical events. A few examples include the Vocaloid opera *The End* hosted by the Yamaguchi Center for Arts and Media in December 2012 and *Vocaloid Opera Aoi* from July 2014, which starred traditional Japanese *bunraku* puppets operated by human puppeteers to a Vocaloid soundtrack. These events can be seen as part of the same cultural impetus that has produced the East Asian subgenre of 2.5D musicals, or live stage shows based on anime, manga, and gaming franchises. Stage adaptations of popular anime and manga have existed in Japan since the Takarazuka Revue's 1973 adaptation of Ikeda Riyoko's manga *The Rose of Versailles*. However, they have taken on a new 2.5D spin in the twenty-first century, starting with

Musical: Prince of Tennis in 2003.[31] Since this time, they have become popular not only in Japan but also in mainland China, Taiwan, and other East Asian nations.[32] 2.5D musicals have become associated with a transnational cultural movement that intertwines the kyara-image, the actor's body, and the audience's interactions with both.

In one way, these live events are among the most intense experiences of Miku and her Vocaloid costars, because, like raves, they generate immense crowd energy. But in another way, they are the most organized or stratified of the events. Unlike the raves Jordan analyzed, there is a strong singular focus for action at a Miku concert: everyone moves in the same direction and repeats the same phrases. The concerts are also commercial, corporate-sponsored events, so they are stratified along lines of class: who has the money, time, and means of transport to attend. Media commentator Anzai Masayuki has noted that the concerts in Japan were originally segregated along gendered lines as well. According to Anzai, although Vocaloid radio programs have a high percentage of teenage female listeners, the concerts were attended almost entirely by thirty- to forty-year-old male otaku at first.[33] Happily, Anzai also notes that this is changing, with more range in terms of age and gender in recent audiences.

Still, concerts are only one means of access. For instance, along with official events, many fan-staged events have featured video screenings and quasi-official promotions, such as the Nerima Vocaloid Festival, a charity event for earthquake relief. Indeed, the Vocaloid program itself has the potential to allow a more free-flowing production of music, art, and videos online, through collaborations among small molecular groups and wider audiences. One person can technically make an animated Vocaloid video, but they would have to be able to write the lyrics, use the Vocaloid software to create the vocals, use another program to compose the backing music, draw the images, and edit them into video—something not many individual users will have the skills to do. Instead, Vocaloid "Producers" (as they call themselves) more often rely on collective collaboration, with one person writing the lyrics, another writing the music, and another creating the art. Once the video is uploaded to Nico Nico, it receives the comments of multiple users, who scroll horizontally across the surface of the video, becoming another visual aspect of the text. Online videos have a much different temporality than concerts, because the video is never finished as long as it is receiving comments. It is always in the process of inciting and circulating the desires of fans. I call this the *temporality of continual processing*: an ongoing, collective production of desiring across time and space. In this way, we might say that the mobile, multiple figure of Hatsune Miku acts less as an idol or object of desire and more as a BwO: the plane where desire is produced and destratified.

That said, Vocaloids continue to be restratified because they are a commercial product and require participation in commercial structures to make. The very collectivity of creation I just described itself became the focus of a 2012 commercial for the Google Chrome web browser, which shows images of people composing or drawing that multiply into a split screen of thousands of participants, triumphantly proclaiming "Hatsune Miku, Virtual Singer; Everyone, Creator." The commercial then urges audience members to "start your own web"—of course, by using Google Chrome. The affective labor of thousands of fans is condensed into a one-minute congratulatory commercial that sells our own process back to us in a stratified form: do your own thing, but use our framework.

This kind of restratification is not unique to Vocaloid producers. It is a dilemma faced by all fans who work with corporately created characters. In the end, if you wish to be a fan, you cannot opt out of today's media. You need to buy the software, watch the videos, and support the creators to keep up. But that does not mean that these texts can never be destratified again. After all, with Vocaloid, we are also talking about a desire to consume what we produce ourselves—and not only through official channels. As Andrea Horbinski and Alex Leavitt have demonstrated, Miku has also been used in videos that criticize government policies, such as the Nonexistent Youth Healthy Development Ordinance, which limits the depiction of sexuality in manga.[34] So, if all the examples and counterexamples given thus far prove anything, it is that "power" is not an object possessed by only one group but a process created by the frictions or tensions of desire as it moves in a continual dance of de- and restratification. As both dynamic kyara and usable programs, Vocaloids like Miku have the potential to become multipurpose, multilayered channels for the circulation of fans' intense need for connection: an alternative economy of desire. To make the Vocaloid kyara a healthy BwO, however, we need to experiment with it, to see how Vocaloids can disrupt the structures of the music and pop culture industries while recognizing its imbrications in them. In order to bring out their full potential, we need only keep asking, What can a Vocaloid do? Where is it limited now, and how can we transform those limits immanently, from within? Indeed, these questions about the affordances and potentials of virtual characters apply not only to Vocaloids but to instances of virtual corporeality and 2.5D culture more broadly.

Lu Yang and the Queer Orientations of the Flesh

Vocaloids are products of popular culture. They are imbricated in the commercial mass media and spread through large-scale fan-oriented platforms, so fans and scholars alike must carefully negotiate the stratifying forces embedded within them to find the potentials for critique that Vocaloids offer. However, alongside popular culture, digital media have also created new potentials for avant-garde artistic experimentation. Stemming from the international video art movements of the 1980s and 1990s, the digital avant-garde has produced a generation of animators and musicians fascinated with issues of virtuality and embodiment. In studies of Chinese new media art, these artists are known as the "post-internet" generation.[35] New media scholar Jihoon Kim defines this trend as "an array of artistic production that focuses its attention to the cultural impact of the internet and digital technologies, attempts to overcome the dualities of the material and the virtual, and translates the technologically-influenced expressions, activities, and identities into multiple forms and experiences."[36] These artists use technology self-reflexively, in posthuman fashion, to interrogate the impacts of that very technology on our fundamental conceptions of body, mind, agency, and self. Of course, new media artists do not exist in a purely intellectual realm separate from late-stage capitalism and the tech industry. They do, however, have different relations to the economic pressures of capital and to popular culture that are equally worth exploring.

While the term *post-internet generation* may seem to imply a break with pre-internet perceptions and theories of embodiment, the younger generation of artists does have commonalities with some of their philosophical forebears, such as an interest in perceptions and experiences of embodiment. Along with Deleuze and Guattari's theories of virtuality and affect, we can understand post-internet artists (and posthuman scholars) through the works of phenomenological philosophers like Merleau-Ponty, another author of the 1960s whose work has had a posthumous resurgence in film and media scholarship of the early twenty-first century. In 1964, Merleau-Ponty argued that "if philosophy is in harmony with the cinema, if thought and technical effort are heading in the same direction, it is because the philosopher and the moviemaker share a certain way of being, a certain view of the world which belongs to a generation."[37] In this quotation, Merleau-Ponty speaks of the way in which media technologies like cinema do not determine the ways we think but rather express modes of being and perception shared by philosophers and media producers alike at a given time—such as the concerns around posthumanism and technology that arose at the turn of the twenty-first century. Without necessarily delimiting analysis to a generational stance, it is productive to ask, What ways of being, viewing, and touching the world were shared by the philosophy of phenomenological posthumanism and new media artists in the 2000s and 2010s? How do these views continue to expand into the 2020s?

To answer these questions, I consider the works of independent new media artist Lu Yang, whose practices include 3D digital modeling, medical imaging, video gaming, and site-specific performance art. Lu Yang's works pose the same question he asks every time he meets with a neuroscientist: "Do you believe that consciousness comes from the brain?" The resulting bioart experiments draw equally on cutting-edge neuroscience, traditional Buddhist iconography, and imagery drawn from Japanese popular culture. Lu Yang's entire oeuvre (as of this publication) is devoted to animating bodies, both as anatomical objects and as what Merleau-Ponty has termed the "flesh," a chiasm or intertwining of body and world, touch and visibility, technology and consciousness. Lu Yang's works illustrate a persistent concern with issues of embodiment and biopower, control and consciousness, and the instability of gender and genetics. They enact a queering of the body in which the links between chromosomes, reproductive organs, and gendered identities are broken and re-formed, refusing to view embodiment as a naturalized or preexisting phenomenon based on the possession of certain organs or physical abilities. As such, they help us to explore how animation can reinforce our sense of "being-in-the-world" as embodied subjects who also live, perceive, and act within various digital media environments in the 2010s and early 2020s.

Lu Yang was born in Shanghai in 1984 and studied at the China Academy of Arts under Zhang Peili, "the founding chair of the [New Media] department and a pioneer of video art in China."[38] Lu Yang is considered a rising star in the Chinese art world and an exemplary new media artist. However, Lu Yang denies that his work has any connection to nationalism, politics, or established art movements like *haipai,* the Shanghai style of video and installation art.[39] Instead, Lu Yang relentlessly pursues a personal vision that questions the place of the body within the modern frameworks of neuroscience and global internet cultures. Along with rejecting national identity, Lu Yang refuses to be bound by binary gender identities. In a 2020 interview published in *Ocula,* journalist Sam Gaskin noted that "Lu Yang is referred to as 'he' in *Material World Knight,* and a recent *ArtNews* profile used the same pronoun, but in most previous interviews Lu Yang has been referred to as 'she.' The artist prefers neither. 'I'd like everyone to just use my name,' Lu Yang said. 'I'm a bit disgusted by gendered titles.'"[40] Indeed, the full name "Lu Yang" (often styled "LuYang") is a major part of the artist's oeuvre, appearing repeatedly in the titles of works like *LuYang the Destroyer* (2021), *Dance Dance LuYang Revolution* (2018), *LuYang Delusional Crime and Punishment* (2016), and *LuYang Delusional Mandala* (2015). Out of respect for this preference, I refer to the artist as Lu Yang whenever possible, rather than by the family name "Lu" or any gendered pronoun. When a pronoun is required for grammatical or stylistic reasons, I use *he,* because as of 2022, Lu Yang uses *he/him* pronouns in the English text on his website. It should be understood, however, that Lu Yang has explicitly rejected binary gender identities and so can be considered a nonbinary artist for the purposes of this study. In addition to statements in interviews, Lu Yang's works have consistently featured asexual, androgynous virtual avatars, including CGI-animated figures with Lu Yang's own face that are naked and have no visible primary or secondary sexual characteristics. Such avatars are explicitly linked to the potentials opened up by the virtual and by digital media; as Lu Yang notes, "In the virtual world, I was able to do things such as choosing my own gender-neutral body and creating an appearance that reflects my own sense of beauty, which are not possible in real life."[41] Along with the transformative potentials of the virtual, Lu Yang's works demonstrate a prolonged grappling with the materiality of the body: the organs, the skeleton, the brain, and the neurochemistry that are the material foundation of our phenomenal experience of the world. So, although these works are idiosyncratic in many ways, they also demonstrate the intersection of embodiment and virtuality that characterizes a "certain way of being, [or] certain view of the world,"[42] emerging among the current generation of media artists and philosophers, particularly in the areas of feminist and queer phenomenology. Before I continue to an analysis of Lu Yang's videos, then, I would like to offer a brief definition of queer phenomenology as explained by Ahmed and suggest ways in which it might intersect with Lu Yang's virtual bodies.

In *Queer Phenomenology,* Ahmed draws on the works of philosophers like Husserl, Heidegger, Merleau-Ponty, Fanon, and others to illustrate the complex interweaving of bodies, dwelling places, lineages, and racial and gendered experiences that attend the term *orientation.* Quoting from Merleau-Ponty's *Phenomenology of Perception,* Ahmed points out that "spatial forms or distance are not so much relations between different points in objective space as they are relations between these points and a central perspective—our body."[43] She goes on to explain that "the 'here' of the body does not simply refer to the body, but to 'where' the body dwells."[44] Many of her examples of dwellings are domestic spaces or objects, such as the table where the work of writing is done, which many philosophers have contemplated as an example of the tangible object of experience. However, orientation in Ahmed's reading is not *only* spatial or based on physical objects. It is also temporal: the table is "before" the philosopher as the preexisting condition that allows the (often elided) labor of writing to take place.

Orientation is also an effect of directionality considered more broadly: which way we face or what we are oriented toward in terms of identities. Ahmed highlights the "Orient" in Orientalist conceptions of the East and looks at how bodies (especially those seen as Oriental) are directed through racial, gendered, and sexual orientations. As these examples might suggest, "orientation" is not conceived as an essentialist property of bodies but rather as a matter of bodies being "in line" or "out of line" with the directions others face within a society. "A key argument in this book," Ahmed says of her work, "is that the body gets directed in some ways more than others."[45] Like Deleuze and Guattari, her approach places the focus more on what bodies *do* than on what they *are.* More precisely, she focuses on how bodies are oriented, which means how they are directed in relation to existing or possible worlds they inhabit and how they can turn to face in other directions, for instance, by refusing the lineages or orientations imposed by compulsory heterosexuality. In her view, "queer tables or queer objects"—that is, the places or platforms that support queer connections—are those that "support proximity between those who are supposed to live on parallel lines, as points that should not meet. A queer object hence makes contact possible. Or, to be more precise, a queer object would have a surface that supports such contact."[46] For Ahmed, this means bodily contact, in the physical, sexual, and social sense. However, digital objects can also work as surfaces that support contact, as I have argued so far in describing Vocaloids as BwOs or surfaces for the circulation of desire. The works of Lu Yang also allow us to see how the "queer table" might include digital and mixed-reality platforms, such as virtual avatars and video games that serve to redirect or reorient both the creator's and the viewers' bodies in queer ways. To demonstrate, I present three examples of Lu Yang's work that create queer embodiment online by "crossing the lines" between seemingly disparate discourses, namely, Western medical science, Buddhist religious thought, and Japanese popular culture.

The Medical and Phenomenal Bodies of Lu Yang

In the 2015 animated short film *LuYang Delusional Mandala,* Lu Yang uses CGI to make a series of comparisons between digital animation, neuroscientific procedures, and experiences of perception, consciousness, and death. In the opening sequence, Lu Yang reveals how the film was created by taking a 3D scan of his own face (at this time, still presented with conventionally feminine-coded features, such as long hair), converting it into data, and using those data to create androgynous, hairless 3D models that the artist could turn in any direction at will. A synthesized Mandarin-language narration track explains the production process in monotonous, robotic tones that contrast with the film's upbeat techno soundtrack, dynamic collage style, and flashing glitch and static effects. In this opening segment, indexicality is both evoked and undermined by digital technologies. The scanned model has a direct connection to the animator's physical body, because its face and shoulders (at the very least) were captured from life. But the plasmatic and animatic quality of the digital character is striking, as it is degendered, cross sectioned, morphed, taken apart, and reconstituted with uncanny ease. From the very start, then, the animator's lived body and the process of CGI animation—which we might see as the digital "table" on which the labor of animation takes place—are inextricably intertwined. Lu Yang does not hide the work of animation but rather reveals it as the point from which a new form of embodiment can emerge.

Once the process of digital imaging has been introduced, the video goes on to build a connection between animation and neurosurgery. One procedure Lu Yang depicts is deep brain stimulation (DBS), through which electrical impulses are applied to key areas of the brain to relieve the symptoms of diseases like Parkinson's and Tourette's. Figure 18 shows Lu Yang's rendering of the stereotactic frame that allows neurosurgeons to implant electrodes into the brain at precise locations using a 3D coordinate system. The fact that 3D modeling and DBS both use a coordinate system suggests a technical parallel between them, as well as a functional parallel: that of controlling bodily movements and facial expressions. Lu Yang illustrates the control aspect of both DBS and animation vividly by having his avatar's face contort into a series of grotesquely exaggerated expressions as needles slide one by one into the stereotactic frame. Here animation and neuroscience are seen as methods of biotechnological control or biopower.

This is a recurrent theme in Lu Yang's oeuvre, which included the early installations *Happy Tree* (2010) and *Reanimation! Underwater Zombie Frog Ballet* (2011), in which live or dead animals were made to spasm and twitch to a techno beat using electrical currents. Lu Yang has since admitted that the exhibitions using animals were unethical and has vowed that they will not be repeated. As a result, the text description accompanying the *Delusional Mandala* video on Vimeo states, "Because of the powerful curse in the content of the work, the artist has to apply the spell to herself to avoid harming others."[47] Basically, the film applies electrical control to Lu Yang's own tortured ("cursed") virtual avatar to explore the ethical issues that arise when the body is framed as an object of technological manipulation, using the artist as test subject rather than "harming others," such as innocent animals.

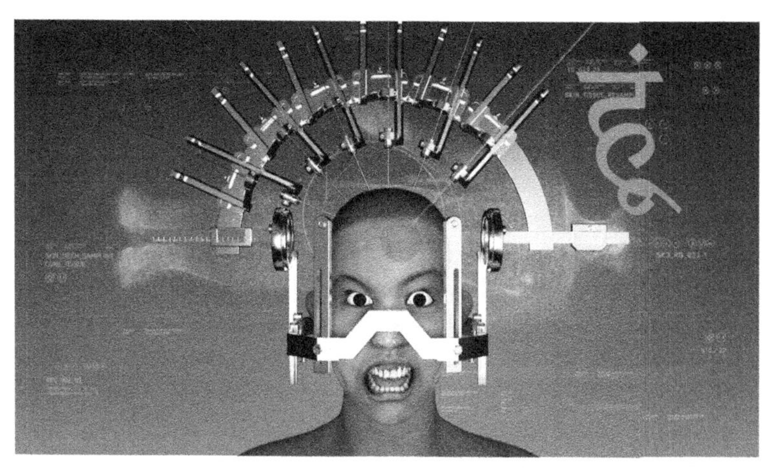

FIGURE 18. Lu Yang's distorted face crowned by the stereotactic frame in *LuYang Delusional Mandala* (2015).

That said, Lu Yang is not mired in the kind of pure scientific empiricism that Merleau-Ponty critiqued, which sees the body as nothing but a biological machine. Lu Yang is equally interested in how perception, consciousness, spirituality, and emotion are related to embodiment and how rigid medical conceptions of the body can be overcome. In *Delusional Mandala,* the stereotactic arc is overtly compared to the "nimbus" or halo of divinity that surrounds religious figures in Buddhist art. In several scenes, Lu Yang is presented as a multiarmed deity or a Christian saint–like figure. The robotic voice-over narration that accompanies these images defines consciousness using both scientific terms and Buddhist religious terms in Sanskrit. This transcendent consciousness, however, is balanced by a visceral return to the mortal body, as the scene in which Lu Yang is deified is followed by a scene about death. Here Lu Yang's avatar goes into seizures while entering a fiery MRI machine and then dies repeatedly, falling, flailing, and crumpling as if dropped from a great height. The avatar is also at points reduced to a skinless column of diseased organs, swaying in a rhythmic dance while the face of Lu Yang grins maniacally from atop a sinuous spinal column. Despite the clinical tone of the robotic narrator's definitions of death, these segments are disturbing in their corporeality. The spasming, falling figures evoke a sympathetic tremor in my own muscles, as if my body not only sees but also sympathetically feels the image. In this way, Lu Yang makes use of the "haptic visuality" described by phenomenological feminist film theorists like Laura U. Marks,[48] as well as the intertwining of consciousness and embodiment in the flesh theorized by Merleau-Ponty and later queer phenomenologists like Ahmed.

In *Delusional Mandala,* Lu Yang's vision of digital being is neither purely spiritual nor empirically biological but is rather a site of crossing over between the lively and the technological. In the final scene, the body of the deceased avatar is placed into an elaborate hearse that becomes a new vehicle for experience. Resembling an elaborate golden pavilion on wheels, the hearse is emblazoned with animated portraits of Lu Yang's mobile face crowned with the stereotactic halo. Even though the character has died, it seems to live on in a new form that is partly organic, partly architectural, partly mechanical, and entirely digital (Figure 19). For the last three minutes of the film, the hearse races from an abstract space dotted with grainy celluloid filters into an animatic rendering of a landscape under a night sky. All the while, its paper lanterns are buffeted as if by strong winds, which gives a vivid physical impression of moving at high speed. Lu Yang's final vision of his own digital self, then, is one that retains embodiment in evoking haptic sensory experiences but also intertwines them with new technological ways of being.

In addressing posthuman embodiment, Lu Yang also engages with the issues of gender, sexuality, and desire that are central to the image of Hatsune Miku as BwO. In Lu Yang's case, however, appealing icons drawn from Japanese popular culture, such as the *bishōnen* (beautiful boy) and the *mahō shōjo* (magical girl), are subject to defamiliarization and queering, as Lu Yang conducts grotesque visual experiments using these familiar generic and gendered tropes.

The 2013 video *Uterus Man* is a perfect example of this approach. In this pop art parody, Lu Yang creates a fictional video game playthrough featuring a male superhero who is also an anthropomorphized uterus. This video utilizes the iconography of Japanese side-scrolling combat video games, such as *Street Fighter,* as well as science fiction anime. There are clear allusions to the iconic 1995 mecha series *Neon Genesis Evangelion,* evident in the blocky white kanji screen text (a hallmark of Studio Gainax animation) and the "Placenta Defense AT field," which the game's robotic voice-over narration defines as an "Absolute Terror field" in homage to the name of a defensive shield in *Evangelion.* The game's protagonist, Uterus Man, is depicted as a slen-

FIGURE 19. Lu Yang as animated hearse in *LuYang Delusional Mandala*.

der, youthful, albino bishōnen, a character design that might remind anime-savvy viewers of *Evangelion*'s red-eyed, silver-haired queer angel, Kaworu. Lu Yang has admitted to being influenced by Japanese anime and its internet community.[49] It is also significant that the references are to *Evangelion* as opposed to any other anime, because this series features themes of body horror and medical experimentation, raising the promise of cyborg empowerment and the threat of biopolitical control. Lu Yang's game focuses even more directly on the medicalized body by comparing its main character's design with the physiological structure of the uterus, often using cuts to documentary footage of ovaries taken with endoscopic cameras, among other medical clips. Rather than being indexed simply as existing organs, however, these anatomical structures are transformed through animation in fantastic machines, such as the "Pelvis Chariot" on which Uterus Man rides.

The fact that this video features a male character representing a female reproductive organ is in itself a queering of epic proportions. Lu Yang dramatically breaks from the heteronormative and transphobic discourse that assumes a natural connection between XY/XX chromosomes, male or female sex organs, and binary gender identities of man and woman. Uterus Man gives birth to a baby through his vaginal feet, and yet he still performs an "XY chromosome attack," with text captions on the screen reminding us that XX genes are female and XY genes are male. Although this character may seem purely fantastical, it should be noted that Uterus Man's look was based partly on a real asexual person: the Japanese artist Mao Sugiyama, who reportedly cut off their own penis, cooked it, and fed it to a paying audience as a piece of performance art. Lu Yang was fascinated with Sugiyama's genital surgery performance piece, and the two artists connected with each other on Twitter, where they "talked a lot about sexual issues" and "became online friends."[50] Lu Yang ended up going to Tokyo for two months to hold photography sessions with Sugiyama that were used in the design of Uterus Man. The resulting anime-style parody of an anatomy lesson prompts us to question the discourses that hold chromosomes, sex organs, and gender identities "in line" and so direct bodies into limiting binaries.

Along with drawing on real people and live-action medical imaging, this video game invites players to "become animated" as Uterus Man themselves. Uterus Man started out as a parody trailer for a nonexistent arcade game, but it eventually became "a professionally developed video game (produced by the Fukuoka Asian Art Museum), [which made] its New York premiere in [an exhibit called] Lu Yang Video Room at Ventana 244."[51] Players were able to align their points of view with Uterus Man, control his motions, and mirror his actions in their own ducking and swerving. The control of motion and point of view is in fact one of the key tropes that carries across all of Lu Yang's works, be they games, installations, or online videos. Though Lu Yang has claimed to be "not terribly enthusiastic about animation,"[52] the videos themselves reveal an obsession with bringing images to life through motion and aligning them in uncanny ways with living bodies, both of which are key features of animation (as I discussed in my analysis of electro swing music videos and dancing in chapter 4). The theme of technological motion control, particularly as depicted through a virtual avatar's dancing body, is highlighted in many of Lu Yang's other works, including 2018's *Electromagnetic Brainology Brain Control Messenger,* a parodic J-pop music video that takes on the classic magical girl figure of anime.

For this video, Lu Yang employed an actress credited as "Chan Momo" to play an alien-fighting magical girl hero, the Brain Control Messenger. It begins with a video game loading screen that introduces the magical girl heroine through a stock transformation sequence or *henshin* (changing forms) scene. This type of scene, in which an ordinary girl becomes her crime-fighting alter ego, is a staple of magical

FIGURE 20. The 2.5D transformation sequence of a medical magical girl in *Electromagnetic Brainology Brain Control Messenger* (2018).

girl anime, such as *Sailor Moon*. Echoing the animetic limited animation style of magical girl shows, Chan Momo is lit with high-key lighting to create a flat, bright, shadowless 2D impression. She is also dressed in an animetic costume that combines mechanical-looking shoulder armor and kneepads with a beribboned sailor-suit school uniform in bold primary colors of white, red, yellow, and blue. Her transformation is choreographed to match the energetic musical intro to her J-pop song, which features a synthesizer repeating a twelve-note riff based on the pentatonic scale, creating an "Oriental" sound. However, she does not dance to the song—at least, not yet. Her movements during the loading and transformation sequence are limited to poses and stylized gestures set against a whirl of 2D animated flames, smoke, and sparkles (Figure 20). As with Hatsune Miku, the character and setting here take on a 2.5D quality as live-action idol performance, gamic screen text, and shōjo anime overlap.

Once transformed, the Brain Control Messenger sings her verses directly to the camera in idol fashion. The song describes experiences of physical suffering, but they are enacted with incongruously cute gestures, such as brushing a curled-up hand under her eye to indicate crying. In the background, her various "weapons," all based on neurosurgical devices, are introduced using rotating CGI models and on-screen text that explains their names and uses. As the video progresses, she fulfills her magical girl hero role by fighting a giant alien with a brain-shaped head that looks like the creatures in the sci-fi comedy *Mars Attacks!* (dir. Tim Burton, 1996). Despite the Hollywood incursion, Lu Yang maintains a strong connection with Japanese pop culture by setting the pair's giant-monster-sized dance battle in a photocollage version of Tokyo, featuring the otaku capital of Akihabara, among other famous sites. Interestingly, Lu Yang grants his giant shōjo the ability to control the city's populace using a video game controller marked with the character for "brain." It seems the Brain Control Messenger's animetic powers come not from magic but from neuroscience. This is also evident in her costume and weapons, as her crown is based on the surgical stereotactic frame featured in *Delusional Mandala,* and her wand is the paddle-shaped emitter for a transcranial magnetic stimulation device, which is used to stimulate nerve cells in the brain with magnetic fields and alleviate depression. Even her headphones are based on galvanic vestibular stimulation (GVS), a procedure that influences the fluids of the inner ear to create sensations of balance or imbalance. The idea that the magical girl represents medical science is reinforced by the lyrics of the J-pop song that plays throughout, which describes a suffering patient who "arrives from the country of pain" and is healed by a mystical blaze that "massages the hippocampus."

Along with creating CGI depictions of biomedical devices, Lu Yang may have employed the actual devices in creating the video. A short making-of documentary for *Electromagnetic Brainology Brain Control Messenger* posted to Lu Yang's Vimeo channel purports to show the actress Chan Momo using a GVS rig to manipulate and control her own proprioceptive senses in preparation for her role in the music video. At the start of the featurette, the actress is shown meeting with a male doctor, who explains in Japanese that she will wear a set of earphones connected to a GVS machine. The machine is identified at the start of the video and remains visible on the desk throughout the opening scenes, resembling a white humanoid figurine on a base that floats upright in a bowl of water, all of which is wired to a set of headphones. Later in the video, Chan puts on the headphones and a brown, purselike bag that presumably contains the GVS apparatus. She lifts the bowl with nervous giggles, asking, "You're absolutely sure it won't hurt, right?" The doctor assures her that it won't hurt and turns it on. She immediately screams and exclaims, "It feels weird *[kimochi warui]*!" and "Scary *[kowai]*!" It seems she can feel the movements of the floating figure in her own body. Soon enough, she gets used to it and tries walking around. The video then cuts to a second segment of GVS test footage, this time accompanied by the upbeat *Brain Control Messenger* song. Here we see her holding a device very like the video console brain controller her character uses, which is attached by a wire to her headset. As she walks around the room, she staggers left or right, moving in the direction of the joystick. This would lead us to believe that Chan Momo was in fact controlling her body with the GVS device, as the "animator" of her own perceptions. It is not clear whether this making-of video is a genuine demonstration of the GVS device or another fictional performance piece, because Lu Yang's Vimeo page also contains some obviously fabricated medical demonstrations framed as scientific "exorcisms." Whether or not the video is authentic, however, it seems that Lu Yang aims to denaturalize the female body by placing it in dialogue with the animetic shōjo archetype and with images of controlling biotechnology. The imagery in *Electromagnetic Brainology Brain Control Messenger* is silly and campy on the surface, but taken in the context of Lu Yang's artistic career, we can see how it comments on issues of great concern to the current generation, namely, how one forms an identity, a sense of conscious agency, or a perception of the world in the age defined by digital media and animated images that intimately manipulate our senses through the operations of biopower and phenopower. The answer shown in *Brain Control Messenger* is to seize the technological means of the production of perception, or to take control of the devices and images that evoke bodily experiences in yourself, for yourself.

Kim argues that films like 2015's *Delusional Mandala* "emblematize Lu Yang's preoccupation with the idea of posthumanism, in that they dramatize the transformation of human bodies through their connection to non-human technological (both physical and virtual) artifacts."[53] Lu Yang's preoccupation with this topic has continued since the publication of Kim's article. Starting in 2020, Lu Yang began working more with real-time motion capture performances in which a human dancer directly controls the movements of a fully rendered computer-animated virtual avatar called DOKU. In keeping with Lu Yang's shift to he/him pronouns, DOKU is a male-presenting figure dressed in a sleek, futuristic black bodysuit reminiscent of science fiction films and anime. This human–avatar hybrid, created by Lu Yang and controlled by professional dancers, has appeared in several live performances and live-streamed events in the early 2020s. Most often, DOKU is shown dancing through scaled-down photocollage city sets so that he appears as a *kaiju* or giant monster figure, much like the giant Brain Control Messenger and her alien foe. The informational text on Lu Yang's website describes the most recent performance, *Gigant DOKU—LuYang the Destroyer* (2021), as "an exploration of the possibilities and limitations of the 'digital body,' produced in collaboration with Russian dancers and electronic musicians."[54] In this way, Lu Yang's works can be seen as part of a global current of thought that addresses posthuman concerns and phenomenological experiences of the body in their imbrications with digital technology.

It would not be accurate to say that Lu Yang has joined a unified "posthumanist movement" or that he has made any direct references to Western phenomenological scholars, such as Merleau-Ponty. Lu Yang's work, like Chinese animation more generally, is rather picking up on transnational currents of thought in animation and new media art. In *Animated Encounters: Transnational Movements of Chinese Animation, 1940s–1970s,* Daisy Yan Du argues that

> in the global history of animation, the invisible interstices between demarcated national borders and historical nationhoods are more significant than the animated film produced within a single national, cultural, or territorial space. This invisible yet animated middle ground generates the movement and life force of animation as a whole art form across national, cultural, spatial, and temporal borders in multiple directions, and subsequently (trans)forms the histories of world animation.[55]

Du calls "this interstice the animated contact zone, the in-between space of dynamic encounters."[56] We might also call it a site of chiasm: a crossing-between or interleaving of cultures, enacted through the flesh of animation. Lu Yang's works can be seen as presenting bodies that cross over between different modes of existence and ways of doing. The body is deliberately medicalized in much of Lu Yang's work, where it is depicted as a material object defined by fixed anatomical structures and subject to the interventions of neurosurgical devices. And yet, even from within this objectifying framework, Lu Yang still shows these bodies "becoming-animated,"[57] suggesting how the technologies of vision and science can create nonbinary and posthuman bodies that we can perceive and inhabit in meaningful ways. DOKU, Uterus Man, and the Brain Control Messenger queer our ideas of sex, gender, and the physiology of the human body, turning the normative discourses of anatomy and liberal humanism both against themselves. As such, they provide parodic pop culture heroes who deliver serious messages about how we can create and recreate ourselves through a vast array of organic, inorganic, and virtual bodies. Ultimately, they call us to recognize a new way of being in the world as subjects enmeshed in systems of biopower, but also as active, intentional agents of the flesh.

Hatsune Miku and the Brain Control Messenger can be seen as two complementary cases of posthuman embodiment. Miku illustrates the BwO, or the virtual and affective potential of collective and collaborative action on the part of creator-fans. Lu Yang's various avatars and parodic superheroes could be said to present organs reoriented into new bodily configurations: Organs without Bodies, in the case of Lu Yang's macabre mass of dancing organs atop a waving spinal column, but also Organs as Entire Bodies, in the case of Uterus Man, or Organs as Technical Affordances, in the case of the Brain Control Messenger. Just as Deleuze and Guattari warn, both the BwO of the Vocaloids and the strange Organic configurations of Lu Yang's oeuvre can become cancerous or reimbricated into a system of Organization that relies on hierarchies and stratification. In Miku's commodification and Lu Yang's ambivalent critique and promotion of medical science, we might see these figures as a return to what Deleuze has termed "societies of control" or what Foucault has termed "biopower." At the same time, however, something in both figures exceeds the mechanisms of control that characterize them. In the case of the Vocaloid phenomenon, the excess is found in the work of fans themselves, which is largely unregulated and leads to an indescribably rich array of identities both for the virtual characters and for the creators themselves. In Lu Yang's works, the excess is generated both visually, in the rapid, glitching, color- and text-saturated imagery, and in the transgression of both Eastern and Western discourses of the body and the soul. Lu Yang's works are more than illustrated anatomy lessons or anime fan videos; they are examples of how queer bodies can "cross the lines," as they cross between modes, styles, media, genders, and national cultures to create something viscerally disturbing that compels the viewer/player to question their own experiences of embodiment in a virtual world.

In many respects, the Vocaloid phenomenon and Lu Yang's performance art are the products of their times. At least, they were created and consumed by people who grew up in an age when the internet could still be regarded optimistically as a frontier or site of limitless potential for individuals to (de)construct themselves. However, they are also early indicators of ways that virtual embodiment could develop in the future: through collective action and critique of the control of digital media, which is of increasing concern in late-capitalist democracies and authoritarian societies alike. As such, the posthuman forms of embodiment I discuss in this chapter are valuable examples, not just as case studies in the ongoing history of media studies, but also as guideposts for the future, in which animated media, however virtual, may be experienced more and more often in the flesh.

CONCLUSION

In *Queer Phenomenology,* Sara Ahmed points out that for Merleau-Ponty, the body is not simply an object but a sensory relation with the world, as "the 'here' of the body does not simply refer to the body, but to 'where' the body dwells."[1] The "where" of the body is also a "when" of the body, as the traces of past labors persist in the marks on tabletops and flesh alike. As I write this conclusion at my old, marked-up desk in early 2023, the larger world in which I find myself dwelling seems like a very different place than it was when I first began my research into animation and embodiment in 2016. The past seven years have seen historic changes on a large scale. From the rise of social justice movements like #MeToo and Black Lives Matter in the United States and United Kingdom to the global Covid-19 pandemic of the early 2020s and the ongoing climate crisis, the world has seen a series of dramatic cultural, economic, and political ups and downs. In fact, it would not be an overstatement to say that our very perception of our place in history has changed as scholars have proposed the planet's entry into the new geological era of the "Anthropocene," a term coined by the Anthropocene Working Group that became current in 2016 to describe the substantial impacts of humanity on the geology and ecosystems of the earth. The start of the twenty-first century, then, marks an era of major changes not only to our concept of the physical world but also to our perceptions of embodiment and life itself. In this conclusion, I provide a brief outline of the changes that have taken place during the time it has taken me to write this book. Then, I explain why it is more important than ever to continue exploring the corporeal dimensions of digital and animated media and how they shape our perceptions of and orientations toward the world in which we dwell.

Since 2016, much of the world has seen major social and political shifts. In North America, identity politics and critical race theory, which have long been the purview of academics and activists, became the talk of the mainstream media in a series of high-profile events between 2017 and 2021. These include the #MeToo movement, started in 2017 to raise awareness of sexual abuse and gender inequality; the anti-trans legislation of the Trump administration and the subsequent increased public awareness of and pushback against transgender rights; and the deaths of African American youths subjected to police brutality, which sparked protests by the Black Lives Matter movement (among others) in 2020. All of these events drew starkly polarized reactions from right- and left-wing commentators—particularly, between Republicans and Democrats in the United States—which were reflected in American mass media and in public discourse on the Anglophone internet. In Commonwealth nations like Canada and Australia, there have also been fraught efforts at attaining "truth and reconciliation" between settler colonizers and Indigenous peoples, which gained a higher profile in Canada in the wake of the discovery of mass graves at historical residential schools in 2021. Europe saw the United Kingdom's "Brexit" from the European Union in 2020. Two years later, Russian president Vladimir Putin's war on Ukraine beginning in March 2022 raised once again the Cold War specter of widespread nuclear annihilation. Meanwhile, in East Asia, China has continued to eclipse Japan in influence both regionally and globally, leading to both new cultural exchanges and sociopolitical frictions. As Frank N. Pieke and Koichi Iwabuchi note in the introduction to their 2021 book *Global East Asia: Into the Twenty-First Century,* "China's state-led globalization and emerging superpower status are fundamentally changing the nature and impact of globalization (or at least contributing materially to such a change)"[2]—a situation reflected in the frictions between global media conglomerates, such as Disney, which seeks to woo Chinese audiences, and protests against both Disney's media imperialism and Chinese political dominance.

Spanning the globe in this time have been two major crises: the climate crisis and the global Covid-19 pandemic, along with the chain reactions of economic disruption, political conflict, and social unrest that have followed from both throughout the world. Following the announcement of the Anthropocene era and the increased awareness of climate crisis brought about by the media and environmental activism, there has been an increase in "climate grief" and "Anthropocene anxiety"[3] related to the mass extinction and resulting loss of biodiversity currently in progress. In March 2023, the United Nations' Intergovernmental Panel on Climate Change released a report claiming that global warming is "nearing the point of no return" and stating that this is our "final warning" to mitigate the dire environmental impacts of average temperature increases above 1.5 degrees Celsius.[4] Along with provoking action among scientists, politicians, activists, and ordinary citizens, the climate crisis has impelled many humanities scholars to seek perspectives on life beyond the anthropocentric, such as posthumanism and ecocriticism. However, humanitarian issues have also returned to the fore with the Covid-19 pandemic. The pandemic's impact has been especially devastating in the developing world, where vaccine roll-outs were initially slow or nonexistent and living conditions were already more precarious. But even those living in wealthy nations and in positions of privilege—including academics like me—felt the psychological and physical pressures created by the loss of work, "pivoting" back and forth between remote and in-person work, going in and out of lockdowns, and being isolated from physical contact with all but a select few people in one's "social bubble" (as it was called in Canada).

I do not have the space, in this brief conclusion, for a detailed analysis of each one of these major events. I also do not want to mimic the catastrophizing rhetoric of many mainstream media outlets with a series of negative "ripped from the headlines" sound bites or "hot button" topics. Suffice to say, each of these events is much larger and more complex than I have represented in this sketch. Still, I am compelled to mention them in my conclusion because they form the background against which this book was written, and my interpretations of animated films and media have been influenced by these events. Inspired by Ahmed, I am endeavoring, however briefly, to bring what was in the background—the conditions of my current orientation in space and time—into the foreground.

All of these serious real-world events may seem disconnected from the animated films and music videos I have analyzed throughout this book. After two years of Zoom meetings, online conferences, remote learning, and family get-togethers conducted over video calls, even I have been tempted at times to think that I was learning more about the ways in which interacting through screens does *not* replace real-world, in-person experience than about the inextricable connections between embodiment and digital images. Watching a digitally animated avatar of myself interacting with the other avatars of scholars in a simulated 3D space at an online conference was simply not the same as traveling to Kyoto, attending live panels, and enjoying conversations over dinner with colleagues in person. However, I did not embark on this project to prove that watching an animated film—or expressing oneself through an animated avatar—is *identical* to having an embodied experience of the spaces or movements shown in that film. Nor do I believe that we can dispense with going outside or seeing others face-to-face so long as we have screens to entertain and connect us. Quite the opposite: I set out to argue that animated media impinge on our perceptions of the world because they evoke within us a set of multisensory embodied experiences and that this relation is, as Merleau-Ponty characterizes the flesh, a mutually entangled and reversible interpenetration. What we see on screens inflects our perceptions of world, body, time, and movement; likewise, the kinds of world, bodies, times, and movements we perform in real life inform how we perceive animated images, both on a prereflective level and through conscious reflection. In this way, animation becomes one of the ways we dwell in the world. The difficulties of the past seven years have informed my reading of phenomenological philosophy and animated media, just as those philosophies and media were themselves informed by the technological advances, scholarly trends, and historical trials of their own generations.

This book has explored a few of the many dimensions of embodiment experienced by those who belong to the generation known in China as the post-internet generation or in North America as the generation of digital natives, namely, those artists and audiences accustomed to integrating digital media into daily life, and engaging with the forms of embodiment they afford. That is not to say that these experiences are open only to those born after 1980; on the contrary, animation has been influencing viewers' lives through anontological moving images for over a century now. However, it has been my task to counter the discourse of digital disembodiment that was current in postmodern scholarship and philosophy of the 1990s and early 2000s, which held that digital cinema and CGI animation are somehow less physical or less "real" because they are not photographic recordings of existing bodies or motions. Although animation undoubtedly has its own (an)ontology that differs from live-action cinema, it is still capable of rousing vivid sensations and varied affects though the unique properties of its own flesh, which in turn impact viewers based in part on their own particular neurological makeup and life experience, including embodied traumas, carnal desires, and historical memories.

The first two chapters of this book defined the titular concept of the "flesh of animation" and showed how 2D hand-drawn cel animation can evoke haptic visuality and embodied affects. These two chapters considered issues of depth, perspective, spatiality, and animated worlds in looking at the cinematic aspects of Japanese anime and the combination of cel animation and live-action footage in hybrid films. The third chapter considered the issue of embodiment and the control of our perceptions in so-called live-action remakes that make extensive use of 3D CGI modeling. The final two chapters considered the temporal and multidimensional elements of animation in more niche-oriented short-form animated videos, including electro swing music videos, Vocaloid performances, and video installation art. Although the case studies in each of these chapters are by no means exhaustive or even representative of all that animation is capable of, I hope they are at least sufficient to illustrate a single point: that animation has a flesh, or a means of entwining visual, haptic, and tactile perceptions (among others), and that this flesh is part of the body that many of us inhabit today as posthuman subjects.

Critics may find that the case studies in this book are not exhaustive or inclusive enough. I will be the first to admit that there is very little about animation from South America, Africa, and South Asia in this book or about animation by Indigenous creators. It may also seem that the case studies have been selected eclectically, with some directors of Japanese anime considered at length, such as Okiura Hiroyuki, and other equally deserving directors whose works depict embodiment in unique and fascinating ways overlooked (for instance, Yuasa Masaaki, whose work I very much wanted to include as an example of embodiment in the animetic style of anime). Because embodiment underlies every work of animation to some degree, I have found it impossible to address all the works that might be relevant within the scope of a single, compact book. Therefore I have tried to take a cross section of works from the areas with which I am most familiar: anime, mainstream Hollywood cinema, music video, and performance arts. My textual selections—like my grasp of recent world events—no doubt reflect the ways in which I have been oriented toward some of the most powerful media producers of my time and place. However, I have also made some effort to include works by creators who refuse or complicate the dynamics of global popular culture, such as Jérémy Clapin's indie art film *I Lost My Body* and the performance art of Lu Yang. I do not claim that this book is a complete portrait of embodiment in animation or a universally applicable theory of queer posthuman phenomenology. It is merely an invitation for future scholars who may also wish to examine embodiment in animation, providing a starting point that builds on as many apt examples by past and present scholars of animation and film phenomenology as I can reasonably include.

It is my hope that this book continues the conversation on the many ways in which our diverse sensory experiences and phenomenal perceptions of the world are expanded by animation, especially in its intersections with digital media technologies. Since the early 1900s, animation has been one of the many ways in which we grasp changes in our world and express them clearly in visual media. As I write, animators continue to evoke bodily impressions and sensory experiences, both human and inhuman, to cope with our rapidly changing world. I hope that in the (likely difficult) years to come, more animated works will be released that address the collective shocks, fears, and hopes we have variously experienced. That is the multidimensional and temporally layered gesture of the flesh of animation: to bring the traces of the past into the present, to transform them through contemporary movements, and to anticipate how they may shape the future of our bodies and our world.

NOTES

Introduction

1. Christian Ferencz-Flatz and Julian Hanich, "Editors' Introduction: What Is Film Phenomenology?" *Studia Phænomenologica* 16 (2016): 13.

2. Linda Williams, "Film Bodies: Gender, Genre, Excess," *Film Quarterly* 44, no. 4 (1991): 2–13.

3. N. Katherine Hayles, *How We Became Posthuman: Virtual Bodies in Cybernetics, Literature, and Informatics* (Chicago: University of Chicago Press, 1999).

4. Scott Balcerzak, "Andy Serkis as Actor, Body and Gorilla," in *Cinephilia in the Age of Digital Reproduction: Film, Pleasure and Digital Culture,* ed. Scott Balcerzak and Jason Sperb (London: Wallflower, 2009), 197.

5. Balcerzak, 198.

6. Shane Denson, "Crazy Cameras, Discorrelated Images, and the Post-perceptual Mediation of Post-cinematic Affect," in *Post-Cinema: Theorizing 21st-Century Film,* ed. Shane Denson and Julia Leyda (Sussex, U.K.: REFRAME Books, 2016), 194.

7. Vivian Sobchack, *Carnal Thoughts: Embodiment and Moving Image Culture* (Berkeley: University of California Press, 2004), 135.

8. Sandra Annett, *Animating Fan Communities: Transcultural Flows and Frictions* (New York: Palgrave Macmillan, 2014).

9. Sylvie Bissonnette, *Affect and Embodied Meaning in Animation: Becoming-Animated* (New York: Routledge, 2019), 30.

10. Torben Grodal, *Embodied Visions: Evolution, Emotion, Culture, and Film* (Oxford: Oxford University Press, 2009).

11. Kate Ince, *The Body and the Screen: Female Subjectivities in Contemporary Women's Cinema* (London: Bloomsbury, 2017); Katharina Lindner, *Film Bodies: Queer Feminist Encounters with Gender and Sexuality in Cinema* (London: I. B. Tauris, 2018); Saige Walton, *Cinema's Baroque Flesh: Film, Phenomenology and the Art of Entanglement* (Amsterdam: Amsterdam University Press, 2016).

12. Lev Manovich, *The Language of New Media* (Cambridge, Mass.: MIT Press, 2000), 294.

13. Spencer Shaw, *Film Consciousness: From Phenomenology to Deleuze* (Jefferson, N.C.: McFarland, 2008), 39.

14. Maurice Merleau-Ponty, "Film and the New Psychology," in *Sense and Non-sense* (Evanston, Ill.: Northwestern University Press, 1964), 58.

15. Deborah Levitt, *The Animatic Apparatus: Animation, Vitality and the Futures of the Image* (Winchester, U.K.: Zero Books, 2018), 59.

16. Levitt, 58.

17. Thomas Lamarre, *The Anime Ecology: A Genealogy of Television, Animation, and Game Media* (Minneapolis: University of Minnesota Press, 2018), 203.

18. Steven Shaviro, "Post-Continuity: An Introduction," in Denson and Leyda, *Post-Cinema*, 60.

19. Laura Mulvey, "Visual Pleasure and Narrative Cinema," *Screen* 16, no. 3 (1975): 6–18.

20. Jean-Louis Baudry, "Ideological Effects of the Basic Cinematographic Apparatus," trans. Alan Williams, *Film Quarterly* 28, no. 2 (1974–75): 39–47.

21. Merleau-Ponty, "Film and the New Psychology," 71.

22. Vivian Sobchack, *The Address of the Eye* (Princeton, N.J.: Princeton University Press, 1992), 219.

23. Sobchack, 205.

24. Scott C. Richmond, *Cinema's Bodily Illusions: Flying, Floating, and Hallucinating* (Minneapolis: University of Minnesota Press, 2016), 6.

25. Richmond, 6.

26. Richmond, 17.

27. Richmond, 1.

28. Steven Shaviro, *The Cinematic Body* (Minneapolis: University of Minnesota Press, 1994), 267.

29. Shaviro, 264.

30. Gilles Deleuze and Félix Guattari, *A Thousand Plateaus: Capitalism and Schizophrenia*, trans. Brian Massumi (Minneapolis: University of Minnesota Press, 1987), 279.

31. Elizabeth Grosz, "From 'Intensities and Flows,'" in *The Body*, ed. Tiffany Atkinson, 142–55 (New York: Palgrave Macmillan, 2005).

32. Judith Butler, "Sexual Ideology and Phenomenological Description: A Feminist Critique of Merleau-Ponty's Phenomenology of Perception," in *The Thinking Muse: Feminism and Modern French Philosophy*, ed. Jeffner Allen and Iris Marion Young (Bloomington: Indiana University Press, 1989), 86.

33. Butler, 93.

34. Shaw, *Film Consciousness*, 25.

35. Maurice Merleau-Ponty, *The Visible and the Invisible; Followed by Working Notes*, ed. Claude Lefort, trans. Alphonso Lingis (Evanston. Ill.: Northwestern University Press, 1968), 251–52.

36. Laura U. Marks, *The Skin of the Film: Intercultural Cinema, Embodiment, and the Senses* (Durham, N.C.: Duke University Press, 2000), xi.

37. Marks, 162–64.

38. Marks, 84.

39. Sobchack, *Address of the Eye*, 302.

40. Sobchack, *Carnal Thoughts*, 170.

41. Sobchack, 170.

42. Markos Hadjioannou, "Tracing an Ethics of the Moving Image," in

From Light to Byte: Toward an Ethics of Digital Cinema (Minneapolis: University of Minnesota Press, 2012), 178.

43. Hadjioannou, 197.

44. Hadjioannou, 203.

45. Hadjioannou, 208.

46. Hayles, *How We Became Posthuman,* 2.

47. Hayles, 18.

48. Hayles, 23.

49. Hayles, 49.

50. Hayles, 199.

51. Hayles, 196.

52. Donna Haraway, *Simians, Cyborgs, and Women: The Reinvention of Nature* (New York: Routledge, 1991), 189–95.

53. Hayles, *How We Became Posthuman,* 199.

54. Ingrid Richardson and Carly Harper, "Corporeal Virtuality: The Impossibility of a Fleshless Ontology," *Body, Space, and Technology* 2, no. 2 (2001), https://core.ac.uk/display/11242216.

55. Jennifer M. Barker, *The Tactile Eye: Touch and the Cinematic Experience* (Berkeley: University of California Press, 2009), 137.

56. Barker, 137, emphasis added.

57. Barker, 45.

58. Barker, 117–18.

59. Barker, 118.

60. Sylvie Bissonnette, *Affect and Embodied Meaning in Animation: Becoming-Animated* (New York: Routledge, 2019), 3.

61. Bissonnette, 62.

62. Dan Torre, *Animation—Process, Cognition and Actuality* (New York: Bloomsbury, 2017).

63. Francesco Casetti, *The Lumière Galaxy: Seven Key Words for the Cinema to Come* (New York: Columbia University Press, 2015), 28.

64. Richmond, *Cinema's Bodily Illusions,* 17.

65. Sianne Ngai, *Ugly Feelings* (Cambridge, Mass.: Harvard University Press, 2005).

66. Sobchack, *Address of the Eye,* 205.

67. Elizabeth Bell, Lynda Haas, and Laura Sells, eds., *From Mouse to Mermaid: The Politics of Film, Gender, and Culture* (Bloomington: Indiana University Press, 1999); Johnson Cheu, ed., *Diversity in Disney Films: Critical Essays on Race, Ethnicity, Gender, Sexuality and Disability* (Jefferson, N.C.: McFarland, 2013).

68. Jane Batkin, *Identity in Animation: A Journey into Self, Difference, Culture and the Body* (London: Routledge, 2017); Joanna Bouldin, "The Body, Animation and the Real: Race, Reality and the Rotoscope in Betty Boop," *Conference Proceedings for Affective Encounters: Rethinking Embodiment in Feminist Media Studies,* ed. A. Koivunen and S. Paasonen, 48–54 (Turku:

University of Turku, School of Art, Literature and Music, Media Studies, 2001).

69. Grodal, *Embodied Visions*, 27–36.

70. Hannah Frank, "Traces of the World: Cel Animation and Photography," *Animation: An Interdisciplinary Journal* 11, no. 1 (2016): 23–39; Mihaela Mihailova, "Collaboration without Representation: Labor Issues in Motion and Performance Capture," *Animation: An Interdisciplinary Journal* 11, no. 1 (2016): 40–58.

71. Suzanne Buchan, "Animation Spectatorship: The Quay Brothers' Animated 'Worlds,'" in *Animated Worlds*, ed. Suzanne Buchan (London: John Libbey, 2007), 102.

72. Buchan, 98.

73. Paul Kanyuk, "Brain Springs: Fast Physics for Large Crowds in WALL•E," *IEEE Computer Graphics and Applications* 29, no. 4 (2009): 19–25.

74. Thomas Lamarre, *The Anime Machine: A Media Theory of Animation* (Minneapolis: University of Minnesota Press, 2009); Lamarre, *The Anime Ecology: A Genealogy of Television, Animation, and Game Media* (Minneapolis: University of Minnesota Press, 2018).

75. Lamarre, *Anime Machine*, 200.

76. Lamarre, 201.

77. Gilles Deleuze, *Cinema 2: The Time-Image* (Minnesota: University of Minnesota Press, 1989).

78. Paul Virilio, *War and Cinema: The Logistics of Perception* (London: Verso, 1989).

79. Stephen Prince, "Through the Looking Glass: Philosophical Toys and Digital Visual Effects," *Projections: The Journal for Movies and Mind* 4, no. 2 (2010): 20.

80. Alan Cholodenko, "(The) Death (of) the Animator; or, The Felicity of Felix. Part 1," *Animation Studies: Animated Dialogues* (2009): 5.

81. Deleuze, *Cinema 2*, 195.

1. Haptic Visuality in Cinematic Anime

1. Lenn E. Goodman, trans., *Avicenna* (London: Routledge 1992), 155.

2. Sobchack, *Carnal Thoughts*, 170.

3. Jean Baudrillard, *Simulacra and Simulation*, trans. Sheila Faria Glaser (1988; repr., Ann Arbor: University of Michigan Press, 1994), 1.

4. Norbert Wiener, *Cybernetics; or, Control and Communication in the Animal and the Machine* (1948; repr., Cambridge, Mass.: MIT Press, 2019), 182.

5. Baudrillard, *Simulacra and Simulation*, 1.

6. David Abram, *The Spell of the Sensuous: Perception and Language in a More-Than-Human World* (New York: Pantheon Books, 1996), 48.

7. Shaw, *Film Consciousness*, 46.

8. Vivian Sobchack, "Animation and Automation, or, the Incredible Effortfulness of Being," *Screen* 50, no. 4 (2009): 378.

9. Sobchack, 390.

10. Roland Barthes, *Camera Lucida: Reflections on Photography* (New York: Hill and Wang, 1980), 96.

11. Sobchack, "Animation and Automation," 390–91.

12. Daniel Yacavone, "Film and the Phenomenology of Art: Reappraising Merleau-Ponty on Cinema as Form, Medium, and Expression," *New Literary History* 47, no. 1 (2016): 159–85.

13. Yacavone, 172.

14. Yacavone, 176.

15. Merleau-Ponty, *The Visible and the Invisible,* 139.

16. Merleau-Ponty, 146.

17. Saige Walton, *Cinema's Baroque Flesh: Film, Phenomenology and the Art of Entanglement* (Amsterdam: Amsterdam University Press, 2016).

18. Abram, *Spell of the Sensuous,* 31–32.

19. Abram, 48.

20. Levitt, *Animatic Apparatus,* 59.

21. Levitt, 58.

22. Levitt, 59.

23. Bissonnette, *Affect and Embodied Meaning in Animation,* 3.

24. Merleau-Ponty, *The Visible and the Invisible,* 139.

25. Pall Wells, *Understanding Animation* (New York: Routledge, 1998), 25.

26. Thomas Looser, "From Edogawa to Miyazaki: Cinematic and Anime-ic Architectures of Early and Late Twentieth-Century Japan," *Japan Forum* 14, no. 2 (2002): 302.

27. Looser, 310.

28. Looser, 319.

29. Lamarre, *Anime Machine,* 19.

30. Lamarre, xxvii.

31. Lamarre, 42.

32. Donald Crafton, *Shadow of a Mouse: Performance, Belief, and World-Making in Animation* (Berkeley: University of California Press, 2012), 22–24.

33. Stevie Suan, *Anime's Identity: Performativity and Form beyond Japan* (Minneapolis: University of Minnesota Press, 2021), 229.

34. Lamarre, 55.

35. Bissonnette, *Affect and Embodied Meaning in Animation,* 123.

36. Lamarre, *Anime Machine,* 82.

37. Drew Ayers, *Spectacular Posthumanism: The Digital Vernacular of Visual Effects* (New York: Bloomsbury, 2019), 205.

38. Ju-yu Catherine Cheng, "Ecological Time in Hayao Miyazaki's Nausicaä of the Valley of the Wind," *NTU Studies in Language and Literature* 75, no. 38 (2017): 75–100; Susan Napier, *Miyazakiworld* (New Haven, Conn.: Yale University Press, 2018); Mark Schilling, "Miyazaki Hayao and Studio Ghibli, the Animation Hit Factory," *Japan Quarterly* 44, no. 1 (1997): 30–40.

39. Andrew Osmond, "A Letter to Momo," *All the Anime* (blog), July 10, 2015, https://blog.alltheanime.com/a-letter-to-momo/.

40. Susan Napier, *The Fantastic in Modern Japanese Literature: The Subversion of Modernity* (London: Routledge, 1996), 100.

41. Michael Dylan Foster, *Pandemonium and Parade: Japanese Monsters and the Culture of Yōkai* (Berkeley: University of California Press, 2009), 6.

42. Foster, 7.

43. Sergei Eisenstein, *Eisenstein on Disney*, ed. and trans. Jay Leyda (London: Seagull Books, 1986).

44. Melek Ortabasi, "(Re)animating Folklore: Raccoon Dogs, Foxes, and Other Supernatural Japanese Citizens in Takahata Isao's *Tanuki Gassen Pompoko*," *Marvels and Tales: Journal of Fairy-Tale Studies* 27, no. 2 (2013): 256.

45. Napier, *Fantastic in Modern Japanese Literature*, 100.

46. Joon Yang Kim, "South Korea and the Sub-empire of Anime: Kinesthetics of Subcontracted Animation," *Mechademia* 9 (2014): 90.

47. Kim, 94–95.

48. Kim, 91.

49. Theron Martin, "My Beautiful Girl Mari [Review]," *Anime News Network*, August 24, 2005, https://www.animenewsnetwork.com/review/my-beautiful-girl-mari.

50. Shaw, *Film Consciousness*, 57.

51. Kim, "South Korea and the Sub-empire of Anime," 95.

52. Kim, 96.

53. Lamarre, *Anime Ecology*, 27.

54. Marks, *Skin of the Film*, 61.

55. Marks, 9.

56. Susan Napier, "Matter out of Place: Carnival, Containment, and Cultural Recovery in Miyazaki's Spirited Away," *Journal of Japanese Studies* 32, no. 2 (2006): 295.

57. Kim, "South Korea and the Sub-empire of Anime," 100–101.

2. Liveliness in the Hybrid Film

1. William D. Routt, "De Anime," in *The Illusion of Life II: More Essays on Animation*, ed. Alan Cholodenko (Sydney: Power, 2007), 174.

2. Giorgio Agamben, *Homo Sacer: Sovereign Power and Bare Life* (Redwood City, Calif.: Stanford University Press, 1998).

3. Kenny K. N. Chow, *Animation, Embodiment, and Digital Media: Human Experience of Technological Liveliness* (New York: Palgrave Macmillan, 2013), 63.

4. Levitt, *Animatic Apparatus*, 58.

5. Sianne Ngai, *Ugly Feelings* (Cambridge, Mass.: Harvard University Press, 2009).

6. "How Disney Combines Living Actors with His Cartoon Characters," *Popular Science*, September 1944, 110, http://www.dix-project.net/rsiDetails.php?rsiID=1164.

7. "How Disney Combines."

8. Frederick S. Litten, "A Mixed Picture: Drawn Animation/Live Action Hybrids Worldwide from the 1960s to the 1980s," April 24, 2011, http://litten.de/fulltext/mixedpix.pdf.

9. Franziska Bruckner, "Hybrid Image, Hybrid Montage: Film Analytical Parameters for Live Action/Animation Hybrids," *Animation* 10, no. 1 (2015): 22–41.

10. Alan Cholodenko, "Who Framed Roger Rabbit, or the Framing of Animation," in *The Illusion of Life: Essays on Animation,* ed. Alan Cholodenko (Sydney: Power, 1991), 210.

11. Cholodenko, 280.

12. Jacques Derrida, *Of Grammatology,* trans. Gayatri Spivak (Baltimore: Johns Hopkins University Press, 1976), 158.

13. Cary Elza, "Alice in Cartoonland: Childhood, Gender, and Imaginary Space in Early Disney Animation," *Animation* 9, no. 1 (2014): 7–26; Bell et al., *From Mouse to Mermaid*; Cheu, *Diversity in Disney Films*; Jennifer A. Sandlin and Julie C. Garlen, eds., *Disney, Culture, and Curriculum* (New York: Routledge, 2016).

14. Khelli R. Willetts, "Cannibals and Coons: Blackness in the Early Days of Walt Disney," in Cheu, *Diversity in Disney Films,* 11.

15. Willetts, 15–16.

16. Willetts, 9.

17. Willetts, 20.

18. Dolores Martinez, "Bodies of Future Memories: The Japanese Body in Science Fiction Anime," *Contemporary Japan* 27, no. 1 (2015): 72.

19. Iris M. Young, "Throwing Like a Girl: A Phenomenology of Feminine Bodily Comportment, Motility and Spatiality," *Human Studies* 3, no. 2 (1980): 137–56.

20. J. P. Telotte, *Animating Space: From Mickey to Wall-E* (Lexington: University Press of Kentucky, 2010), 149.

21. Telotte, 149–50.

22. Tellotte, 149.

23. Ngai, *Ugly Feelings,* 91.

24. Eisenstein, *Eisenstein on Disney,* 70.

25. *Oxford English Dictionary* (Oxford: Oxford University Press, 2022), s.v. "incorporation."

26. Deleuze and Guattari, *A Thousand Plateaus,* 163.

27. Brian Massumi, "Translator's Foreword: The Pleasures of Philosophy," in Deleuze and Guattari, *A Thousand Plateaus,* xvi.

28. Grodal, *Embodied Visions,* 20.

29. Ngai, *Ugly Feelings,* 20.

30. Ngai, 19–20.

31. Ngai, 91.

32. Ngai, 102–3.

33. Ngai, 107.

34. Ngai, 116.

35. Karl F. Cohen, *Forbidden Animation: Censored Cartoons and Blacklisted Animators in America* (Jefferson, N.C.: McFarland, 2013), 54.

36. Harold Martin, "'Song of South' Wins High Praise," *Atlanta Constitution,* October 15, 1946, 9, https://ajc.newspapers.com/image/398022472/.

37. Martin, 9.

38. Jason Sperb, *Disney's Most Notorious Film: Race, Convergence, and the Hidden Histories of "Song of the South"* (Austin: University of Texas Press, 2012), 96.

39. Sperb, 69.

40. Bosley Crowther, "Spanking Disney; Walt Is Chastised for 'Song of the South,'" *New York Times,* December 8, 1946.

41. Sperb, *Disney's Most Notorious Film,* 69–70.

42. Sperb, 15.

43. Jeremy Blum, "'Song of the South' Trends as Fans Debate Legacy of 'Disney's Most Notorious Film,'" *Huffington Post,* June 10, 2020, https://www.huffpost.com/entry/song-of-the-south-disney_n_5ee0f564c5b66552b9a6de28.

44. Alison Durkee, "A Year after Disney Said It Would Revamp Racist Splash Mountain, It's Still Open and Company Won't Say When Work Will Start," *Forbes,* August 11, 2021, https://www.forbes.com/sites/alisondurkee/2021/08/11/a-year-after-disney-said-it-would-revamp-racist-splash-mountain-its-still-open-and-company-wont-say-when-work-will-start/.

45. Sperb, *Disney's Most Notorious Film,* 209.

46. Franz Fanon, *Black Skin, White Masks, trans.* Charles Lam Markmann (London: Pluto Press, 1986), 111–12.

47. Ngai, *Ugly Feelings,* 335.

48. https://www.imdb.com/title/tt0093101/plotsummary.

49. Susan Napier, *Anime from Akira to Howl's Moving Castle: Experiencing Contemporary Japanese Animation* (New York: St. Martin's, 2005), 31.

50. Richard Harrington, "Twilight of the Cockroaches (NR)," *Washington Post,* October 6, 1989, https://www.washingtonpost.com/wp-srv/style/longterm/movies/videos/twilightofthecockroachesnrharrington_a0aacd.htm.

51. David Morley and Kevin Robins, "Techno-Orientalism: Japan Panic," in *Spaces of Identity: Global Media, Electronic Landscapes and Cultural Boundaries,* 147–73 (London: Routledge, 1995).

52. Susan Sontag, "Notes on Camp," in *Camp: Queer Aesthetics and the Performing Subject—a Reader,* ed. Fabio Cleto (1964; repr., Ann Arbor: University of Michigan Press, 1999), 59.

53. John R. Dilworth, "The Cockroaches of Joe's Apartment," *Animation World Network* 1, no. 6 (1996), http://www.awn.com/mag/issue1.6/articles/diljoe1.6.html.

54. Geoff King, *Film Comedy* (London: Wallflower Press, 2002), 65.

55. Mulvey, "Visual Pleasure and Narrative Cinema."

56. Kristoffer Noheden, "Magic Art and Minor Myths: Jan Švankmajer's Transmutation of Material Reality," in *Surrealism, Cinema, and the Search for a New Myth*, 159–216 (Cham, Switzerland: Palgrave Macmillan, 2017).

3. Phenopower in Live-Action Remakes

1. "The Journey to The Lion King," *The Lion King*, DVD/Blu-ray (Burbank, Calif.: Walt Disney Home Entertainment, 2019).
2. Jody Duncan, "The Lion King: A Moon-Shot Movie," *Cinefex* 166 (August 2019). My thanks to Mihaela Mihailova for bringing this quotation to my attention.
3. Levitt, *Animatic Apparatus*.
4. Josh Rottenberg, "'The Lion King': Is It Animated or Live-Action? It's Complicated," *LA Times*, July 19, 2019, https://www.latimes.com/entertainment-arts/movies/story/2019-07-19/the-lion-king-remake-animation-live-action-photo-real.
5. Yohana Desta, "Is the New Lion King Animated or Live-Action? Even Jon Favreau Isn't Sure," *Vanity Fair*, May 30, 2019, https://www.vanityfair.com/hollywood/2019/05/lion-king-animated-or-live-action-jon-favreau.
6. Chris Pallant, "Disney-Formalism: Rethinking 'Classic Disney,'" *Animation* 5, no. 3 (2010): 341–52.
7. Elizabeth Stephens, "Sensation Machine: Film, Phenomenology and the Training of the Senses," *Continuum* 26, no. 4 (2012): 529.
8. Prince, "Through the Looking Glass," 20.
9. Prince, 20.
10. Prince, 20–21.
11. Manovich, *Language of New Media*, 305.
12. Barker, *Tactile Eye*, 69.
13. Christopher Holliday, *The Computer-Animated Film: Industry, Style and Genre* (Edinburgh: Edinburgh University Press, 2018), 14.
14. Stephens, "Sensation Machine," 529.
15. Stephens, 536.
16. Stephens, 536.
17. Lamarre, *Anime Ecology*, 200.
18. Baudry, "Ideological Effects."
19. Lamarre, 203.
20. Lamarre, 91.
21. Denson, "Crazy Cameras," 194.
22. James L. Hodge, *Sensations of History: Animation and New Media Art* (Minnesota: University of Minnesota Press, 2019), 8–10.
23. Hodge, 15, emphasis original.
24. Wells, *Understanding Animation*, 25.
25. Holliday, *Computer-Animated Film*, 39.
26. Holliday, 15.
27. Holliday, 40.
28. Masahiro Mori, "The Uncanny Valley: The Original Essay by Masahiro

Mori," 1970, trans. Karl F. MacDorman and Norri Kageki, *IEEE Spectrum*, June 12, 2012, https://spectrum.ieee.org/the-uncanny-valley; Nicholas Bestor, "The Technologically Determined Decade: Robert Zemeckis, Andy Serkis, and the Promotion of Performance Capture," *Animation* 11, no. 2 (2016): 176.

29. Bestor, "Technologically Determined Decade," 174.

30. Bestor, 176.

31. Balcerzak, "Andy Serkis as Actor, Body and Gorilla," 210.

32. Bestor, "Technologically Determined Decade," 182.

33. Rocío Carrasco, quoted in Mihailova, "Collaboration without Representation," 48.

34. Drew Ayres, *Spectacular Posthumanism: The Digital Vernacular of Visual Effects* (New York: Bloomsbury, 2019), 80–81.

35. Mulvey, "Visual Pleasure and Narrative Cinema."

36. Jacques Derrida, *Of Grammatology*, trans. Gayatri Chakravorty Spivak (Baltimore: Johns Hopkins University Press, 1974), 157–62.

37. Holliday, *Computer-Animated Film*, 61.

38. Bérénice Bonhomme, "Disney, remakes et reprises," *Mise au point* 10 (2018): para. 6.

39. Bonhomme, para. 9.

40. Pamela McClintock, "Disney and the New Science of a Fairy-Tale Remake," *Hollywood Reporter* 421, no. 8 (2015): para. 1.

41. Adam B. Vary, "'Bambi' Is Next Up for Disney 'Live-Action' Remake," *Variety*, January 24, 2020, https://variety.com/2020/film/news/bambi-disney-remake-1203479063/.

42. Nicholas Benson, "All Hail Disney: Establishing Corporate Authorship through Industrial Intertextuality," *Quarterly Review of Film and Video* 37, no. 1 (2020): 26.

43. Djao Wei, "Opinion Status as Ethnic Identity in the Chinese Diaspora," *Journal of Contemporary Asia* 32 (2002): 363.

44. Mingwu Xu and Chuanmao Tian, "Cultural Deformations and Reformulations: A Case Study of Disney's *Mulan* in English and Chinese," *Critical Arts* 27, no. 2 (2013): 191.

45. Ariel Dorfman and Armand Mattelart, *How to Read Donald Duck: Imperialist Ideology in the Disney Comic* (Nicaragua: International General, 1971).

46. Xu and Tian, "Cultural Deformations and Reformulations," 203.

47. Zhuoyi Wang, "Cultural 'Authenticity' as a Conflict-Ridden Hypotext: *Mulan* (1998), *Mulan Joins the Army* (1939), and a Millennium-Long Intertextual Metamorphosis," *Arts* 10 (July 2020): 1–16.

48. Wang, 5.

49. Wang, 78.

50. Joseph M. Chan, "Disneyfying and Globalizing the Chinese Legend Mulan," in *In Search of Boundaries: Communication, Nation-States, and Cul-*

tural Identities: A Study of Transculturation, ed. Joseph Man Chan and Bryce Telfer McIntyre (Westport, Conn.: Ablex, 2002), 241.

51. Jingan Young, "The Problem with Mulan: Why the Live-Action Remake Is a Lightning Rod for Controversy," *Guardian*, September 7, 2020, https://www.theguardian.com/film/2020/sep/07/mulan-disney-live-action-remake-hong-kong-china.

52. Chan, "Disneyfying and Globalizing," 243.

53. Chan, 228.

54. Chan, 228.

55. Xu and Tian, "Cultural Deformations and Reformulations," 190.

56. Wang, "Cultural 'Authenticity,'" 228, emphasis added.

57. David Bordwell, "Intensified Continuity: Visual Style in Contemporary American Film," *Film Quarterly* 55, no. 3 (2002): 24.

58. Bruce Isaacs, "The Mechanics of Continuity in Michael Bay's Transformers Franchise," *Senses of Cinema* 75 (2005): paras. 3, 7, http://www.sensesofcinema.com/2015/michael-bay-dossier/michael-bay-transformers-continuity/.

59. Denson, "Crazy Cameras."

60. Eric C. Mullis, "Martial Somaesthetics," *Journal of Aesthetic Education* 47, no. 3 (2013): 97.

61. Mullis, 108.

62. Mullis, 110.

63. Mullis, 101.

64. Mullis, 98.

65. Rebecca Ratcliffe, "Pro-democracy Boycott of Disney's Mulan Builds Online via #milkteaalliance," *Guardian*, September 4, 2020, https://www.theguardian.com/world/2020/sep/04/pro-democracy-boycott-of-disneys-mulan-builds-online-via-milkteaalliance.

66. Kōichi Iwabuchi, *Recentering Globalization: Popular Culture and Japanese Transnationalism* (Durham, N.C.: Duke University Press, 2002).

67. Marc Steinberg, *Anime's Media Mix: Franchising Toys and Characters in Japan* (Minneapolis: University of Minnesota Press, 2012), viii.

68. Marc Steinberg, *The Platform Economy: How Japan Transformed the Consumer Internet* (Minneapolis: University of Minnesota Press, 2019), 10.

69. Hitomi Yoshida, "The Localisation of the Hana Yori Dango Text: Plural Modernities in East Asia," *New Voices* 4 (2011): 78–99.

70. Ian Ang, *Watching Dallas: Soap Opera and the Melodramatic Imagination*, trans. Della Couling (1982; repr., London: Routledge, 1989).

71. Northrop Davis, *Anime and Manga Go to Hollywood* (New York: Bloomsbury, 2015).

72. Matthew Giles, "We Talked to the 'Ghost in the Shell' Director about Weed, Whitewashing, and Cyberpunk," *Vice*, March 31, 2107, https://www.vice.com/en/article/538qnn/ghost-in-the-shell-director-rupert-sanders.

73. James Rendell, "'I Am (Not) Major': Anti-fan Memes of Paramount

Pictures' *Ghost in the Shell* Marketing Campaign," *New Review of Film and Television Studies* 19 (2021): 13–14.

74. Sandra Annett, *Anime Fan Communities: Transcultural Flows and Friction* (New York: Palgrave Macmillan, 2014).

75. Matt Hills, "Transnational Cult and/as Neoliberalism: The Liminal Economies of Anime Fansubbers," *Transnational Cinemas* 8, no. 1 (2017): 82–83.

76. Nick Valdez, "Detective Pikachu Director Hopes to Please Hardcore Pokemon Fans," *comicbook*, May 7, 2019. https://comicbook.com/anime/news/detective-pikachu-hardcore-pokemon-fans-rob-letterman-comments/.

77. "Pokémon: Detective Pikachu," Box Office Mojo, http://www.boxofficemojo.com/release/rl2827781633/weekend/.

78. Lamarre, *Anime Ecology*, 81.

79. Lamarre, 91.

80. Anne Allison, *Millennial Monsters: Japanese Toys and the Global Imagination* (Berkeley: University of California Press, 2006); David Buckingham and Julian Sefton-Green, "Structure, Agency, and Pedagogy in Children's Media Culture," in *Pikachu's Global Adventure*, ed. Joseph Tobin, 12–33 (Durham, N.C.: Duke University Press, 2004); Christine R. Yano, "Panic Attacks: Anti-Pokémon Voices in Global Markets," in Tobin, *Pikachu's Global Adventure*, 108–40.

81. Lamarre, *Anime Ecology*, 87.

82. Peter Dionne, "How 'Pokémon Detective Pikachu' Was Animated," *Movies Insider*, June 1, 2019, https://www.businessinsider.com/how-pokemon-detective-pikachu-was-animated-ryan-reynolds-vfx-2019-5.

83. Sharon L. Snyder and David T. Mitchell, "Re-engaging the Body: Disability Studies and the Resistance to Embodiment," *Public Culture* 13, no. 3 (2001): 367–89.

84. Oona McGee, "Pokémon: Detective Pikachu Movie Trailer Surprises Fans with First Look at Live-Action Characters," *Sora News 24*, November 13, 2018.

85. Joey Paur, "First Reactions to DETECTIVE PIKACHU Have Rolled In and People Seem to Love It!," *Geek Tyrant*, April 24, 2019, https://geektyrant.com/news/the-first-reactions-to-detective-pikachu-have-rolled-in-and-people-seem-to-love-it.

86. Kristen M. Daly, "Cinema 3.0: The Interactive-Image," *Cinema Journal* 50, no. 1 (2010): 81–82.

87. Hayles, *How We Became Posthuman*, 1.

88. Daniel Yacavone, "Film and the Phenomenology of Art: Reappraising Merleau-Ponty on Cinema as Form, Medium, and Expression," *New Literary History* 47, no. 1 (2016): 182–83.

4. Time and Reanimation in Electro Swing Music Videos

1. Deleuze, *Cinema 2*, 3.

2. Deleuze, 195.

3. Donald Crafton, *Before Mickey: The Animated Film 1898–1928* (1982; repr., Cambridge, Mass.: MIT Press, 1993), 25.
4. Hodge, *Sensations of History,* 27.
5. Deleuze, *Cinema 2,* 12.
6. Deleuze, 189.
7. Deleuze, 265, emphasis added.
8. Deleuze, 267, emphasis added.
9. Daly, "Cinema 3.0."
10. Shaviro, "Post-continuity."
11. Sergi Sánchez, "Towards a Non-Time Image: Notes on Deleuze in the Digital Era," in Denson and Leyda, *Post-Cinema,* 183.
12. Denson, "Crazy Cameras."
13. Hodge, *Sensations of History,* 30.
14. Hodge, 15.
15. Deleuze, *Cinema 2,* 99.
16. Sandra Annett, "The Nostalgic Remediation of Cinema in Hugo and Paprika," *Journal of Adaptation in Film and Performance* 7, no. 2 (2014): 172.
17. Susanne Scheibe, Alexandra M. Freund, and Paul B. Baltes, "Toward a Developmental Psychology of Sehnsucht (Life Longings): The Optimal (Utopian) Life," *Developmental Psychology* 43, no. 3 (2007): 778–95.
18. Deleuze, *Cinema 2,* 194.
19. Jason Sperb, *Flickers of Film: Nostalgia in the Time of Digital Cinema* (New Brunswick, N.J.: Rutgers University Press, 2016).
20. Kristin McGee, *Remixing European Jazz Culture* (New York: Routledge, 2020), 210.
21. Nick Wiltsher, "The Aesthetics of Electronic Dance Music, Part I: History, Genre, Scenes, Identity, Blackness," *Philosophy Compass* 11, no. 8 (2016): 415–25.
22. Wiltsher, 416.
23. Wiltsher, 417.
24. Wiltsher, 417.
25. Gabriela Jiménez, "'Something 2 Dance 2': Electro Hop in 1980s Los Angeles and Its Afrofuturist Link," *Black Music Research Journal* 31, no. 1 (2011): 131–44.
26. Chris Inglis, "Electro Swing: Re-introduction of the Sounds of the Past into the Music of the Future," in *Popular Music in the Post-digital Age: Politics, Economy, Culture and Technology,* ed. Ewa Mazierska, Les Gillon, and Tony Rigg (New York: Bloomsbury, 2019), 193.
27. Inglis, 193.
28. McGee, *Remixing European Jazz Culture,* 173–74.
29. McGee, 172.
30. Scheibe et al., "Toward a Developmental Psychology of Sehnsucht," 778.
31. Scheibe et al., 778.
32. Scheibe et al., 781.

33. Deleuze, *Cinema 2,* 195.

34. Rhea Vichot, "Listen to the Plastic Beat: Anglophonic Fandom of City Pop Music and Sehnsucht," paper presented at the Mechademia Asian Conference: Ecologies, virtual conference, Kyoto Manga Museum, Kyoto, Japan, June 5–6, 2021.

35. Cribblingdepression, "warm nights in tokyo [city pop/シティポップ]," YouTube video, May 26, 2019, https://www.youtube.com/watch?v=GOVPpLtJUIg.

36. Robin James, quoted in Wiltsher, "Aesthetics of Electronic Dance Music, Part I," 421.

37. Wiltsher, "Aesthetics of Electronic Dance Music, Part I," 421.

38. Wiltsher, 421.

39. Wiltsher, 422.

40. Cache McClay, "Why Black TikTok Creators Have Gone on Strike," BBC News, July 15, 2021, https://www.bbc.com/news/world-us-canada-57841055.

41. "Acknowledging the Black Roots of Swing and Jazz," Swing Patrol, https://mel.swingpatrol.com/resource/acknowledging-the-black-roots-of-swing-and-jazz/.

42. Alan Cholodenko, "'First Principles' of Animation," in *Animating Film Theory,* ed. Karen Beckman (Durham, N.C.: Duke University Press, 2014), 98–110.

43. Jacques Derrida, *Life Death: The Seminars of Jacques Derrida,* ed. Pascale-Anne Brault and Peggy Kamuf, trans. Pascale-Anne Brault and Michael Naas (Chicago: University of Chicago Press, 2020).

44. Cholodenko, "Death (of) the Animator," 5, emphasis original.

45. Jay David Bolter and Richard A. Grusin, *Remediation: Understanding New Media* (Cambridge, Mass.: MIT Press, 1999), 14–15.

46. Henry Jenkins, quoted in Wells, *Understanding Animation,* 153.

47. Haraway, *Simians, Cyborgs, and Women,* 189–95.

48. Arjun Appadurai, *Modernity at Large: Cultural Dimensions of Globalization* (Minneapolis: University of Minnesota Press, 1996), 30.

49. Appadurai, 31.

50. Andreas M. Baranowski and Heiko Hecht, "The Auditory Kuleshov Effect: Multisensory Integration in Movie Editing," *Perception* 43, no. 10 (2017): 1061–70.

51. Sandra Annett, "World War Cute," in *Anime Fan Communities: Transcultural Flows and Frictions,* 49–76 (New York: Palgrave Macmillan, 2014).

52. Carlito Pablo, "Protest Planned against Vancouver Gig of Chinese Man Hip-Hop Band from France," *Georgia Straight,* March 28, 2018, https://www.straight.com/news/1050036/protest-planned-against-vancouver-gig-chinese-man-hip-hop-band-france.

53. Carol Vernallis, *Experiencing Music Video: Aesthetics and Cultural Context* (New York: Colombia University Press, 2004), x.

54. Vernallis, 97.

55. Vernallis, 97, emphasis added.

56. McGee, *Remixing European Jazz Culture,* 201.

57. McGee, 212.

58. Caravan Palace, "Caravan Palace—Supersonics—Making-of Video," YouTube video, 00:30, February 11, 2021, https://www.youtube.com/watch?v=Gw0qzA8U5zE.

59. Deleuze, *Cinema 2,* 195.

60. Deleuze, 195.

61. Idoall, "Supersonics—Discussion Thread," Reddit, August 16, 2019, http://www.reddit.com/r/CaravanPalace/comments/cr485z/supersonics_discussion_thread/.

62. Nick Wiltsher, "The Aesthetics of Electronic Dance Music, Part II: Dancers, DJs, Ontology and Aesthetics," *Philosophy Compass* 11, no. 8 (2016): 426.

63. Wiltsher, 427.

64. Merleau-Ponty, *The Visible and the Invisible,* 142.

65. Bissonnette, *Affect and Embodied Meaning in Animation.*

66. TakeSomeCrime, "Parov Stelar—Catgroove (TSC—Forsythe)," YouTube video, 00:30, February 20, 2010, https://www.youtube.com/watch?v=twqM56f_cVo.

67. Wiltsher, "Aesthetics of Electronic Dance Music, Part II," 433.

68. Wiltsher, 433.

69. Vernallis, *Experiencing Music Video,* 97.

5. Virtual (Idol) Corporeality and the Posthuman Flesh

1. Hayles, *How We Became Posthuman,* 5.

2. Bissonnette, *Affect and Embodied Meaning in Animation.*

3. Nakamuraya Yotarō, ed., *Bokarohihyōshū VOCALOCRITIQUE* [Vocalo criticism collection VOCALOCRITIQUE] (Tokyo: White Note, 2012).

4. Itō Hiroyuki, "Interview: Kuriputon Fyūchā Media daihyōtorishimariyakushachō Itō Hiroyuki-shi" [Interview: Crypton Future Media representative director and president Mr. Itō Hiroyuki], in *Hatsune Miku to nakamatachi* [Hatsune Miku and friends] (Tokyo: Yamaha Music Media Corporation, 2012).

5. "Hatsune Miku 'bōkaroido arubamu' ga Tokunaga wo sae, hatsushui" [Hatsune Miku "Vocaloid album" overtakes Tokunaga, reaches #1 for the first time], *Oricon Style,* May 25, 2010, http://www.oricon.co.jp/news/76554/full/.

6. Bamboo Dong, "Hatsune Miku to Open for Lady Gaga," *Anime News Network,* April 16, 2014, https://www.animenewsnetwork.com/interest/2014-04-16/hatsune-miku-to-open-for-lady-gaga.

7. Rachel Tackett, "Wanna Sleep Next to Hatsune Miku? There's an App for That!," *Sora News* 24 (October 8, 2013), https://soranews24.com/2013/10/08/wanna-sleep-with-hatsune-miku-theres-an-app-for-that/.

8. Miyazaki Toshiki, "AI Love You: Japanese Man Not Alone in 'Marriage' to Virtual Character," *Mainichi*, April 18, 2020, https://mainichi.jp/english/articles/20200417/p2a/00m/0na/027000c.

9. Akiko Sugawa-Shimada, "Emerging '2.5-Dimensional' Culture: Character-Oriented Cultural Practices and 'Community of Preferences' as a New Fandom in Japan and Beyond," *Mechademia: Second Arc* 12, no. 2 (2020): 124.

10. Sugawa-Shimada, 124.

11. Deleuze and Guattari, *A Thousand Plateaus*, 165.

12. Saitō Tamaki, *Sentō bishōjo no seishin bunseki* (Tokyo: Ōta Shuppan, 2000), trans. J. Keith Vincent and Dawn Lawson as *Beautiful Fighting Girl* (Minneapolis: University of Minnesota Press, 2011), 163.

13. Azuma Hiroki, *Dōbutsuka suru posutomodan: otaku kara mita nihon shokai* (Tokyo: Kōdansha Gendai Shinsho, 2001), trans. Jonathan E. Abel and Shion Kono as *Otaku: Japan's Database Animals* (Minneapolis: University of Minnesota Press, 2009), 87.

14. Deleuze and Guattari, *A Thousand Plateaus*, 154.

15. Deleuze and Guattari, 257.

16. Tim Jordan, "Collective Bodies: Raving and the Politics of Gilles Deleuze and Felix Guattari," *Body and Society* 1 (1995): 125–44.

17. Patrick Galbraith, "Moe: Exploring Virtual Potential in Post-millennial Japan," *electronic journal of contemporary japanese studies*, October 31, 2009, Article 5, http://www.japanesestudies.org.uk/articles/2009/Galbraith.html.

18. Jordan, "Collective Bodies," 138.

19. Kohki Watabe, "Characters' Amnesia in 2.5D Culture: Affective Reception of Bronze Statues of Anime and Manga Characters and Public Sculptures," *Mechademia: Second Arc* 15, no. 2 (2023): 98.

20. Watabe, 98.

21. Watabe, 99.

22. Watabe, 101.

23. Terazawa Kaoru, "'Moe' kara hajimaru fantashii—fujoshi katari" [Moé-born fantasy: The story of fujoshi], *Jidō Bungei* 56, no. 2 (2004): 28–31.

24. Azuma Hiroki, Itō Gō, and Natsume Fusanosuke, "'Kyara/kyarakutaa' gainen no kanōsei" [The possibility of the concepts "kyara/kyarakutaa"], in *Kontentsu no shisō—manga, anime, raito noberu* [The ideology of contents: Manga, anime, light novels], ed. Azuma Hiroki (Tokyo: Seidosha, 2007), 131.

25. Daniel Black, "The Virtual Ideal: Virtual Idols, Cute Technology and Unclean Biology," *Continuum: Journal of Media and Cultural Studies* 22, no. 1 (2008): 40.

26. Black, 42.

27. Levitt, *Animatic Apparatus*, 96.

28. Levitt, 96.

29. Crypton Future Media, "Miku Expo History," https://mikuexpo.com/history.

30. Nate, "MIKU BREAK ver.0.9 Livestream Announcement!," Vocaloid News Network, November 29, 2021, https://www.vocaloidnews.net/miku-break-ver-0-9-livestream-announcement.

31. Iwashita Hosei, "*The Prince of Tennis* in 2- and 2.5D: Character Growth and Growth into Character," trans. Brian Bergstrom, *Mechademia: Second Arc* 15, no. 2 (2023): 32–46.

32. Akiko Sugawa-Shimada, "Emerging '2.5-Dimensional' Culture," 124–39.

33. Anzai Masayuki, "Boku no moeru shigoto" [My work with "MOE"], *Eizō jōhō media shakaishi* 66, no. 1 (2012): 60.

34. Alex Leavitt and Andrea Horbinski, "Even a Monkey Can Understand Fan Activism: Political Speech, Artistic Expression, and a Public for the Japanese Dōjin Community," in *Transformative Works and Fan Activism*, ed. Henry Jenkins and Sangita Shresthova, special issue, *Transformative Works and Cultures* 10 (2012): para. 5.13, http://journal.transformativeworks.org/index.php/twc/article/view/321/311.

35. Jihoon Kim, "Digital and Postdigital 3D Animation in the Contemporary Chinese Art Scene: Miao Xiaochun and Lu Yang," *Journal of Chinese Cinema* 11, no. 3 (2017): 227–42.

36. Kim, 229.

37. Merleau-Ponty, "Film and the New Psychology," 59.

38. Robin Peckham, "Tortuous Visions of Lu Yang: The Bioart in China," *Digimag* 52 (March 2010): para. 10, http://digicult.it/digimag/issue-052/tortuous-visions-of-lu-yang-the-bioart-in-china/.

39. Peckham, para. 7.

40. Sam Gaskin, "Lu Yang Destroys Self in Motion Capture Performance," *Ocula Magazine*, November 13, 2020, para. 11, https://ocula.com/magazine/art-news/lu-yang-destroys-self-through-motion-capture/.

41. Gaskin, para. 9.

42. Merleau-Ponty, *Film and the New Psychology*, 56.

43. Merleau-Ponty, quoted in Ahmed, *Queer Phenomenology*, 8.

44. Ahmed, *Queer Phenomenology*, 8.

45. Ahmed, 15.

46. Ahmed, 169.

47. Lu Yang, *LuYang Delusional Mandala*, Vimeo, September 30, 2015, https://vimeo.com/141005910.

48. Marks, *Skin of the Film*, xi.

49. Barbara Pollack, *Brand New Art from China: A Generation on the Rise* (London: Bloomsbury, 2018), 139.

50. Chris Coleman, "Lu Yang Interview," Chinese Animation and Game Network, March 7, 2017, http://luyang.asia/2017/03/07/cagn-lu-yang-interview/.

51. Xin Wang, "Uterus Man, Pelvis Chariot, and the Irreverent Video Games of Lu Yang," *Hyperallergic,* November 21, 2014, https://hyperallergic.com/164210/uterus-man-pelvis-chariot-and-the-irreverent-video-games-of-lu-yang/.

52. Peckham, "Tortuous Visions of Lu Yang," para. 22.

53. Kim, "Digital and Postdigital 3D Animation," 234.

54. Lu Yang, "Gigant DOKU—LuYang the Destroyer," Luyang.asia, June 12, 2021, http://luyang.asia/2021/06/12/gigant-doku-luyang-the-destroyer/.

55. Daisy Yan Du, *Animated Encounters: Transnational Movements of Chinese Animation, 1940s–1970s* (Honolulu: University of Hawai'i Press, 2019), 21.

56. Du, 21.

57. Bissonnette, *Affect and Embodied Meaning in Animation,* 3.

Conclusion

1. Ahmed, *Queer Phenomenology,* 8.

2. Frank N. Pieke and Koichi Iwabuchi, "Introduction: The Many Faces of Global East Asia," in *Global East Asia: Into the Twenty-First Century,* ed. Frank N. Pieke and Koichi Iwabuchi (Berkeley: University of California Press, 2021), 5.

3. Thomas Bristow and Rachel C. Harkes, "The New World Order: Anthropocene Anxiety, Climate Grief, Solastalgia," *Global Journal of Archaeology and Anthropology* 5, no. 1 (2018): 1–3.

4. "'Point of No Return': UN Report to Provide Stark Climate Warning," *Al Jazeera,* March 20, 2023, https://www.aljazeera.com/news/2023/3/20/point-of-no-return-un-report-to-provide-stark-climate-warning; Fiona Harvey, "Scientists Deliver 'Final Warning' on Climate Crisis: Act Now or It's Too Late," *Guardian,* March 20, 2023, https://www.theguardian.com/environment/2023/mar/20/ipcc-climate-crisis-report-delivers-final-warning-on-15c.

SELECTED FILMOGRAPHY

A Letter to Momo, dir. Okiura Hiroyuki (Tokyo, Japan: Production I.G., 2011). GKIDS (2014), DVD/Blu-ray, 120 min.

Ban Dan'emon's Monster Hunt at Shōjōji, dir. Kataoka Yoshitarō, 1935. *The Japanese Anime Classic Collection,* disc 3 (Tokyo, Japan: Digital Meme, 2007), DVD, 4 discs, 10 min.

"Black Swamp Village," performed by the Speakeasies Swing Band. YouTube video, 7:45, March 17, 2012, https://www.youtube.com /watch?v=Hc5_S7z5RJk.

Boogie Doodle, dir. Norman McLaren (National Film Board of Canada, 1941). https://www.nfb.ca/film/boogie-doodle/. Streaming video, 3 min.

"Clap Your Hands (Official Video)," performed by Parov Stelar. YouTube video, 3:17, May 13, 2014, https://www.youtube.com/watch?v =EHs7Av5TZhQ.

Cool World, dir. Ralph Bakshi (Los Angeles, Calif.: Bakshi Animation/ Paramount Studios, 1992). Amazon Prime streaming video, 82 min.

"Dark Woods Circus [VOCALOID] Eng Sub," performed by MachigeritaP. YouTube video, 4:00, April 9, 2009, https://www .youtube.com/watch?v=OsjTBdiPq8o.

Electromagnetic Brainology Brain Control Messenger, dir. Lu Yang. Vimeo video, 10:08, January 31, 2018, https://vimeo.com/253722161.

Electromagnetic Brainology Brain Control Messenger_Documentary, dir. Lu Yang. Vimeo video, 14:12, February 2, 2018, https://vimeo.com /253985996.

Gertie the Dinosaur, dir. Winsor McCay (New York: Winsor, 1914). *Winsor McCay: The Master Edition* (Chatsworth, Calif.: Milestone Film and Video, 2004), DVD, 12 min.

Gigant DOKU—LuYang the Destroyer @GarageMuseum, dir. Lu Yang. Vimeo video, 19:12, May 31, 2021, https://vimeo.com/557309137.

Howl's Moving Castle, dir. Miyazaki Hayao (Tokyo, Japan: Studio Ghibli, 2004). Walt Disney Home Entertainment (2006), DVD, 119 min.

I Lost My Body (J'ai perdu mon corps), dir. Jérémy Clapin (Paris: Xilam Studios, 2019). Netflix streaming video, 81 min.

"I've Got That Tune—OFFICIAL VIDEO," performed by Chinese Man. YouTube video, 4:30, November 12, 2009, https://www.youtube.com/watch?v=kqjeNSNuNPM.

Joe's Apartment, dir. John Payson (Hollywood, Calif.: Geffen Film Company/MTV Productions, 1996). Amazon Prime streaming video, 79 min.

"Jolie Coquine," performed by Caravan Palace. YouTube video, 3:46, February 29, 2012, https://www.youtube.com/watch?v=9BoaOsvZmpw.

Jurassic Park, dir. Steven Spielberg (Universal City, Calif.: Amblin Entertainment, 1993). Universal Pictures Home Entertainment (2000), DVD, 127 min.

Jurassic World, dir. Colin Trevorrow (Universal City, Calif.: Amblin Entertainment/Legendary Pictures, 2015). Universal Pictures Home Entertainment (2015), DVD/Blu-ray, 124 min.

The Lion King, dir. Roger Allers and Rob Minkoff (Burbank, Calif.: Walt Disney Studios, 1994). Walt Disney Home Entertainment (2003), DVD, 88 min.

The Lion King, dir. Jon Favreau (Burbank, Calif.: Walt Disney Studios, 2019). Disney+ streaming video, 118 min.

LuYang Delusional Mandala, dir. Lu Yang. Vimeo video, 16:27, September 30, 2015, https://vimeo.com/141005910.

Mulan, dir. Tony Bancroft and Barry Cook (Burbank, Calif.: Walt Disney Studios, 1998). Walt Disney Home Entertainment (2000), DVD, 87 min.

Mulan, dir. Niki Caro (Burbank, Calif.: Walt Disney Studios, 2020). Disney+ streaming video, 115 min.

My Beautiful Girl Mari, dir. Lee Sung-Gang (Seoul, South Korea: Siz Entertainment, 2002). ADV Films (2005), DVD, 80 min.

"Parov Stelar—Catgroove (TSC—Forsythe)," performed by Forsythe. YouTube video, 3:59, February 20, 2010, https://www.youtube.com/watch?v=twqM56f_cVo.

Pokémon: Detective Pikachu, dir. Rob Letterman (Burbank, Calif.: Legendary Pictures, 2019). Netflix streaming video, 104 min.

Pom Poko, dir. Takahata Isao (Tokyo, Japan: Studio Ghibli, 1994). Walt Disney Home Entertainment (2005), DVD, 119 min.

Red Hot Riding Hood, dir. Frederick Bean "Tex" Avery (Culver City, Calif.: MGM Cartoon Studio, 1943). *Tex Avery Screwball Classics,* vol. 1 (Warner Bros. Home Entertainment, 2020), DVD, 7 min.

Ryan, dir. Chris Landreth (National Film Board of Canada, 2004).

Available on YouTube, 13:57, https://www.youtube.com/watch?v=nbkBjZKBLHQ.

"Shoot Him Down! (Official Video)," performed by Alice Francis. YouTube video, 3:47, August 28, 2013, https://www.youtube.com/watch?v=-xE6nONHbV4.

The Skeleton Dance, dir. Walt Disney (Los Angeles, Calif.: Disney Brothers Cartoon Studios, 1929). *Walt Disney Treasures Silly Symphonies—The Historic Musical Animated Classics*, disc 2 (Walt Disney Home Entertainment, 2001), DVD, 2 discs, 5.5 min.

Snow-White, dir. Dave Fleischer (New York: Fleischer Animation Studio, 1933). *Betty Boop: The Essential Collection*, disc 4 (Olive Films, 2015), DVD, 4 discs, 7 min.

Song of the South, dir. Harve Foster and Wilfred Jackson (Burbank, Calif.: Walt Disney Studio, 1946). Internet Archive, https://archive.org/details/song-of-the-south. Streaming video, 94 min.

"St. James Ballroom (Official Video)," performed by Alice Francis. YouTube video, 3:51, November 1, 2013, https://www.youtube.com/watch?v=Rz2XRqoQqoA.

"Supersonics (Out Come the Freaks Edit) (Official Video)," dir. Bechir "Jiwee" Jouini, performed by Caravan Palace. YouTube video, 3:00, December 10, 2020, https://www.youtube.com/watch?v=57fY0LeESQY.

"Swingin Man HD," performed by Jazzbit. YouTube video, 3:15, July 31, 2013, https://www.youtube.com/watch?v=uv_h4C6fb1k.

The Three Caballeros, supervising dir. Norman Ferguson (Burbank, Calif.: Walt Disney Studio, 1944). *Classic Caballeros Collection* (Walt Disney Home Entertainment, 2008), DVD, 72 min.

"Thrift Shop (Bart & Baker Electro Swing Remix)—Postmodern Jukebox," performed by Bart & Baker. YouTube video, 3:45, May 8, 2013, https://www.youtube.com/watch?v=bDlC9m1FDo4.

"Thrift Shop (Vintage 'Grandpa Style' Macklemore Cover)," performed by Postmodern Jukebox, featuring Robyn Adele Anderson. YouTube video, 3:04, February 11, 2013, https://www.youtube.com/watch?v=4Cnm0tdkJEU.

Twilight of the Cockroaches, dir. Yoshida Hiroaki (Tokyo, Japan: Madhouse Inc., 1987). Bad Movie Mang YouTube channel streaming video, 85 min.

Uterus Man, dir. Lu Yang. Vimeo video, 11:20, December 18, 2013, https://vimeo.com/82164043.

Who Framed Roger Rabbit, dir. Robert Zemeckis (Burbank, Calif.:

Touchstone Pictures, 1988). Buena Vista Home Entertainment (2003), DVD, 104 min.

"World Is Mine," performed by supercell, featuring Hatsune Miku. YouTube video, 4:13, December 14, 2008, https://www.youtube.com/watch?v=EuJ6UR_pD5s.

INDEX

Page numbers in italics refer to figures and tables.

SANDRA ANNETT is associate professor of film studies at Wilfrid Laurier University, Canada. She is author of *Anime Fan Communities: Transcultural Flows and Frictions* and coeditor-in-chief of the journal *Mechademia: Second Arc* on East Asian popular cultures.

Printed and bound by CPI Group (UK) Ltd, Croydon, CR0 4YY

09/05/2024

14500138-0003